Doing Critical Research in Education

From Theory to Practice

Kathryn Bell McKenzie and Linda Skrla

TEACHERS COLLEGE PRESS

TEACHERS COLLEGE | COLUMBIA UNIVERSITY
NEW YORK AND LONDON

We dedicate this book to all our former students, whose probing questions motivated us to write this book.

Published by Teachers College Press,® 1234 Amsterdam Avenue, New York, NY 10027

Copyright © 2023 by Teachers College, Columbia University

Front cover art by Susan Wilkinson / Unsplash.

Library of Congress Cataloging-in-Publication Data

Names: McKenzie, Kathryn Bell, author. I Skrla, Linda, author.
Title: Doing critical research in education : from theory to practice / Kathryn Bell McKenzie and Linda Skrla.
Description: New York, NY : Teachers College Press, 2023. I Includes bibliographical references and index. I Summary: "This user-friendly guide explains difficult concepts with examples of applications for anyone who wants to engage in critical research to address some of the most pressing issues in education, as well as all areas in which there is oppression or marginalization of students and their communities"—Provided by publisher.
Identifiers: LCCN 2022055171 (print) I LCCN 2022055172 (ebook) I ISBN 9780807768129 (paperback) I ISBN 9780807768136 (hardcover) I ISBN 9780807781616 (ebook)
Subjects: LCSH: Action research in education. I Critical pedagogy—Reseach.
Classification: LCC LB1028.24 .M388 2023 (print) I LCC LB1028.24 (ebook) I DDC 370.72—dc23/eng/20230120
LC record available at https://lccn.loc.gov/2022055171
LC ebook record available at https://lccn.loc.gov/2022055172

ISBN 978-0-8077-6812-9 (paper)
ISBN 978-0-8077-6813-6 (hardcover)
ISBN 978-0-8077-8161-6 (ebook)

Printed on acid-free paper
Manufactured in the United States of America

Contents

PART II: INTERSECTIONAL AND IDENTITY-BASED CRITICAL RESEARCH IN EDUCATION

PART III: ADDITIONAL TYPES OF CRITICAL
RESEARCH IN EDUCATION

Preface

Nearly 20 years of teaching the course *Introduction to Systems of Human Inquiry* led us to write this book. *Systems of Human Inquiry* is a doctoral-level course in educational research that addresses the various paradigms that guide the way research is thought of and thus conducted. One of the paradigms is research guided by critical theories, which many of our students were drawn to—possibly because the educational research we have engaged in for our entire careers was situated within the critical paradigm. This may also be why students wanted to learn and work alongside us. Combined, we have served as committee members or chairs of nearly 200 student dissertations, not including masters theses, at four universities. Whether in class or working on their dissertations, students wanted to know if there was one book that explained the theories of critical research in education and then showed how to conduct research guided by these theories. There wasn't, so we thought it would be a service to them, and the students and researchers to come, to write one.

This book is organized in three parts. The first part, **Background of Critical Research in Education**, includes Chapters 1–3. In Chapter 1, "Isn't Research Just Research? An Overview of Systems of Human Inquiry," we provide an overview of systems of human inquiry, including the necessary terminology for understanding these systems. We follow that with a brief history of social science as well as the two research paradigms—positivism and interpretivism—and conclude by introducing critical theory, its history, and its place in educational research. We also provide in this chapter a research paradigm chart adapted from two previous versions, one from Patti Lather (1991) and the other from Lincoln and Guba (2000). We used this chart in our *Systems of Human Inquiry* classes, and it became the students' go-to resource. Chapter 2, "Research Considerations in Critical Research in Education," does not in any way address all the issues surrounding research that one needs to keep in mind. What it does do is discuss several of the issues that are often overlooked or not addressed in depth but that are vital to doing critical research. These are assuring quality, ethical considerations, reflexivity and positionality, and the theoretical framework. Then in Chapter 3, "Traditional Critical Theory in Education," we introduce the format we follow for the remaining chapters of the book, excluding Chapter 14, "The Future of Critical Research in Education." We begin with the background or history; continue with the notable theorists and researchers;

and when needed, address important concepts or terminology, as well as any other issues particular to the chapter topic.

Possibly the most helpful contribution of this chapter, and the others that follow this format, is the use of a published peer-reviewed journal article to explain the research components associated with the critical research paradigm, such as critical feminist research, which is addressed in Chapter 6. For each journal article we begin by discussing the statement of the research problem, the purpose of the research, and the research question/s. We next move to the theoretical framework, followed by the methodology and methods, and then the analysis and results/findings,[1] and conclude with the discussion and recommendations. It's important to note that we were deliberate in our choice of our example articles, paying attention to each author's discipline, race/ethnicity, gender, university affiliation, academic rank, and the journal in which the articles were published. All the articles, of course, are critical and address issues related to education, but they are also varied, as are the authors' disciplines. For example, we include teacher education professors as well as social epidemiologists who research issues in education. The authors are diverse in their race/ethnicity and gender. They come from an array of doctoral universities, including Very High Research Activity (R1), High Research Activity (R2), and Doctoral/Professional Universities (D/PU) both inside and outside the United States. The articles represent 10 different journals. For example, one article was published in *Educational Administration Quarterly*, and another was published in *The International Journal of Community Music*.

Part II of the book, **Intersectional and Identity-Based Critical Research in Education**, includes Chapters 4–10 and addresses some of the most important topics in critical research in education, as well as some of the most controversial. Controversy, however, should not make one shy away from doing this important research, but it needs to be done mindfully, honestly, and well. In this part we address Critical Race Theory (CRT) (in general), Critical Race Theory in Education, Critical Feminist Research in Education, LGBTQ Studies and Queer Theory in Education, Indigenous/Tribal Critical Research in Education, Latinx Critical Research in Education, and Critical Disability Studies in Education. You may notice that sometimes we use "research" in the chapter titles, and sometimes we use "theories" or "studies." We use the terminology that is most frequently used or accepted in the subfield of critical theory we are writing about.

Part III, **Additional Types of Critical Research in Education**, mostly adheres to the same format as the previous chapters in Part II, except for Chapter 14. The chapters in this section, though, veer from the intersectional and identity-based focus of the previous section. We begin with Chapter 11, "Critical Policy Studies in Education," which has been an area of study since the 1940s. Following this chapter, we introduce two fairly recent areas of study in education: Chapter 12, "Critical Quantitative Studies in Education," and Chapter 13, "Critical Social Epidemiological Studies in Education." Chapter 14, "The Future of Critical Research in Education," offers our projections as to where critical research in education may go next.

What this book does not do is go into great detail about the various theoretical frameworks, methodologies, methods, or analytical techniques and strategies of the critical theories in education we discuss. There are plenty of books and articles about these issues that are good and very specific, and we've cited them heavily so that readers can find them. In our book, however, we set out to address specifically and pedagogically the various types of critical research in education that exist today. We do this knowing that even more types and variations of critical research in education may be in existence once this book is completed and in print. The field is always expanding.

We wrote this to be the book we wished we'd had when teaching *Systems of Human Inquiry* and could have used with our doctoral students just beginning their research journey. Actually, we would have liked to have had it as a guide when doing our own critical research in education. We hope it is of use to you whether you are a doctoral student, a researcher (including practitioners who research), or a professor who wants a course text that is clear, comprehensive, and pedagogical.

Acknowledgments

This work wouldn't be as good without the help and support from Kathryn's life and work partner, Dr. Martyn Gunn, who is a scientist and academic in a field (biochemistry) far from ours. He was the perfect person to read this book with a "beginner's mind." Martyn applied his inexhaustible curiosity to the task. He read the entire book word for word several times, editing as he went, and posing questions that made us clarify concepts and ideas we took for granted.

As always, I appreciate the love and support from my partner, Martyn, and our children Kelsey, Kolter, Sophie, and their families.
    —Kathryn

Thanks to my family for their love and support: my sister Lily, and my sons Steve, Scott, and Eric.
    —Linda

Part I

BACKGROUND OF CRITICAL RESEARCH IN EDUCATION

CHAPTER 1

Isn't Research Just Research?

An Overview of Systems of Human Inquiry

I, Kathryn, will never forget the embarrassment of presenting what I thought was appropriate research to the students and professor in my first doctoral class, *Anthropology of Education*. I had conducted a survey with teachers. It was the only way I knew to do research. The professor, a well-known ethnographer, was annoyed, and my fellow students were probably entertained. I was a former elementary teacher and, at that extraordinarily embarrassing moment, an assistant principal. My understanding of research or inquiry was what I had taught my elementary students—the scientific method—and, as a school administrator, the data analysis involved in understanding standardized test scores and the surveys we did of faculty, staff, and parents. I did not formally know about ethnography or naturalistic research even though as an educator I had been doing it for years—observing and interviewing students, taking anecdotal records of students in literature discussion groups or journal writing, and so forth. I didn't know this was research—I thought of it as just teaching. I didn't know there were systems of inquiry, paradigms, that rely on ontological, epistemological, and axiological assumptions to inform the methodology and methods one employs in research. In fact, I had never heard of ontology, epistemology, or axiology. A year or so later I took a course called *Systems of Human Inquiry*, and as Patti Lather might say, I got a little smarter and a little lost. I eventually came to teach *Systems of Human Inquiry* at my universities, and now, having taught it over 20 times, I'm still learning and hopefully getting smarter as new fields of inquiry are emerging.

For this chapter, then, we begin by defining the needed terms and provide an example of their use in research by contrasting the traditional paradigms of positivism and interpretivism, using a recent research article. Next, we provide a brief overview of the historical context within which these paradigms emerged. Finally, to address the focus of this book, "doing critical research in education," we move on to the nontraditional paradigm, critical theory. For critical theory, we offer a more thorough history, return to the research article to provide a contrast between critical theory and the traditional paradigms of positivism and interpretivism, and explain the use of critical theory specifically in education.

TERMINOLOGY

Paradigm

Paradigm is not as easy to define as one might think. Paradigm was introduced in English in the late 15th century and referred to the Greek notion of pattern, model, or example. Most of us became familiar with it, along with the concept of paradigm shift, from Thomas Kuhn's 1962/1996 landmark book *The Structure of Scientific Revolutions*. However, "a number of philosophers have complained that Kuhn's conception of a paradigm is too imprecise to do the work he intended for it" (Audi, 1999, p. 642). Answering the critique, Kuhn (1996), in the postscript to the 3rd edition of his book, stated that:

> the term "paradigm" is used in two different senses. On the one hand, it stands for the entire constellation of beliefs, values, techniques, and so on shared by the members of a given community. On the other, it denotes one sort of element in that constellation, the concrete puzzle-solutions which, employed as modes or examples, can replace explicit rules as a basis for the solution of the remaining puzzles of normal science. (p. 174)

Defining paradigm succinctly, Lincoln and Guba (1985) stated that "paradigms represent a distillation of what we think about the world (but cannot prove)" (p. 15). The definition we prefer, though, is offered by Denzin and Lincoln (2005), drawing from Guba:

> The *net* [emphasis added] that contains the researcher's epistemological, ontological, and methodological premises may be termed a paradigm or an interpretive framework, a "basic set of beliefs that guides action" (Guba, 1990, p. 15). All research is interpretive; it is guided by the researcher's set of beliefs and feelings about the world and how it should be understood and studied. Some beliefs may be taken for granted, invisible, only assumed, whereas others are highly problematic and controversial. Each . . . paradigm makes particular demands on the researcher, including the questions the researcher asks and the interpretations he or she brings to them. (p. 22)

Habermas (1968/1972) would add interests and purposes to the *net*. He proposed three types of human interests—technical, practical, and emancipatory. If the interest is technical, then the purpose is instrumental—that is, to find causal explanations. This is positivism. If the interest is practical, then the purpose of the inquiry is to understand. This is interpretivism. If the interest is emancipatory, then the purpose is to emancipate. This is critical theory (see Table 1.1). We will return to these interests and purposes and apply them to the example below.

It is also important to understand the components subsumed in the *net*, the paradigm: ontology, epistemology, methodology, and, we would add, axiology

Table 1.1. Paradigm Chart

Interest	Technical	Practical	Emancipatory
Purpose	Instrumental	Understand	Emancipate
Paradigm	*Positivism[1]	*Interpretivism Naturalistic Constructivist Phenomenological Hermeneutic	*Critical theory Critical race theory Critical White studies Neo-Marxism Feminist LatCrit Gay and lesbian studies, etc.[2]
Ontology	Naive Realism: Reality is objective and found. The world is as we see it without interpretation or subjective construction.	Reality is subjective and constructed. Not everyone sees or understands things in the same way.	Historical Realism: "virtual reality shaped by social, political, cultural, economic, ethnic, and gender values crystallized over time into social structures that are taken to be real" (p. 193)[3]
Epistemology	Naive Empiricism: There is one and only one truth or probability to truth.	Multiple truths that are constructed and co-constructed. Knowledge is not discovered but created.	"Subjectivist, formed between the researcher and the researched, and aims for emancipation from oppression" (p. 89).[4]
Axiology	Knowledge is arrived at objectively, free from values.	Values the lived-experiences of the individual, value-laden.	"More than value-laden, prompted and guided by the researcher's values" (p. 89).[5]
Methodology	The scientific method	Participant observation Case study Ethnography Phenomenology Grounded theory Action research, etc.	Critical Ethnography Critical Historiography Participant Action Research, etc.[6]

(*continued*)

Table 1.1. Paradigm Chart (continued)

Interest	Technical	Practical	Emancipatory
Purpose	Instrumental	Understand	Emancipate
Methods	Conducting experiments, making models, conducting surveys	Observing, interviewing, analyzing documents, narrative analysis, etc.	Observing, interviewing, analyzing documents, narrative analysis, etc.

1. *Indicates the term most commonly used. The terms that follow are examples, not an exhaustive list.

2. Some include queer theory as a critical theory, and some, like Patti Lather, include it in the poststructural paradigm.

3. Guba & Lincoln (2005).

4. Lincoln & Guba (2013).

5. Lincoln & Guba (2013).

6. It should be noted that critical research is continuing to evolve, and researchers are now using quantitative methodologies and methods that align with CRT. See the tenets proposed in Chapter 13.

and methods. Beginning with ontology, it, like epistemology, is a field of philosophy. One could spend a lifetime studying each of these fields, but for this chapter we will use simplified definitions for each of the paradigm components, as the goal is to understand the various paradigms and how they influence our research.

Ontology

Plainly stated, *ontology* is the "philosophical study of the nature of existence, being, or reality" (Schwandt, 2015, p. 221). Ontology asks the questions, What is existence? What does it mean to be? What is the nature of reality? These questions, and the ones associated with the other paradigmatic components like epistemology, speak directly to the previous statement from Denzin and Lincoln that research is guided by a "set of beliefs and feelings about the world and how it should be understood and studied" (2005, p. 22). Depending on the paradigm in which your research is positioned—positivism, interpretivism, critical—the answers to the philosophical questions will be different.

To clarify, we will begin with the two contrasting paradigms of positivism and interpretivism, defining the components of each. For positivism, the answer to the ontological question "What is the nature of reality?" would be reality is "out there," made up of parts that can be studied, leading to prediction and thereby control (Lincoln & Guba, 1985). Or said another way, there is an objective reality that can be found. It is not dependent on human perception. This is often called *naive* realism. For example, in a recent volume of *Educational*

Researcher there was a positivistic study of the effects of principal quality on student attendance, "Principal Quality and Student Attendance" (Bartanen, 2020). The interest was technical—Does the quality of the principal have an effect on student attendance? The purpose was instrumental, to find a causal explanation. The ontological assumption was a reality "out there"—that is, students are often absent in school. This reality was made up of parts, different factors that could be causing the absences. These parts could be teased out and studied, like the principal's effect on absenteeism. And from this study, predictions could be made resulting in control; one could predict which schools would have more or less absenteeism depending on the principal and could then make the necessary changes to decrease absenteeism.

In interpretivism, or naturalistic research, the answer to the ontological question "What is the nature of reality?" would be that there are multiple realities that are constructed and subjective. So if an interpretivist or naturalistic researcher were to study student absenteeism, their interest would be practical—that is, in-the-field experiences—and their purpose would be to understand. Thus, the researcher might choose a high school to study and then interview students, teachers, parents, and principals about why they think students are absent and what might improve attendance. The researcher would be interested in the lived experiences of the people closest to the situation or phenomenon, to their truths, their realities. The goal would not be to predict and control but rather to understand. From this understanding, recommendations for additional research, policy, or practice could be offered. Thus, you can see the ways ontology, or one's beliefs about the nature of reality, influences research depending on the paradigm the research is situated within.

Epistemology

Whereas ontology is the study of reality, *epistemology* is the study of knowledge. In other words, what can one know and how can one know it? This may sound silly. You may think either you know or you don't know something, but it's more complicated than that. Philosophers from the time of Plato, and possibly before, have been debating the various types of knowledge: for example, a posteriori knowledge and a priori knowledge, propositional knowledge and nonpropositional knowledge. There is also debate about the conditions of propositional knowledge or what constitutes knowing: for example, the belief condition—whether one has to believe something to know it; the truth condition—whether something has to be true to know it; and the justification condition—whether adequate evidence must exist to believe something is true in order to know it. This is called justified true belief. As you can see, it's complicated.

Continuing to compare positivism with interpretivism, the epistemology in positivism is that there is one truth, or a probability of truth, that is out there and can be discovered, unaffected by a knower. Using our research example, our positivist researcher would contend that the quality of the principal either does or does not have an effect on student attendance, whereas in interpretivism there are multiple truths and truth is not found; it is constructed. There is a relationship between the knower and the known. Therefore, our interpretivist researcher would look at the truths constructed by students, teachers, and principals as to why students are absent and come to an understanding of the situation.

On the first day in my *Systems of Human Inquiry* class, I, Kathryn, began by posing two questions to the students. I asked students to take a few minutes and jot down the answer to this question: What do you know? Then I asked: How do you know this? This began a robust discussion about ontology—what students believe about the nature of reality; about epistemology—what is "true," what can be known; as well as axiology, methodology, and methods. Of course, most students, except possibly those with a degree in philosophy, did not realize this is what we are discussing. That came later in the course, but the activity ignited the students thinking about these issues. As the course went on and as we discussed the varying paradigms, additional epistemological questions were introduced. For example: Who is a knower? Does some knowledge count more than others? Whose knowledge gets privileged and whose gets marginalized?

Axiology

Axiology, also called value theory, is "the branch of philosophy dealing with ethics, aesthetics, and religion" (Guba & Lincoln, 2005, p. 200). The inclusion of religion in axiology, however, resulted in axiology being "defined *out* [emphasis added] of scientific inquiry" (p. 200), leaving only ontology, epistemology, and methodology. Presumably this was because of the relationship between religion and science in the Enlightenment, or Age of Reason. However, Guba and Lincoln (2005), as well as others like Heron and Reason (1997) and Indigenous scholars like Roxanne Struthers (2001), have called for axiology to be included in paradigms of inquiry in that "the axiological question asks what is intrinsically valuable in human life, in particular what sort of knowledge, if any, is intrinsically valuable" (Heron & Reason, 1997, p. 277). A positivist, therefore, would find knowledge arrived at objectively to be valuable, whereas an interpretivist would value the knowledge derived from lived experiences, the researcher's and the researched—in other words, subjective knowledge. Our positivist researcher, then, would value the results derived from the statistical model employed, and our interpretivist researcher would value the data from the interviews with the students, teachers, and principals.

Methodology and Methods

Often the terms *methodology* and *methods* are conflated. There are, however, distinctions. According to Pascale (2011), methodology is "the logical frameworks of research design" and methods are "techniques for acquiring data" (p. 2). Crotty (1998/2003), being more specific, states that methodology is

> the strategy, plan of action, process or design lying behind the choice and use of particular methods and linking the choice and use of methods to the desired outcomes . . . [whereas methods are] the technique or procedures used to gather and analyze data related to some research question or hypothesis. (p. 3)

Like ontology, epistemology, and axiology, one's methodology and thus methods depend on the paradigm. In positivism the methodology would be experimental or survey research, seeking to find objective reality using mainly quantitative methods like controlled experiments or surveys. Conversely, in interpretivism the methodology might, for example, be case study or participant observation, among others, and the methods would be observing, interviewing, performing document analysis, and more. Therefore, our positivist researcher's methodology would be experimental, and the method would be model-making. In the example study, our positivist researcher used econometric and regression analyses. Our interpretivist researcher's methodology might be participant observation, engaging with study participants, being in the field, and employing methods like conducting observations and interviews.

BRIEF HISTORY OF SOCIAL SCIENCE, POSITIVISM, AND INTERPRETIVISM

Having introduced the concept of paradigm and the components (ontology, epistemology, axiology, methodology, and methods), we will provide a brief, although incomplete, summary of the history of social science, specifically the emergence of positivism and interpretivism as ways to study the social world, before moving on to critical theory. Some believe that science began with the scientific revolution in the 16th century, but the legacy of scientific thought goes back before recorded history. People have been trying to understand and predict or control the natural world around them for thousands of years, engaging in myths, magic, alchemy, astronomy, medicine, zoology, and biology. However, the terms *science* and *scientist* did not exist. Those attempting to study nature were called natural philosophers, although some have called Ibn al-Haytham (who was born in 965 CE in what we now call Iraq and who developed the scientific method emphasizing experimental data and replicability) the world's "first true scientist" (Al-Khalili, J., 2009, p. 1). The term scientist, however, was not coined until 1833 by William Whewell (*Stanford Encyclopedia of Philosophy*, n.d.).

The advent of "modern" science occurred during what is now called the scientific revolution in the 16th and 17th centuries. It brought about the following shifts:

the reeducation of common sense in favour of abstract reasoning; the substitution of a quantitative for a qualitative view of nature; the view of nature as a machine rather than as an organism; the development of an experimental, scientific method that sought definite answers to certain limited questions couched in the framework of specific theories; and the acceptance of new criteria for explanation, stressing the "how" rather than the "why" that had characterized the Aristotelian search for final causes. (Brush et al., 2019, Scientific Revolution section)

In the early 19th century Auguste Comte introduced the term *positivism*, applying it to sociology, or the study of society. He proposed that "human beings and their institutions must be viewed as 'neutral objects' which can be investigated in more or less the same way as any other scientific object" (Held, 1980, p. 161). He was attempting to make the study of society more scientific, more certain, more positive. In other words,

> applying lawlike regularities to explain social life . . . characterized by three core beliefs:
>
> (1) the world exists as an objective entity and is (at least in principle) knowable in its entirety;
> (2) science can study *only* phenomena that can be directly observed (empiricism); and
> (3) the work of science is to construct general laws that express relationships between observed phenomena. (Pascale, 2011, p. 47)

In sum, the world is as we see it without interpretation or subjective construction (naive realism), there is one and only one truth or probability of truth (naive empiricism), and the scientific method is the way to get to truth.

Interpretivism, initially known as antipositivism, emerged in the late 19th and 20th centuries as a critique of positivism. Lincoln and Guba (1985), drawing from Rom Harre (1981), compared this new postpositivist paradigm to its predecessor:

> Where positivism is concerned with surface events or appearances, the new paradigm takes a deeper look. Where positivism is atomistic, the new paradigm is structural. Where positivism establishes meaning operationally, the new paradigm establishes meaning inferentially. Where positivism sees its central purpose to be prediction, the new paradigm is concerned with understanding. Finally, where positivism is deterministic and bent on certainly, the new paradigm is probabilistic and speculative. (p. 30)

That is, the social world cannot be studied or understood like the natural world, using the scientific method, because the social world is understood through interpretations that are subjective and constructed; that is to say, there are multiple truths, not one and only one truth. An array of methodologies guides interpretivist inquiry, such as participant observation, case study, ethnography, and grounded theory, to name a few.

CRITICAL THEORY

Marx, Marxism, and the Institute of Social Research/ The Frankfurt School

Critical theory, in contrast to the traditional theories of positivism and interpretivism, is not about maintaining the status quo while attempting to make it work better (i.e., reform). Rather, critical theory is born out of a call for revolution and is about transforming, not reforming, society by eliminating oppression. It is concerned with creating a more just society through interpretation and transformation (Held, 1980).

Marx and Marxism. The original critical theorists were inspired by Marxism, the philosophy of Karl Marx. Marxism is both a philosophical system and a methodology that aims "to arrive at a scientific analysis of modern economic life" and "capitalism as a system" (Little, n.d., Introduction section), albeit a critical analysis. It is often misunderstood, and historically was appropriated and misused. Marx himself, responding to what he considered misinterpretations and misuse of his principles, said that "ce qu'il y a de certain c'est que moi, je ne suis pas Marxiste," translated as "If anything is certain, it is that I myself am not a Marxist" (Engels, 1882, p. 353).

Marx was a member of the Communist League, an international political party that met in London in 1847 and commissioned Marx and Friedrich Engels to write the *Communist Manifesto* to publicly express the Communists' views, aims, and tendencies (Marx & Engels, 1848). In addition, Marx and Engels addressed directly the critiques of communism and offered their critiques of what they termed reactionary socialism, conservative socialism, and critical-utopian socialism and communism. Additionally, they critiqued the earlier models of transforming society put forth by the critical Socialists and Communists, calling their proposals "purely utopian in character" (Marx & Engels, 1848, p. 19). In contrast, Marx and Engels (1848) believed revolution, an uprising of the proletariat, was necessary and ended the manifesto saying

> the Communists disdain to conceal their view and aims. They openly declare that their ends can be attained only by the forcible overthrow of all existing social conditions. Let the ruling classes tremble at a Communist revolution. The proletarians have nothing to lose but their chains. They have a world to win. Workingmen of all countries, unite! (p. 20)

There is much to understand in Marx's writings and subsequently Marxism, including what some call the philosophies and others the methodologies of dialectical and historical materialism and the concomitant theories: "the labor theory of value, the theories of class conflict and exploitation, the theory of the forces and relations of production, or the theory of the mode of production" (Little, n.d., p. 1).

What is important for this discussion of critical theory, however, is the main idea that Marx posited: namely, people's lives are affected by the material conditions they live in. Here he is talking specifically about economic and political systems of production like industrial capitalism, which was the result of the Industrial Revolution that brought about private ownership of production for profit. Capitalism, according to Marx, created modern classes—the bourgeoisie, those who own the means of production, and the proletariat, those who do the work—and class struggle. Marx believed that class struggle, conflict, was what propelled history and brought about new forms of social structure; this was his dialectical materialism. Specific to capitalism, he believed class struggle would lead to the destruction of capitalism and then reconstruction into socialism and ultimately to communism. This struggle, the struggle of the proletariat, was marked by (1) alienation from work—becoming just a cog in a machine, commodified, and dispensable; and (2) exploitation—whereby, for example, the first 4 hours of the workday pays for the worker's labor (what it takes to provide food, shelter, and clothes) and the next 4 hours are profit for the employer, profit the worker does not share in. However, this is not all that capitalism does; it also instills an ideology. According to Marx and Engels,

> the ideas of the ruling class are in every epoch the ruling ideas, i.e. the class which is the ruling material force of society, is at the same time its ruling intellectual force. The class which has the means of material production at its disposal, has control at the same time over the means of mental production . . . and those who lack the means of mental production are subject to it. (Marx, 1846, Ruling class and ruling ideas section)

The Institute of Social Research/The Frankfurt School. Moving on from the discussion of Marx and Marxism to critical theory, the Institute of Social Research was established in 1923 in Frankfurt, Germany to advance studies in Marxism. The key figures associated with the Institute were an eclectic group of scholars, including philosophers, sociologists, psychologists, economists, and political scientists. Included in the Institute was the Frankfurt School, whose predominant scholars included Max Horkheimer, Theodor Adorno, Herbert Marcuse, Walter Benjamin, Erich Fromm, and later Jürgen Habermas. Important to note, there are distinctions between the first generation of critical theorists, those of the Institute of Social Research in 1923, and the second generation led by Habermas in the 1970s. Further, there is a third generation of the Institute directed now by Ferdinand Sutterlüty. For this discussion, however, the focus will be on the first and second generations:

> In a nutshell, the first and founding generation of the Frankfurt School attempted to actualize Marx's critique of capitalism. This project not only involved the need to

account for capitalism's continued existence, but also for the rise of fascist as well as state-capitalist systems of totalitarian domination. Marx's critique thus needed to be expanded to explain the susceptibility of the masses, including the working class, to nationalist propaganda, the fascist cult of leadership, or the (equally disabling) complacency with the existing order of injustice via consumerism and the culture industry. (Garlitz & Kögler, 2015, p. 381)

When Hitler became chancellor in 1933, the Institute was forced to move from Germany to the United States and later returned to Germany in 1950, although several of its members stayed in the United States.

To restate, the events of the 1920s and 1930s, including the rise of Nazism and fascism, proved counter to Marx's predictions. There was not an awakening by the proletariat. They did not shed their false consciousness and come to understand that capitalist ideology was alienating and exploitative. They did not revolt, capitalism didn't fall, and socialism didn't emerge. Why was this? Answering this question was the task of the Frankfurt School through a research program that reexamined Marxist theory and advanced an interdisciplinary theory of society. When Horkheimer, who studied philosophy, sociology, and psychology, took over the directorship of the school in 1930, the focus shifted from economic theory to social science theory, later termed critical theory, concerned with "the conditions which make possible the reproduction and transformation of society, the meaning of culture, and the relation between the individual, society and nature" (Held, 1980, p. 17).

Habermas, who led the second generation of the Frankfurt School, became its director in 1984. His influence included defending the normative rationality of the Enlightenment, the Age of Reason, and promoting a normative critical social theory, which was contrary to his predecessors, who saw Enlightenment reason as instrumental reason. "Instrumental reason, as Horkheimer understood it, was devoted to determining the means to an end, without reasoning about ends in themselves" (Jeffries, 2016, p. 366), efficiency without regard to personal costs. However, Habermas saw the Enlightenment, modernity, as an unfinished program that offered advances in science, technology, economic growth, and more. He also knew the destructive consequences of the Enlightenment, like the "objectivating science" and "the universalistic foundations of morality and law" (p. 366). What he offered was the theory of communicative action. Within this theory he posited two spheres: one, the lifeworld and two, the system. The lifeworld is the

everyday world of family and household, of shared meanings and understandings, of the unconstrained conversations that take place in the public spheres. The system by contrast means structures and patterns of instrumental rationality and action, notably money and power, whose chief function is the production and circulation of goods and services. The system then includes the economy, state administration and state-sanctioned political parties. The relationship between lifeworld and system is important for Habermas: the former, which is the home of communicative reason and action, risks being colonized by the latter, which is the home of instrumental reason. (Jeffries, 2016, p. 367)

Habermas believed that there was power in ordinary everyday communication that influences thoughts, actions, beliefs, norms, and even identities. This is the lifeworld. However, this communication and the power derived from it can be disrupted (colonized) by the system and result in "social pathologies such as alienation, anomie, and social conflict" (Parkin, 1996, p. 424). Critical theory, as defined by Habermas, allows for "an empirical political analysis that exposes the subtle ways that a given state and economic structure function to systematically exclude citizens from decision-making, and to restrict public political argument, participation, and mobilization" (p. 424). This can be seen today in efforts across the United States to suppress both voting, particularly in communities of color, and public protest.

Habermas retired as the director of the Institute for Social Research in 1993. That led to the emergence of the third generation of the Frankfurt School, who are extending their reach and creating international relationships and furthering interdisciplinary relationships. Throughout the history of the Frankfurt School there has not been a consensus on theory or methodology; in fact, there has been much disagreement. However, there has always been a unity in purpose that cleaves to the words of Marx and that are inscribed on his tombstone: "The philosophers have only interpreted the world, in various ways. The point, however, is to change it."

CRITICAL THEORY AND EDUCATION

To change the world continues to be the ambition of critical theory, to change it by addressing oppression, discrimination, and alienation both theoretically and practically. Today that includes racism, sexism, classism, heterosexism, ageism, ableism, nativism, and any and all other expressions, systemic and otherwise, of injustice. Speaking specifically to education,

> throughout US history, education policies, practices, and politics have been described and tested to yield empirical data [positivism and interpretivism], often with little attempt to place findings in a larger theoretical infrastructure that could provide them with increased explanatory, critical, or even liberatory power. (Anyon, 2009, p. 10)

Anyon (2009) offered clarity regarding the interplay of theory and research. First, she cautioned that "one cannot understand or explain x by merely describing x. One must look exogenously at non-x—particularly the context and social forces in which the object of study is embedded" (p. 2). She then offered two analogies:

> Trying to understand a school in East Los Angeles or South Bronx, New York . . . without accounting for the context of poverty in which the schools exist is like trying to explain the flattened landscape after a hurricane without noting the velocity of the wind. One would miss explanatory principles that caused the hurricane's damage; and one would be in danger of ignoring the pitfalls and possibilities that inhere in preparations for the future. (p. 3)

And:

> A pebble on the beach is just a stone until it is studied, say, as an intricate instantiation of the theory of atomic structure. And the color of the stone is not merely a pretty sight; it exemplifies modern theories of energy and light . . . [so] an urban school may present as a collection of harried teachers and unmotivated students, until it is studied as an institutional repository of the effects of discriminatory macroeconomic, political, and racial policies and social forces. (Anyon, 2005, as cited in Anyon, 2009, p. 4)

That is, you cannot just study schools and the workings of schooling as isolated phenomena. You must also study the economic, political, social, racial, and cultural values that over time have created the structures wherein schools are nested.

Having previously described the paradigm components of positivism and interpretivism, now would be an appropriate time to describe them for critical theory. Returning to Habermas's human interests, critical theory is interested in emancipation, and its purpose, then, is to emancipate. In this historical epoch, critical theory encompasses Critical Race Theory, Feminist Theory, LatCrit, Gay and Lesbian Studies, Critical Policy Studies, and more. It should be noted that some include LGBTQ+ studies in critical theory, and some include it in poststructuralism. Critical theory's ontology is historical realism, that is, "virtual reality shaped by social, political, cultural, economic, ethnic, and gender values crystallized over time into social structures that are taken to be real" (Guba & Lincoln, 2005, p. 193).

So, returning to our example research article, the critical theorist with an ontology of historical realism would see student absenteeism as a possible indicator of the social, political, cultural, racial, and ethnic values inherent in the current society. The axiology in critical theory is value-laden and "prompted and guided by the researcher's values" (Lincoln & Guba, 2013, p. 89). The epistemology is "subjectivist, formed between the researcher and the researched, and aims for emancipation from . . . oppression" (p. 89). Applying these components to our example article, regarding student absenteeism the critical researcher would want to look at who is absent and why. For example, are the students who are most often absent those who have historically been marginalized: students living in poverty, or students of color, or students who learn differently, or LBGTQ+ students? Are students not attending school because they have to stay home and take care of a sick sibling because the parents are hourly workers who do not have paid leave to stay home and take care of a sick child, and staying would mean a loss of wages, money needed for rent or food? Are students missing school because they are victims of harassment or oppressive policies? In other words, what are the taken-for-granted social structures based on the social, political, cultural, racial, and ethnic values that could be affecting student absenteeism? The methodology might be a case study of a school and school community employing methods to determine which students and student groups are absent most frequently. This would be followed by interviewing and observing students, teachers, and school leaders, as well as families in the community, regarding why they think students are absent. The difference, then, between critical theory and traditional paradigms is that it situates and analyzes educational issues within the larger context of social structures imbued with the dominant, albeit oppressive, values of our time.

In the following chapters, we introduce a variety of critical approaches; most use qualitative methodologies, and others do not use or do not solely use qualitative approaches. For each approach we provide its background, where it is located in the field of education, and the unique features that contrast it to the other approaches. Most importantly, we provide guidance through research examples on how to design and conduct a study within each of these approaches.

CHAPTER 2

Research Considerations in Critical Research in Education

In this chapter we address topics that are often confusing for, or overlooked by, beginning researchers but that are paramount for conducting research that is trustworthy, ethical, and self-reflexive, particularly when doing critical research. Critical researchers "show the world what it is really fighting for, and consciousness is something that it *has to* acquire, even if it does not want to" (Marx, 1843, para. 9).

ASSURING QUALITY

Researchers using quantitative, qualitative, mixed-method, practitioner-action, arts-based, or other established methods for educational research have plentiful sources that discuss means for increasing the likelihood that one's results are accurate and believable. Depending on the type of research methods, these might take the form of reliability or validity measures, means for establishing trustworthiness and credibility, disclosing conflicts of interest, and so forth.

Adding a critical lens to the research process, whatever form one is using, such as critical feminist research, adds additional considerations and responsibilities for which the researcher must hold themselves accountable. At the core of critical philosophical viewpoints and, thus, critical research methods, is the stance that human society is constructed in ways that distribute power and resources unequally along racial, economic, gender, sexual orientation, ability, language, tribal, geographic, and other lines. Therefore, critical researchers studying such inequities in educational settings must design and conduct their research in ways that take this into account. This is the case for all types of critical research, those using qualitative methods *and* those using quantitative ones.

For qualitative research, Lincoln and Guba laid out a comprehensive and well-elaborated set of principles for assuring trustworthiness and credibility in their 1985 book *Naturalistic Inquiry*. These principles and their accompanying procedures, such as member-checking, triangulation, and peer debriefing, have become standard practice in the great majority of qualitative studies in education.

Even these well-established safeguards, however, have the potential to be conducted in performative rather than in substantive ways that cause the research to fall short of critical aims. As Denzin and Lincoln (2008) pointed out, when addressing critical research in Indigenous settings, "Critical theory's criteria for self-determination and empowerment perpetuate neocolonial sentiments while turning the indigenous person into an essentialized 'other' who is spoken for" (p. 6). In other words, no amount of attention to trustworthiness and credibility safeguards will help if the researcher fails to grasp the problems of combining grand social theory with research in contemporary, localized educational settings. Denzin and Lincoln further claimed that

> critical theory must be localized, grounded in specific meanings, traditions, customs, and community relations that operate in each indigenous setting. Localized critical theory can work if the goals of critique, resistance, struggle, and emancipation are not treated as if they have "universal characteristics that are independent of history, context, and agency" (L. T. Smith, 2000, p. 299). (p. 6)

This is just one example of the type of quality assurance issue that researchers must attend to when conducting critical research in education.

Whereas in the past quantitative studies were not usually associated with critical research, Stage and Wells (2014) made the case that quantitative methods could be combined with critical sensibilities to accomplish specific kinds of research. They described their work and drew from two preeminent critical researchers, Kincheloe and McLaren:

> We used quantitative work, not to *prove* the relevance of grand theories, but rather to add to knowledge about the students and faculty whom we studied, and specifically those who were underrepresented and/or oppressed. Kincheloe and McLaren's (1994) description of critical work was useful to us as we attempted to describe our view of our own work:
>
> - Thought is mediated by socially and historically created power relations.
> - Facts cannot be isolated from values.
> - The relationship between concept and object is never fixed and is often socially mediated.
> - Language is central to the formation of subjectivity.
> - Certain groups in society hold privilege over others that is maintained if subordinates accept their status as natural.
> - Oppression has many faces that must be examined simultaneously.
> - Mainstream research practices generally reproduce class, race, and gender oppression.
>
> We acknowledged qualitative approaches as central in critical inquiry, but argued that quantitative approaches had a contribution to make beyond what had been known as traditional quantitative scholarly inquiry. (p. 2)

For Stage and Wells (2014), then, doing quantitative research in service of critical inquiry required keeping critical principles in mind while designing and conducting their work.

Gillborn et al. (2018) added that combining critical principles with quantitative methods meant rejecting ideas of numeric neutrality and accepting that every part of the research process involved human judgment. They explained:

> Statistics do not simply lie around waiting for interested citizens to pick them up and use them. *Numbers are no more obvious, neutral, and factual than any other form of data.* Statistics are socially constructed in exactly the same way that interview data and survey returns are constructed i.e. through a design process that includes, for example, decisions about which issues should (and should not) be researched, what kinds of question should be asked, how information is to be analyzed, and which findings should be shared publicly. Even given the very best intentions (and notwithstanding the opportunity for game-playing and "creative book-keeping" . . .) at every stage there is the possibility for decisions to be taken that obscure or misrepresent issues that *could* be vital to those concerned with social justice. (p. 163)

This point is a vital one for those interested in designing and conducting critical research in education to keep in mind—at every stage, despite best researcher intentions, the possibility exists of misrepresenting, obscuring, overlooking, or erasing issues related to social justice.

In sum, for researchers designing and conducting critical research in education, regardless of methodology, additional responsibilities for assuring quality research exist. Both quantitative and qualitative methods have their own established set of actions for researchers to take, including reliability, validity, trustworthiness, and credibility criteria. However, when doing critical research attention must be paid to other issues as well; for example, local history and context, positionality of the researcher, the problematic nature of "emancipation" goals, and numerical neutrality.

ETHICAL CONSIDERATIONS

Numerous researchers before us and doubtless after us have and will grapple with the question of how to conduct critical research in education ethically. Our discussion here is about special ethical considerations that arise for today's critical education researchers that are beyond the scope of standard ethical practice assurances that are in place such as institutional review boards (IRBs), codes of ethics from professional organizations, and institutional policies covering disclosures and conflicts of interest. As Sikes (2013) pointed out:

> Cannella and Lincoln argue for a critical approach to the social sciences which "requires a radical ethics, *an ethics that is always/already concerned about power*

and oppression even as it avoids constructing 'power' as a new truth" (2011, 81). Referencing Spivak, they call for research relations which "address contemporary political and power orientations by recognising that the investigator and the investigated (whether people, institutions, or systems) are subjects of the presence or aftermath of colonialism" (2011, 83). (p. 516)

The kind of ethics we are talking about, then, means always/already being concerned about power and oppression at every step of the process from conceptualization to dissemination.

Sikes (2013) also provided a useful list of the types of ethical concerns researchers contemplating critical research in education might consider:

When different cultural groups and peoples with different mores, beliefs, values, practices, worldviews and experiences are involved, the potential problems are exponentially multiplied. This is particularly so when reviewers do not include members of communities where the proposed research is to be conducted. Ethical perspectives/positions are variously described and defined and, in effect, will often be combined to form hybrids. In my own practice (not, I suspect, uncommonly), I tend to take a bricolage or melange [sic] approach and primarily draw on:

- (Kantian) deontological concerns with the duties and responsibilities of researchers (such as respecting persons and not doing any harm) and the rights of research participants (for instance, to withdraw from a project);
- consequentialist concerns about the likely immediate and long-term effects of being involved or in any way touched by a particular research project;
- (Aristotelian) virtue ethics, where the concern is with advancing the general good (although who is defining the good raises inevitable questions about power);
- a situational and contextual awareness that different situations and cultural settings generate their own research-related ethical questions and issues that demand unique and contextual answers and treatment;
- principalist ethics, where the emphasis is on respect for autonomy, beneficence, non-maleficence and justice (following Jean Sieber's [1993] much quoted statement that "ethics has to do with the application of moral principles to prevent harming or wronging others, to promote the good, to be respectful and to be fair" [14]); and
- (Buberian) relational ethics, which acknowledges interpersonal relationships, connectedness and a responsibility to care for each other (see also Noddings [1984] and Gilligan [1982] on the ethics of care);
- community-generated ethics developed by indigenous and local groups involved in or touched by research (for example, Maori Kaupapa ethics, see Tuhiwai Smith [1999]); and

- critical radical and emancipatory ethics, which explicitly seek to advance social justice and equity through a communitarian approach (cf. Christians 2007; Freire 1970, 1973). (pp. 519–520)

Clearly, Sikes's list may appear long and daunting, especially for novice researchers. The types of ethics to be considered and the sources cited, though, could be highly useful to scholars as they conceptualize and carry out critical research studies in education.

The central point we are making here is that researchers claiming a critical orientation for their research have many ethical issues to think through. Most decisions to be made in the design and implementation of critical research in education involve complicated ethical situations. We have included this section in the book near the beginning to highlight the importance of the ethical work that must be done when attaching the word *critical* to research in education.

REFLEXIVITY AND POSITIONALITY

Novice researchers may be confused by the terms *reflection* and *reflexivity*. Reflection is to give something serious thought or consideration, whereas reflexivity is the "turning in upon ourselves" (Chiseri-Strater, 1996, p. 115). It is an "ongoing conversation about experience while simultaneously living in the moment" (Hertz, 1997, p. viii). With regard to research, this conversation "requires an explicit self-consciousness and self-assessment by the researcher about their views and positions [some easily identified and some not] and how these might, may, or have, directly or indirectly influenced the design, execution, and interpretation of the research" (Holmes, 2020, p. 2). In other words, it is through reflexivity that one's positionality is revealed.

A discussion of reflexivity and positionality is needed herein, as

critical theory is an umbrella term to denote those theorists that take up the task described by Marx as the self-clarification of the . . . struggles and wishes of the age. As such, two elements are crucial for it: (1) a connection to social and political struggles of emancipation; and (2) self-reflexivity. (Freyenhagen, 2018, p. 1)

However, "most researchers use reflexivity without defining how they are using it, as if it is something we all commonly understand and accept as standard methodological practice for critical qualitative research" (Pillow, 2003, p. 176). The same can be said about positionality. It is often understood and written about theoretically, but little is written about its application (Soedirgo & Glas, 2020). Positionality indicates a location—in other words, where one "stands" in reference to the world and others. Positionality describes

an individual's world view . . . or "where the researcher is coming from" [and relates to] ontological assumptions (an individual's beliefs about the nature of social reality and what is knowable about the world), epistemological assumptions (an individual's beliefs about the nature of knowledge) and assumptions about human nature and agency (individual's assumptions about the way we interact with our environment and relate to it). (Holmes, 2020, p.1)

These assumptions reflect one's gender, race, ethnicity, social status, religious faith, life experiences, geographical location, abilities, education, and so forth (Chiseri-Strater, 1996; Holmes, 2020) in that "our positionality is not reducible to [just] demographic characteristics (e.g., race, age, gender, and class); it is also informed by our personal and professional experiences, our political and ideological stances, and offered aspects of our social biography, or 'lifeworld'" (Soedirgo & Glas, 2020, p. 528).

To address Pillow's call for researchers to define how they use reflexivity, Soedirgo and Glas (2020) offered strategies for doing "active reflexivity," which they described as

a triple movement consisting of ongoing interrogations of (1) our positionality; (2) how our positionality is read by others, given their own social location and the contexts in which we interact; and (3) the assumptions about our conclusions in the first two stages. (p. 527)

They offered four strategies. The first is recording reflections and assumptions throughout the research process, including the design stage. During this stage they encourage scholars to interrogate and document assessments of "their positionality, that of the presumptive other, and of the relationship between researcher and participants" (p. 529). As the research proceeds, however, these assumptions will surely be challenged. The second strategy "is to systematize reflections into a pre-interview record . . . that outline[s] the expectations of positionality, the presumed effects, and the logic underlying these appraisals" (p. 530). In other words, the document should analyze "how the researcher expects positionality to operate in practice during the research interactions [and] should be updated after each research interaction to record whether or not it unfolded according to expectations" (p. 530). The third strategy is to include others in the process: "Our experiences and those of others make clear that there are limits to reflexivity. Colleagues and research assistants, for example, offer potential avenues for further reflexivity" (p. 530). And the fourth strategy speaks to making the work public. "Whenever possible, scholars should show their reflexivity work when publishing their research. There is value in making clear the assumptions guiding our scholarly interests; our work in the field; and when, why, and how we update and question our assumptions as our investigations progress" (p. 530).

Soedirgo and Glas (2020) cautioned, however, against assuming that one's positionality is essentialist and static and called for reflexivity that is deep and ongoing. And Spivak (1988), as cited in Pillow, 2003, warned that "making positions transparent does not make them unproblematic" (p. 6).

THEORETICAL FRAMEWORK

One of the issues that students and novice researchers find most con⌐
doing research is the definition and use of a theoretical framework,
in qualitative research. There is good reason for this. Like many things in aca-
deme, there is no consensus.

Let's start with the *definition* of theoretical framework. Having reviewed
books and articles on research in general, and educational research specifically,
we found few authors who actually defined theoretical framework. Of those
who did, there was no agreement as to its definition. Most discussed the use of
the theoretical framework, leaving the definition up to the reader. There were
a few authors, however, who directly addressed the definition.

> Acknowledging that the term does not have a clear and consistent definition, we
> define theoretical frameworks as any empirical or quasi-empirical theory of social
> and/or psychological processes, at a variety of levels (e.g., grand, mid-range, and
> explanatory), that can be applied to the understanding of phenomena. (Anfara &
> Mertz, 2006, p. xxvii)

Merriam and Tisdell (2016) defined theoretical framework as the "body
of literature, the disciplinary orientation that you draw upon to situate your
study," which they say will include "concepts, terms, definitions and theories.
This framework in turn will generate the 'problem' of the study, specific research questions, data collection and analysis techniques and how you will
interpret your findings" (p. 86).

Others did not directly address theoretical frameworks but rather theory.
Dimitriadis and Kamberelis (2006) stated that "theories are abstract sets of assumptions and assertions used to interpret and sometimes to explain psychological, social, cultural, and historical processes. Theories are tools to help us
think about things in new ways" (p. vii). And Anyon (2009) provided the most
extensive definition of theory:

> From the Latin and Greek, where theory referenced speculation and contempla-
> tion; from the modern tenet of theory as a model and a set of statements and
> rules of inference; and from our concern and experience with discursive and social
> systems that produce injustice, we derive our notion of theory as an architecture
> of ideas—a coherent structure of interrelated concepts—whose contemplation and
> application (1) help us to understand and explain discursive and social phenomena
> and (2) provides a model of the way that discourse and social systems work and
> can be worked upon. (p. 3)

Moving on to the *use* of theoretical frames, Anfara and Mertz (2006) in
Theoretical Frameworks in Qualitative Research discussed the various camps
regarding theoretical frameworks and their use. These camps are "Theory as
Nearly Invisible, Theory as Related to Methodology, and Theory as More"

(pp. xx–xxv). Theory as Nearly Invisible includes those who write about educational research in general, but when discussing qualitative research either do not mention theory at all (e.g., Gay & Airasian, 2003) or discuss it using quantitative terminology (e.g., Best & Kahn, 2003; Gall et al., 1996).

Theory as Related to Methodology includes those whose write specifically about theory in qualitative research and link it to methodology, as well as epistemologies, methods, and paradigms. These authors include Lincoln and Guba (1985), Guba (1990), Denzin and Lincoln (2003a, 2003b), Patton (1990), Crotty (1998), Yin (1994), and Creswell (1994, 1998). Among these scholars there were, however, disagreements as to terminology and the direction of the linkages between theory and methodology. For example, Crotty considered positivism and interpretivism as theoretical perspectives, whereas Lincoln and Guba categorized them as paradigms. Crotty also contended that research starts with a consideration of the methodology and methods. He asked, "First, what methodologies and methods will we be employing in the research we propose to do? Second, how do we justify this choice and use of methodologies and methods?" (Crotty, 2003, p. 2). Lincoln and Guba (1985, as cited in Anfara & Mertz, 2006, p. xxi) contended the researcher "approaches the world with a set of ideas, a framework (theory, ontology) that specifies a set of questions (epistemology) that he or she then examines in specific ways (methodology, analysis)." Although there were disagreements in terminology and the order in which one approaches research, all the authors believed that theory plays a part in qualitative research, because "without theory, our data on school experience or social phenomena do not go very far, and do not tell us very much that is not already obvious" (Anyon, 2009, p. 3).

Merriam (1998), Becker (1993), Miles and Huberman (1994), Maxwell (1996), Schram (2003), Bentz and Shapiro (1998), Flinders and Mills (1993), and Schwandt (1993) make up the Theory as More camp. Although the various authors used different terms to describe what we call theoretical framework— terms such as *conceptual framework, theory, conceptual context, conceptual scheme, theoretical commitments,* and *theoretical conceptions*—they all agreed that theory guides qualitative research and is pervasive in all aspects of it. In other words, the theoretical framework "affects every aspect of the study, from determining how to frame the purpose and problem, to what to look at and for, to how we make sense of the data that are collected" (Anfara & Mertz, 2006, p. xxiv, drawing from Merriam, 1993).

Additional issues surrounding the use of theory in qualitative research have been going on for decades. Some believe you do not begin research having a theory in that theory emerges from the data (Creswell, 1994). This is the purely inductive method, starting at the ground, the particular, and moving up to the general. Others say that theory, explicit or implicit, is always present and "atheoretical research is impossible" (Schwandt, 1993, p. 6). We always have notions of what might be happening—that is to say, a theory. It is impossible to be a tabula rasa.

Lather (1986) spoke of the "reciprocal relationship b
ry. Data must be allowed to generate propositions in a c
permits use of a priori theoretical frameworks, but wh
framework from becoming the container into which the
(p. 267). Simply put, one starts with a theory but shou
that the theory may need to be modified or thrown ou
the data reveal. Lather cautioned that it would ! ~ a m
a theory and attempt to make the data fit the theory. T
the to-and-fro conversation between the data and the initial (a priori) theory,
which may result in a completely new theory. This aligns with Eisner's (1993)
statement that theory

> not only reveals, it conceals. The theoretical constructs with which we work de-
> fine in large measure the features of the universe we are likely to see. The visions
> that we secure from the theoretical portholes through which we peer also obscure
> those aspects of the territory they foreclose. And foreclose they do. Thus, the di-
> lemma. Without categories and patterns, we have little utility. With categories and
> patterns, we secure utility but risk obscuring what is individual, unique, specific.
> (p. viii)

As this discussion illustrates, there continues to be disagreement as to the
definition and use of theoretical frameworks. For us, no research is atheoretical; it is always guided knowingly or unknowingly by theory. Research begins
with a working theory—What's going on here and how can it be explained?
This leads you to the literature, asking, What have others said about this issue
and what explanations (theories) have they offered? And the questions continue:
What is missing in these theories? What further explanations could there be?
What contradictions are there in the explanations? This is usually referred to
as the gap in the literature or the statement of the problem. For example, the
problem is we don't know x; therefore the purpose of your study is x, which
leads you to your research question.

We need to digress here to briefly address the statement of the problem or
problem statement; both terms are used. For us, statement of the problem is
what is missing in the literature. However, it is not always taught that way.
Some consider it the phenomenon to be addressed, the overall issue like student absenteeism. Lincoln and Guba (1985), speaking to the statement of the
problem, claimed that

> While such a statement is not, strictly speaking, a part of the design, it does serve as
> a major criterion for judging its quality and utility and for guiding its development.
> If the design is usefully conceived as a statement of *means*, its appropriateness is
> best assessed against a statement of *ends*. Typically, the statement of the problem . . .
> includes a justification ("Why is it important to do this?") and ends with a state-
> ment of the objectives [we use purpose] to be achieved by the inquiry. (p. 222)

.ing the question, "Why is it important to do this?," it is because there .thing about the situation we don't know or understand, something that .ne yet has written about. Creswell (1994) said the problem is "the issue .at exists in the literature, theory, or practice that leads to a need for the study. By asking oneself, What is the rationale for the study? The problem begins to become clear" (p. 50). In the articles we've chosen to use as examples to illustrate the components of research, some discuss statement of the problem as a gap in the literature, answering the questions, "Why is it important to do this?" Others, however, do not frame it this way or do not address it at all.

Returning to theory, it informs your problem statement, the purpose of your study, and your research question, and it will inform your data collection and analysis of the data. Be prepared that the problem you think you identified may change during data collection, leading to a change in your purpose, research question, and the theory guiding your research. That is the nature of research, and it's fine. What isn't fine, as Lather (1986) cautioned us, is to stick with a theory because you started with it and try to make the data fit the theory instead of using theory to explain what the data reveal.

CONCLUSION

In this chapter we have discussed four areas that we feel are important for critical researchers in education to take into consideration at the beginning stages of their work that also need to be kept in the foreground throughout the project—assuring quality, ethical considerations, reflexivity and positionality, and theoretical framework. We have done so because these are areas that we have seen undertheorized and underattended throughout our careers as practitioners, professors, advisers, editors, and mentors. To put it another way, it is easy enough for researchers to claim a critical stance for their research. It is much more difficult to design and implement a research project that maintains continuity with the critical stance claimed. Though the issues raised in this chapter on research considerations are not a complete or exhaustive treatment of everything critical researchers should pay attention to, we hope this chapter serves to raise awareness among critical researchers in education and triggers deeper thought and investigation of the issues we raise.

CHAPTER 3

Traditional Critical Theory in Education

In this chapter we begin with the background of traditional critical theory in education. This is followed by the major critical theorists and the concepts associated with them. We conclude by using a journal article to explain the research components of traditional critical theory: statement of the problem, purpose, and research question; methodology and methods; analysis and results/findings; and discussion and recommendations.

BACKGROUND OF CRITICAL THEORY IN EDUCATION

Chapter 1 examined the origins of critical theory, writ large, and the various research approaches that are informed by it, such as critical theories of race and critical feminist theories, among others. Initially, though, critical theory, or what we call traditional critical theory, was more closely aligned with Marx's thoughts on capitalism, specifically the industrial capitalism of the 19th century. Marx contended that capitalism created conflict between the classes. The working class (the proletariat) struggled to get their material needs met—food, shelter, clothing—whereas the capitalist, the factory owners, made money off the labor of the working class, resulting in injustice and oppression (Marx, 1848).

Marx proposed a theory not only to analyze economic relations but also to analyze "those values and viewpoints [ideologies] created by industrial capitalism that affect ostensibly nonpolitical endeavors such as education, religion, literature, and other cultural products and practices" (Dimitriadis & Kamberelis, 2006, p. 31). A current example specific to our topic of education would be the beliefs and practices that uphold the ideology of meritocracy—the naive notion promoted by Daniel Bell (1972) that achievement is only dependent on natural abilities, motivation, and effort and that all students, with the requisite natural abilities or intelligence, have an equal opportunity to excel (McKenzie & Phillips, 2016).

Yet all of us who have worked in or with schools know that not all students come to school with the same opportunity. There is an opportunity gap. Some students come from homes and communities that are rich with resources. Their communities are safe, with little exposure to crime and violence. They live in homes free of toxins like lead paint. They have access to healthy, fresh foods and green spaces for play, and they can easily access and pay for necessities like health care. Furthermore, they have enough resources to provide not only the necessities but also the luxuries, like vacations and trips to museums, piano lessons, soccer clubs, and on and on. Other students come from homes and communities that may be rich with love and care but where economic resources are scarce. Families have to work harder just to make ends meet, and students have to work harder in school to make up for the opportunities they are not afforded (McKenzie et al., 2020). This reality unravels the idea of meritocracy that all students start on equal ground and that those who excel do so on their own through hard work and effort, ignoring the advantages they have been given.

Topics such as the above are the grist of traditional critical theory, as it "tends to focus on the analysis of social class" (Merriam & Tisdell, 2016, p. 60) and the economic conditions that create it. It "points to holistic, rather than piecemeal, solutions to educational problems like low achievement. Holistic theory provides schema for action and social change that address the entire nexus of relevant issues or problems" (Anyon, 2009, p. 15). In line with Marx's analytic principles and goals, it is participatory, does not accept the status quo, and aims to critique, expose, and change things for the better.

We offer here a limited discussion of selected theorists—Marxist, neo-Marxist, and post-Marxist—who influenced traditional critical theory in education and some of the concepts they coined and/or advanced. For a deeper understanding, we suggest you turn to the primary sources. Beyond the primary sources, we draw here from the work of Isaac Gottesman (2016), an educational historian, who provided an account of the different critical turns in educational studies. Like everything in history, there is no clear linear path; there are twists and turns, and the story itself depends on the teller. And so it is with the history of traditional critical theory.

NOTABLE CRITICAL THEORISTS AND THEIR CONCEPTS

Paulo Freire

Concepts:

> praxis
> critical pedagogy
> banking model of schooling
> *conscientização*

Paulo Freire's seminal work *Pedagogy of the Oppressed* was published in 1970 and was well received but did not significantly influence U.S. education scholarship until the mid-1980s. This, according to Gottesman (2016), was because (a) Freire's work focused on adult literacy in postcolonial contexts, and the United States was focused on K–12 education; (b) Freire promoted revolutionary change, whereas U.S. scholars in the conservative Reagan era abandoned notions of revolution and radical reconstruction and advocated for structural reform; and (c) Freire assumed all knew and accepted the "unjust social order" and therefore would support movements to overturn it. The U.S. scholars knew that many were blind to the injustices in the United States and therefore pushed for "the development of nuanced descriptive and explanatory social theory" (2016, p. 25); in other words, theory that would unmask the injustices.

Freire (1970/2002) was a Marxist and embraced the goals of change, liberation, and revolution. According to him, "Liberation is a *praxis* [emphasis added]: the action and reflection of men and women upon their world in order to transform it" (p. 79). Freire was also a teacher, and many attribute the term *critical pedagogy* to him, although he never used it. Critical pedagogy encourages learners, adult and young, to critically examine the social, political, and economic structures that maintain the status quo and create inequity and oppression. According to Giroux (2010),

> Critical pedagogy opens up a space where students should be able to come to terms with their own power as critically engaged citizens; it provides a sphere where the unconditional freedom to question and assert is central to the purpose of public schooling and higher education, if not democracy itself. (p. 717)

Freire may not have introduced critical pedagogy, but he did introduce the concepts of the *banking model of schooling* and *conscientização*. Freire (1970/2002) saw schooling as a didactic or narrative process, with the teacher as the narrator and the students as "listening objects," thus becoming

> receptacles to be filled. Education thus becomes an act of depositing, in which the students are the depositories and the teacher is the depositor . . . In the banking concept of education, knowledge is a gift bestowed by those who consider themselves knowledgeable upon those whom they consider to know nothing . . . The more completely they accept the passive role imposed on them, the more they tend simply to adapt to the world as it is and to the fragmented view of reality deposited in them. (pp. 71–73)

Given Freire's critique of the banking model of schooling, the goal of his literacy project, then, was to develop *conscientização*, which he defined as "learning to perceive social, political, and economic contradictions, and to take action against the oppressive elements of reality" (p. 36, footnote 1).

Bowles and Gintis

Concept:

correspondence theory of schooling

In between the time that Freire wrote *Pedagogy of the Oppressed* in 1970 and when it drew the attention of social and educational scholars, others advanced traditional critical theory, or what is most often now called critical pedagogy when applied to education. For example, in 1976 the economists Bowles and Gintis published *Schooling in Capitalist America*, where they proposed their *correspondence theory of schooling*, a social reproduction theory (Bourassa, 2019; Giroux, 1980) that posits a direct correlation exists between the ways schools function and the ways the workplace functions. Schools, then, are teaching students, explicitly or implicitly, how to be the workers the society needs while maintaining the social order:

> The educational system helps integrate youth into the economic system, we believe, through a structural correspondence between its social relations and those of production. The structure of social relations in education not only inures the student to the discipline of the work place, but develops the types of personal demeanor, modes of self-presentation, self-image, and social-class identifications which are the crucial ingredients of job adequacy. Specifically, the social relationships of education—the relationships between administrators and teachers, teachers and students, students and students, and students and their work—replicate the hierarchical division of labor . . . By attuning young people to a set of social relationships similar to those of the work place, schooling attempts to gear the development of personal needs to its requirements. (Bowles & Gintis, 1976, p. 131)

While Bowles and Gintis's work was seen by some as "an extraordinary and ambitious endeavor to penetrate and interconnect history, political economy, education, social theory, and political strategy" (Hogan as quoted in Gottesman, 2016, p. 46), they were, according to Apple, Giroux, and others, "scholars to move past instead of scholars to build off of" (Gottesman, 2016, p. 48). Thus, there was a turn to

> a cultural Marxist lens [also described as neo-Marxist] that looked at the ideological structure [thought/belief systems] and content [curriculum] of schooling as opposed to the political economic Marxist lens that theorized capital and assessed quantifiable inputs and outcomes of schooling's reproductive tendencies. (p. 47)

Michael Apple

Concepts:

> hidden curriculum
> ideology
> hegemony

One of the key figures in this turn toward cultural or neo-Marxism was Michael Apple. He is often credited with coining the term *hidden curriculum*, but it was actually Philip Jackson who coined the term in 1968 in his book *Life in Classrooms*. In this work, Jackson wrote of two curricula that are taught in schools: the official academic curriculum, and the hidden curriculum that is "the norms and values that are implicitly, but effectively, taught" and that demand adherence to a set of acceptable behaviors (Apple, 1971, p. 27).

Apple (1971) expanded the definition of hidden curriculum in his article "The Hidden Curriculum and the Nature of Conflict" to address not just the norms and values that are tacitly taught that normalize behaviors but also the curriculum that was being taught. In the opening paragraph of this work, he wrote,

> there has been, so far, little examination of how the treatment of conflict in the school curriculum can lead to political quiescence and the acceptance by students of a perspective on social and intellectual conflict that acts to maintain the existing distribution of power and rationality in a society. (p. 27)

He gave as an example the social studies curriculum:

> The perspective found in schools leans heavily upon how all elements of a society, from the postman and fireman in first grade to the partial institutions in civics courses in high school, are linked to each other in a functional relationship, each contributing to ongoing maintenance of society. Internal dissension and conflict in a society are viewed as inherently antithetical to the smooth functioning of the social order . . . More often than not, a social reality is pictured that tacitly accepts "happy cooperation" as the normal if not the best way of life. (p. 33)

This skewed view of the nature and benefits of conflict promotes acceptance of the current norms and social institutions and does not allow for "individuals and groups to be innovative and creative in bringing about [needed] changes in institutional activities" (Apple, 1971, p. 35). Apple cautioned that if educators are not aware of these assumptions, they "run the very risk of continuing to let values work through them" (p. 39).

In addition to the hidden curriculum, two other concepts that Apple advanced in his earliest works were *ideology* and *hegemony*. All three concepts were focused on in his text *Ideology and Curriculum*, published in 1979. In the chapter "The Hidden Curriculum," Apple used "Gramsci's idea of hegemony" as "a conceptual apparatus to structurally locate struggles over the curriculum in a broader social landscape of ideological struggle" (Gottesman, 2016, p. 68). Gramsci's notion of hegemony or cultural hegemony is that the ruling class uses cultural institutions like schools to advance an ideology that is taken for granted and not resisted. In other words, it is not the case of rule by force but rather rule by ideas. In a review of *Ideology and Curriculum*, Henry Giroux wrote, "in brief, the theoretical basis of Apple's critique begins with the notion that domination does not proceed through the traditional use of force; instead, it has a new form, and that form is predominantly ideological" (1979a, p. 90).

Apple's thinking continued to develop, and in *Education and Power* (1982) he offered a critique of his previous work:

> It saw schools and especially the hidden curriculum, as successfully corresponding to the ideological needs of capital; we just needed to see how it was really accomplished. What was now more obviously missing in my formulations at this time was an analysis that focused on contradictions, conflicts, mediations and especially resistances, as well as reproduction. (Apple as quoted in Gottesman, 2016, p. 70)

His thinking about the relationship between schools and society has continued to evolve. His most current works address developing "critically democratic education," as well as critical citizens and teachers, and takes on "neoliberals, neoconservatives, authoritarian populist religious movements and new managerial regimes of authority" (Apple, 2018, p. 4).

Henry Giroux

Concepts:

> critical pedagogy
> theory of resistance

We now turn to Giroux and move into the 1980s and 1990s. Although many credit Freire with the term *critical pedagogy*, Gottesman (2016) contends that it should actually be credited to Giroux and emerged in his work in the 1970s and 1980s. Although Freire had the greatest influence on Giroux's work, Giroux (1979b) found problems applying Freire's postcolonial orientation to the United States: "Freire's pedagogy has been developed and used in Third World countries that bear little resemblance to the advanced industrial countries of the West" (p. 258).

As discussed previously, Freire accepted that there was dominance and oppression in the "Third World" nations and developed his approach accordingly, whereas Giroux (1979b) pointed out that in North America most Americans did not believe there was domination: "The very fact of domination has to be proven to most Americans. In North America technology and science have been developed so as to create immeasurably greater conditions for the administration and manipulation of individuals" (p. 267). Due to the significant contextual differences between the United States and the Third World countries of Freire's work, there was a need to develop a critical theory of education, a "'radical pedagogy,' that would specifically address the complex relationship between structure and agency within the United States" (Gottesman, 2016, p. 79). Giroux, therefore, set out to develop "theoretical tools capable of illuminating the context of schooling in America" (Gottesman, 2016, p. 79).

In his efforts to develop these tools, Giroux (1983) in "Theories of Reproduction and Resistance in the New Sociology of Education: A Critical

Analysis" first analyzed and critiqued the theories associated with the concepts of reproduction and resistance as they applied to schooling. His critique of the reproduction theories was that "by downplaying the importance of human agency and the notion of resistance, reproduction theories offer little hope for challenging and changing the repressive features of schooling" (p. 259). The reproduction theories included the economic-reproductive model associated with Bowles and Gintis, the cultural-reproduction model associated with Bourdieu and Passeron (1977), and the hegemonic-state reproductive model associated with the works, for example, of Roger Dale (1982), Martin Carnoy (1982), and Michael Apple (1971).

Resistance theories were a response to the theories of reproduction. Giroux (1983) provided the rationale for this response:

> Beneath a discourse primarily concerned with the notions of domination, class conflict, and hegemony, there has been a structured silence regarding how teachers, students, and others live out their daily lives in school. Consequently, there has been an overemphasis on how structural determinants [the reproduction theories] promote economic and cultural inequality and an underemphasis on how human agency accommodates, mediates, and resists the logic of capital and its dominating social practices. (p. 282)

Resistance theories, in contrast to reproduction theories, represent "a significant critique of school as an institution and points to social activities and practices whose meanings are ultimately political and cultural" (Giroux, 1983, p. 282).

Giroux did not categorize the resistance theories as he did the reproduction theories, but rather referred us to neo-Marxist social ethnographic studies that employ resistance theories. Ethnographic studies are qualitative firsthand field studies that focus on culture, "the beliefs, values, and attitudes that structure the behavior patterns of a specific group of people" (Merriam & Tisdell, 2016, p. 29). These studies included the work of Paul Willis's *Learning to Labor*, Harry Wolcott's *The Man in the Principal's Office*, Angela McRobbie and Trisha McCabe's *Feminism for Girls*, and Stephen Ball's *Beachside Comprehensive: A Case Study of Secondary Schooling*.

Giroux (1983) offered four criticisms of these works. First, he said that although the studies represent resistance by subordinate groups,

> what is missing . . . are analyses of those historically and culturally mediated factors that produce a range of oppositional behaviors, some of which constitute resistance and some of which do not. Simply put, not all oppositional behavior has "radical significance," nor is all oppositional behavior a clear-cut response to domination. (p. 285)

Second, race and gender were rarely taken into account. Third, these theories focused "primarily on overt acts of rebellious student behavior" and overlooked the less obvious forms of resistance, thus "limiting their analysis" (p. 287). And fourth, "they have not given enough attention to the issue of how domination reaches into the structure of personality itself. . . . [Ignored is] the question of needs and desires in favor of issues that center around ideology and consciousness" (p. 288). In other words, for Giroux these works were descriptive but lacked the needed theoretical nuance.

Subsequently, Giroux (1983) proposed his own *theory of resistance*, which is too involved to discuss here but is worthy of reading. The essence is captured in his concluding remarks:

> In short, the bases for a new radical pedagogy must be drawn from a theoretically sophisticated understanding of how power, resistance, and human agency can become central elements in the struggle for critical thinking and learning. Schools will not change society, but we can create in them pockets of resistance that provide pedagogical models for new forms of learning and social relations—forms which can be used in other spheres more directly involved in the struggle for a new morality and view of social justice. (p. 292)

In his later works, Giroux took on a post-Marxist stance and shifted "his work away from a focus on educational institutions and teachers to a broader engagement with social policies and the influence of media on youth . . . in what has become known as a 'cultural turn'" (Besley, 2012, p. 595).

As is apparent in this discussion of traditional critical theory/critical pedagogy, there are missing voices, specifically women and scholars of color. Late in the 1980s, feminist scholars challenged critical pedagogy. The most well-known came from Elizabeth Ellsworth, who, after teaching a university course that did not go well and was grounded in critical pedagogy literature, wrote the essay "Why Doesn't This Feel Empowering? Working Through the Repressive Myths of Critical Pedagogy." Ellsworth (1989) argued that "key assumptions, goals, and pedagogical practice fundamental to the literature on critical pedagogy—namely, 'empowerment,' 'student voice,' 'dialogue,' and even the term 'critical'—are repressive myths that perpetuate domination" (p. 298). The essay was criticized by many, including Henry Giroux. However, she was not alone in her critique of critical pedagogy. Feminists, including Kathleen Weiler, Patti Lather, Deborah Britzman, among others, joined in. In Chapter 6, we will engage in a more in-depth discussion of feminist scholars' contributions to critical research in education.

RESEARCH COMPONENTS OF EXAMPLE ARTICLE

Most of the literature on traditional critical theory or critical pedagogy is theoretical, such as the majority of the works described above. There are few published articles, particularly in the last few decades, describing empirical

research conducted in schools. In fact, one of the cri[...]
scholars of critical pedagogy was that they needed to[...]
ply their theories (McKenzie & Scheurich, 2004; McN[...]

Additionally, critical educational studies has taken [...]
of the work now addresses issues of race, gender, ethnici[...]
have historically been marginalized. These will be addre[...]
follow. In each chapter, we provide illustrations from en[...]
research components associated with the research approach[...]
traditional critical theory/critical pedagogy, we use the wc[...] [...]ark-
house, an associate professor in the Department of Teachi[...]g and Learning at
Virginia Commonwealth University. We draw from both her dissertation, *Critical
Pedagogy in US History Classrooms: Conscientization and Contradictory
Consciousness* (2016), and her article "Pedagogies of Naming, Questioning,
and Demystification: A Study of Two Critical U.S. History Classrooms" (2018),
which was taken from her dissertation. Parkhouse conducted a study of two
11th-grade history classrooms in different schools. She studied "various approaches to critical pedagogy" and "by integrating observational data with
teacher and student interviews to illuminate how the teachers and students together resist traditional forms of schooling in the US" (2016, p. iii).

Statement of the Problem, Purpose, and Research Question

Parkhouse (2018) agreed that much of the literature on critical pedagogy is theoretical. Drawing from Duncan-Andrade and Morrell (2018), she stated,

> while this body of work has illuminated innumerable issues in education, teachers
> inspired by the idea of emancipatory education have little guidance on how the
> theory speaks to their daily instruction. . . . In addition, "the ways in which critical
> practice is produced in real schools are much more complex than the ways that
> critical theories of schooling are elaborated in the academy" (Niesz, 2006, p. 343).
> (p. 281)

The studies that have been done focus on specific projects, or specific student
groups, "rather than observations in classrooms or interviews with students"
(p. 281). Some research has been done in English classes, but few have focused
on the social studies. Therefore, Parkhouse identified the research problem,
the gap in the literature, saying, "research is needed, therefore, on the various
forms critical pedagogies may take within history classrooms, as well as their
impact on students" (2018, p. 283). Her purpose, then, was to fill the gap in
the literature and examine the forms critical pedagogies can take in history
classes and how they affect the students. And her research question was "What
general approaches and specific practices do two critical U.S. History teachers
use to help their students develop critical consciousness of social realities?"
(p. 283).

Framework

In her dissertation, Parkhouse (2016) explained that she originally planned to use critical pedagogy as articulated by Freire and postcolonial theory as her theoretical frame. However, as is often the case, once she began conducting her research, she needed to change her approach. Lather (1986) cautions that "data must be allowed to generate propositions in a dialectical manner that permits use of a priori theoretical frameworks, but which keeps a particular framework from becoming the container into which the data must be poured" (p. 267). Thus, heeding Lather's advice, Parkhouse noted that

> although postcolonial theory could help illuminate the ways in which students' identities—particularly immigrant students subject to neocolonialism and Latin@ and Black students subject to internal colonialism (Maseman, 2013)—are constructed and deconstructed by discourses (Smith & Riley, 2009), it was the class's commonly held perceptions of social issues such as race and gender, rather than constructions of individual identities, that more compellingly answered the question of how students developed critical consciousness. Secondly, although critical pedagogy remained a central lens for my interpretations, these commonly held perceptions required some additional theoretical constructs for analysis. Such constructs included *false consciousness, contradictory consciousness,* and *mystification,* among others, which led me to revise my theoretical framework to expand upon Post-Marxist *critical theory,* which is a school of thought from which critical pedagogy emerged. (p. 5)

Thus, for Parkhouse, traditional critical theory proved to be the better theoretical framework for her dissertation research than the descendants of traditional critical theory (postcolonial theory and critical pedagogy) that she had envisioned at the proposal stage. However, in the article published from her dissertation, "Pedagogies of Naming, Questioning, and Demystification: A Study of Two Critical U.S. History Classrooms," the analytical frame from which she analyzed her data was predominantly critical pedagogy.

Methodology and Methods

Postcritical ethnography was the methodology Parkhouse used for her study of "teaching practices that [were] grounded in critical pedagogy" (2016, p. 35). She explained that

> critical pedagogy stems from critical theory, and critical ethnography has been described as "critical theory in action" (Noblit, Flores & Murillo, 2004, p. 15). In other words, critical ethnography includes research practices that are grounded in the underlying tenets of critical theory. In addition, critical pedagogues acknowledge the inherently political nature of teaching (Kincheloe, 2008), and critical ethnographers acknowledge the inherently political nature of research (Adkins &

Gunzenhauser, 1999). From the perspective of critical pedagogy, thematic investigation and education should be dialogic, reflexive, and done *with* others, rather than *to* or *for* them. This aligns well with the suggestions of postcritical ethnographers that our research ought to be tempered through self-reflexivity and non-exploitation (Gunzenhauser, 2004). Thus, postcritical ethnography complements both critical theory and critical pedagogy in that it acknowledges participants as co-constructers of knowledge and commits to a critique of "self, interpretation, and representation (Anders, 2012, p. 100)." (p. 36)

Since this was qualitative research, Parkhouse's methods consisted of purposeful sampling. Parkhouse (2018) stated that she selected "two high school U.S. History teachers that I knew from our prior work together had a critical orientation and were interested in co-investigating this research question with me" (p. 283). Her data sources included classroom observations and student and teacher interviews. Acknowledging students and teachers as co-constructers of knowledge, Parkhouse interviewed students, asking their opinions of the United States and "whether their U.S. History class has had any influence on their opinions" (p. 286), specifically related to issues of power, inequity, and agency. She asked teachers about their teaching goals, whether they taught students such that they would develop a critical consciousness, and if there were risks in teaching about "power imbalances or injustices" (p. 315). She also asked the teachers whether they saw evidence of students developing critical awareness. In a second interview with teachers, she asked them to read the students' interview transcripts, which were anonymous, and reflect on whether their goal to help the students develop a critical consciousness was met, and if not, to identify the constraints that kept them from meeting the goal.

Analysis and Results/Findings

Consistent with postcritical ethnography, Parkhouse (2018) focused on local contexts, the history classes, and local knowledge (the teachers and students) and "incorporated the teachers' analyses of their own pedagogies and student responses," involving them as co-constructors of knowledge (p. 286). Parkhouse (2016) also spoke to her positionality and self-reflexivity:

> As highlighted by Noblit, Flores, and Murillo (2004), "postcritical ethnographies require the interrogation of the power and politics of the critic himself/herself as well as in the social scene studied" (p. 19). Therefore, I interrogated how my background, my experiences as a history teacher, my privileged position as a researcher, and my activist stance influenced and limited my understanding (Noblit, 1999). (p. 39)

The findings were thematized and described the different critical pedagogies employed by the two teachers. Ms. Ray employed "a pedagogy of naming": "Ms. Ray felt it was important that she explicitly name racism and other injustices so that students would know they could do so without fear that she may find the issue too controversial to discuss in class" (2018, p. 289). She also named "other forms of oppression and their intersections," like sexism, heterosexism, and others (2016, p. 290). "In addition to modeling that it was okay and even important to call an action or perspective racist, sexist, or otherwise oppressive, Ms. Ray also designed opportunities for students to practice naming oppression" (2018, p. 291). Lastly, and a tenet of all critical theories, she involved the students in praxis by having them name "forms of action," that encourage "justice-oriented political action" (2016, p. 291).

Ms. Bowling applied "a pedagogy of questioning":

> Much like Ms. Ray, Ms. Bowling described her aim as a U.S. History teacher as trying to get students to think "critically about . . . how past events have influenced future events, but also [to] realize that they have the power to change the future." (Parkhouse, 2018, p. 294)

She encouraged students to critically examine their own opinions, "particularly those shaped more by cultural norms or ideologies than critical considerations" (p. 295). They also questioned the dominant ideologies and narratives of the United States and the responsibility they have to engage in political action—for example, "staying informed, voting, and writing representatives" (p. 298). Both teachers employed "pedagogies of demystification," like critical analysis of media messaging and stereotyping.

Discussion and Recommendations

In answering her research question, "What general approaches and specific practices do two critical U.S. History teachers use to help their students develop critical consciousness of social realities?," Parkhouse (2018) found that although both teachers, Ms. Ray and Ms. Bowling, were critical in their orientation to teaching and employed critical pedagogy, there were areas in which they converged and areas in which they diverged. The teachers converged on their *aims* and their *attention to students' immediate realities*. The aims they shared were consistent with critical pedagogy. They wanted their students to

> gain a complex understanding of history, appreciation for multiple perspectives, and sense of the connection of events and trends across time . . . to apply all of those skills as they come to understand the roots of current injustices and recognize their capacity to effect change. (p. 301)

Regarding attention to students' immediate realities, both teachers centered the students, instead of the curriculum. That did not mean they did not address the required curriculum, "but rather [treated] it as one of many resources available for understanding contemporary conditions" (p. 302).

The areas in which the teachers diverged were "*direct versus indirect approaches to critical consciousness*" (p. 303) and "*promoting activism, or not*" (p. 305), both of which, again, are tenets of critical pedagogy. Ms. Ray used the direct approach to raise students' critical consciousness: "She noticed that her students hesitated to discuss racism, so she prioritized candid conversations about race in order to normalize this discourse and prepare students for challenging racism outside of the classroom" (p. 303). Ms. Bowling, however, used the indirect approach: "She provided opportunities for students to question and learn from each other, and in doing so, perhaps reconsider their preconceived notions" (p. 304).

With regard to *promoting activism, or not*, "Ms. Ray was more explicit in her discussions of oppression than Ms. Bowling was, but Ms. Bowling was more explicit in her calls to action" (p. 305). Freire considered critical reflection a type of action, so "students in both classrooms in this way were engaged in action in the forms of naming injustices, questioning common sense ways of thinking," and revealing the injustices in the world (p. 305).

Parkhouse (2018) acknowledged that the ways in which teachers incorporate critical pedagogy into their practice to raise students' consciousness are dependent on the context of their classrooms and communities. In other words, they would be different for each teacher. Citing Darder, Parkhouse reminded us that "there does not exist a formula or homogenous representation for the universal implementation of any form of critical pedagogy (Darder et al., 2009, p. 9)" (p. 303).

Addressing recommendations, Parkhouse did not include any in her 2018 article, but she did include an entire table of recommendations in her dissertation. For example, in the table she first identified the "bottlenecks" that prevent students from developing a critical consciousness, for example, "hesitancy to name racism." Second, she provided an example of hesitancy to name racism—"substituting 'some people' for 'people of color.'" Third, she gave the suggested "critical pedagogy method" for addressing the bottleneck (hesitancy to name racism), which was to "explain that it is not impolite or offensive to call something racist, particularly because racism is a structural and institutionalized issue, not just a problem within individuals" (2016, p. 190).

CONCLUSION

Traditional critical theory has taken several turns over the last few decades from Marxism, to neo-Marxism, to post-Marxism. It has addressed the economic theories of Marx; the critical pedagogy of Freire and Giroux; the correspondence theory of Bowles and Gintis; the hidden curriculum, ideology and hegemony of Apple; and the resistance theory of Giroux. What has remained the same, however, is the commitment to reject the status quo and to critique, expose, and change things for the better. Our coverage of these topics in this chapter is meant to be illustrative rather than exhaustive. There are other theorists who contributed to this literature, and there are other approaches to actually conducting the work. In Parkhouse's work we have provided one example of research that exemplifies these commitments.

INTERSECTIONAL AND IDENTITY-BASED CRITICAL RESEARCH IN EDUCATION

CHAPTER 4

Critical Race Theory

This chapter diverges from the others in Part II in that it is not focused on education, specifically, but rather on the legal system, from which critical race theory (CRT) emerged. It is most closely aligned to the discussion of critical theory in Chapter 1. Therefore, we do not include an example of an empirical research article to demonstrate the research components of CRT. We do, however, devote the next chapter to CRT in education and include an explanation of research components using a sample CRT research article.

We begin this chapter with a definition of CRT and a brief history of its emergence. Next, we discuss three of the most prominent CRT theorists and their concepts and end with a list of the essential elements of CRT in general. Here again in this chapter, we offer hors d'oeuvres rather than the main dish and suggest you read the primary sources, specifically *Critical Race Theory* (1995) edited by Kimberlé Crenshaw, Neil Gotanda, Gary Peller, and Kendall Thomas. We draw significantly from this text as it is a collection of the key writings, published previously in the foremost journals by the predominant scholars of the 1970s–1990s, that led to the critical race theory movement.

THE EMERGENCE OF CRITICAL RACE THEORY

Critical race theory is referred to as both a theoretical framework and an intellectual movement. It emerged in the 1980s out of a critique of the U.S. legal system, predominantly by legal scholars of color "whose work challeng[ed] the ways in which race and racial power are constructed and represented in American legal culture and, more generally, in American society as a whole" (Crenshaw et al., 1995, p. xiii).

CRT began with critique of the liberal ideology of the civil rights movement of the 1950s and 1960s. That critique argued that "civil rights lawyers and other activists too greatly emphasized court-focused strategies aimed at achieving what would turn out to be pyrrhic 'civil' rights victories—i.e., gains solely in 'formal' equality in requirements enshrined in law as to how the state *should* [emphasis added] treat its citizens" (Carle, S., 2009, p. 1479). In other words, the battle for civil rights might have been won in the courts, but the costs were too great and had deleterious long-term effects on the people it was trying to help. There is the law, seen as sacrosanct, guided by blind justice and equality under the law, but then there is the actual lived experiences of those affected by the law.

In the 1970s and early to mid 1980s there were three legal scholars who, with others, became originators of the Critical Race Movement: Derrick Bell, Richard Delgado, and Kimberlé Crenshaw (Crenshaw et al., 1995). We will focus primarily on these "race crits," as they were called, during the genesis of CRT. Other legal scholars, however, were equally instrumental in the movement. These include Mari Matsuda, Kendall Thomas, Linda Greene, Neil Gotanda, Alan Freeman, Cheryl Harris, Charles Lawrence, and Patricia Williams.

Bell, Delgado, and Crenshaw, although respectful of the accomplishments of the civil rights movement, critiqued its liberal ideology. They contended that although the movement addressed "formal equality," such as the "prohibition against explicit racial exclusion, like 'whites only' signs" (Crenshaw et al., 1995, p. xiv), it did not address the systemic social practices that perpetuated injustice. Therefore, it put these social practices "beyond the scope of critical examination or legal remediation" (p. xv). Crenshaw referred to Whites-only restrooms, drinking fountains, cemeteries, and so forth as symbolic subordination, the "formal denial of social and political equality to all blacks, regardless of their accomplishments" (Crenshaw, 1988/1995, p. 114). She juxtaposed this to material subordination: "the ways that discrimination and exclusion economically subordinated blacks to whites and subordinated the life chances of blacks to those of whites on almost every level" (p. 114), that is, discrimination that affected the material conditions of Black lives. In other words, should the law merely protect individual rights, or should it promote them? There is a difference between legally protecting everyone's right to own a home and ensuring nondiscriminatory fair housing practices—one protects and one promotes.

Furthermore, racism during the civil rights era was seen as acts of prejudice and discrimination by individual actors. Alan Freeman (1978/1995) explained this as the "perpetrator perspective" that

> sees racial discrimination not as conditions but as actions, or series of actions, inflicted on the victim by the perpetrator. The focus is more on what particular perpetrators have done or are doing to some victims than on the overall life situation of the victim class. (p. 29)

This allows society at large, and the legal system, to "acknowledge the fact of racism and, simultaneously, to insist on its irregular occurrence and limited significance" (Crenshaw et al., 1995, p. xiv) and precludes a deeper analysis of the ways in which the social structures of the United States privileges Whites and marginalizes "others." Hence, protection from an individual perpetrator can be enforced, but this does not afford an examination of the structures that victimize a whole class of people.

Bell, Delgado, and Crenshaw also critiqued the efforts of the scholars within critical legal studies (CLS), called simply the "crits." These were a group of professors, students, and lawyers, mainly White, who in the late 1970s challenged the legal system that they believed "helped create, support, and legitimate America's present class structure" (Crenshaw, 1988/1995, p. 108). The CLS crits believed "that the law contains deep conflicts; that the legal system is frequently unjust; that the wealthy are more likely to receive justice than the poor; [and] that legal education is imperfect" (Ewald, 1988, p. 670). Like Bell, Delgado, and Crenshaw, the CLS crits also critiqued the antidiscrimination stance of the civil rights movement that upheld a legal rights discourse that they argued was a color-blind approach that did not promote action. In other words, equal treatment under the law does not ensure equal results—to believe that it does ignores history. The goal of the CLS crits was to expose "the way in which legal ideology has helped to create, support, and legitimate America's present class structure" (Crenshaw, 1988/1995, p. 110).

Crenshaw, along with other race crits, attended the CLS conferences of the late 1970s and were in agreement with the CLS crits' contention that "the law was neither apolitical, neutral, nor determinate" (Crenshaw et al., 1995, p. xxii). The race crits did, however, disagree with the CLS crits on several other issues. First, the race crits disagreed with the omission of race and racial power in the CLS crits' legal analysis and agenda, and with the CLS crits' lack of engagement with the lived experiences of people of color. And second, the race crits disagreed with the CLS crits' critique of rights under the law, a critique of the notion that because all are seen as equal under the law that there can be no inequality. According to Crenshaw et al. (1995),

> crits of color [race crits] agreed to varying degrees with some dimensions of the [rights] critique—for instance, that rights discourse was indeterminate. Yet [they] sharply differed with [CLS crits] over the normative implications of this observation. To the emerging race crits, rights discourse held a social and transformative value in the context of racial subordination that transcended the narrower question of whether reliance on rights could alone bring about any determinate results. Race crits realized that the very notion of a subordinate people exercising rights was an important dimension of Black empowerment during the civil rights movement, significant not simply because of the occasional legal victories that were garnered, but because of the transformative dimension of African-Americans re-imagining themselves as full, rights-bearing citizens within the American political imagination. (pp. xxiii-xxiv)

These disagreements moved Crenshaw (1988/1995) to conclude that

> for blacks the task at hand [was] to devise ways to wage ideological and political struggle while minimizing the costs of engaging in an inherently legitimating discourse. A clearer understanding of the space we occupy in the American political consciousness is a necessary prerequisite to the development of pragmatic strategies for political and economic survival . . . we must create conditions for the maintenance of a distinct political thought that is informed by the actual conditions of black people. Unlike the civil rights movement [and the CLS crits' agenda], this new approach should not be defined and thereby limited by the possibilities of

dominant political discourse; rather, it should maintain a distinctly progressive outlook that focuses on the needs of the African-American community. (p. 119)

To this end, Crenshaw, along with other race crits, held a retreat and asked themselves the following: "We had launched simultaneous critiques—of CLS, on the one hand, and of liberal race theory on the other; in doing so, were we actually setting forth something that could be fashioned into a theory in its own right?" (Crenshaw, 2002, p. 1360). They recalled that Crenshaw (2002)

> began to scribble down words associated with our objectives, identities, and perspectives, drawing arrows and boxes around them to capture various aspects of who "we" were and what we were doing. The list included: progressive/critical, CLS, race, civil rights, racism, law, jurisprudence, theory, doctrine, and so on. Mixing them up and throwing them together in various combinations, one proposed combination came together in a way that seemed to capture the possibility we were aiming to create. Sometime toward the end of the interminable winter of 1989, we settled on what seemed to be the most telling marker for this peculiar subject. We would signify the specific political and intellectual location of the project through "*critical*," the substantive focus through "*race*," and the desire to develop a coherent account of race and law through the term "*theory*" [emphasis added] . . . So the name critical race theory, now used as interchangeable for race scholarship as Kleenex is used for tissue, was basically made up, fused together to mark a possibility. (pp. 1360–1361)

NOTABLE CRITICAL RACE THEORISTS AND THEIR CONCEPTS

Derrick Bell

Concepts:

> interest convergence
> constitutional contradictions
> price of racial remedies

Stepping back to 1954, the *Brown v. Board of Education* decision by the U.S. Supreme Court made racial segregation illegal in schools, citing it as a violation of the equal protection clause of the 14th Amendment of the Constitution. This ruling set legal precedent for overturning segregation in other facilities as well. Resistance to the decision ignited the civil rights movement and ultimately led to the passage of the Civil Rights Act of 1964, the Voting Rights Act of 1965, and the Fair Housing Act of 1968.

However, the *Brown* ruling that led to efforts to integrate the schools was not without controversy. Derrick Bell, the first African American tenured professor at Harvard, criticized the "liberal ideology of the mainstream civil rights movement" (Crenshaw et al., 1995, p. 2) and pointed to the effects of integration on the Black community. He contended that what Black communities wanted was not necessarily to have their children educated with White students but rather to have schools in their communities that had, for example, facilities and resources comparable to the White schools so that they could provide their children a high-quality education. Bell's contention was that the liberal well-meaning White attorneys who were dedicated to integration did not understand and represent the desires of the communities they represented. Their commitment to integration blinded them to the real issues of the Black communities they were engaged to serve. To illustrate, in 1975 a coalition of Black community groups in Boston wrote in response to the Boston School Committee desegregation plan:

> In the name of equity, we . . . seek dramatic improvement in the quality of the education available to our children. Any steps to achieve desegregation must be reviewed in light of the black community's interest in improved pupil performance as the primary characteristic of educational equity. We define educational equity as the absence of discriminatory pupil placement and improved performance for all children who have been the objects of discrimination. We think it neither necessary, nor proper to endure the dislocations of desegregation without reasonable assurances that our children will instructionally profit. (Bell, 1975/1995, p. 5)

Bell contended that beyond the commitment that Whites held to integration as a moral obligation to eliminate racial inequality, there were three practical considerations as well that benefited White policymakers who could see the political benefits of *Brown* both at home and abroad. To illustrate the first, Ruth Bader Ginsberg, in a 2004 speech titled *Brown v. Board of Education in International Context* before the Columbia University School of Law, cited an amicus brief filed in the *Brown* case for the United States, where the Attorney General put forth that

> the existence of discrimination against minority groups in the United States has an adverse effect upon our relations with other countries. Racial discrimination furnishes grist for the Communist propaganda mills, and it raises doubts even among friendly nations as to the intensity of our devotion to the democratic faith. (para. 5)

Second, there were the Black veterans who fought and died in World War II who returned home to a still-unaccepting nation and faced discrimination and violence. This, too, soiled the United States's reputation abroad. And third, "there were whites who realized that the South could make the transition from a rural plantation society to the sunbelt with all its potential and profit only when it ended its struggle to remain divided by state-sponsored segregation" (Bell, 1975/1995, p. 23). Bell contended then that "the interest of blacks in achieving racial equality [would] be accommodated *only* when it converge[d] with the interests of whites" [emphasis added] (p. 22). He labeled this concept *interest convergence*.

Bell also wrote about *constitutional contradiction*, which he did cleverly in his 1989 book *And We Are Not Saved*. The book is 10 chronicles, metaphorical tales, in which the fictitious lead character, Geneva Crenshaw, who had been a civil rights lawyer at the NAACP Legal Defense Fund, has a nervous break-down and is institutionalized. During that time, she mentally "time-travels" and is confronted with situations that reveal the U.S. treatment of race within society and the law. She then discusses these issues with the book's narrator.

In the chapter "The Real Status of Blacks Today, the Chronicle of the Constitutional Contradiction," Geneva traveled to the Constitutional Convention of 1787. She introduced herself as a 21st-century woman, and it was apparent to the delegates that she was also a Black woman. This caused quite an uproar, and she was told to leave. Geneva was not deterred, and because she was also encased in a protective bubble that did not allow her to be harmed or removed, she began questioning and debating with the delegates. They were not pleased but did engage with her for a while. Geneva attempted to point out to the fram-ers the contradictions in the discussions about slavery leading up to the draft-ing of the Constitution. She invoked Thomas Jefferson, who along with most of the delegates to the Constitutional Convention was a slave holder, and the words of the Declaration of Independence—"We hold these truths to be self-evident, that all men are created equal, that they are endowed by their Creator with certain unalienable Rights, that among these are Life, Liberty and the pursuit of Happiness." In the end, however, the framers did not embrace the words of Jefferson and chose slavery, which they saw as property necessary to maintain the country's economy, over human rights.

In discussing her time travel, her visions, the narrator asked Geneva what she learned from her debate with the framers. She replied

> that they would not, or could not, take seriously themselves or their ideals. The men who drafted the Constitution, however gifted or remembered as great, were politicians, not so different from the politicians of our own time and like them, had to resolve by compromise conflicting interests in order to preserve both their fortunes and their new nation. What they saw as the requirements of that nation prevented them from sustaining their rhetoric about freedom and rights with constitutional provisions—and thus they infringed on the rights and freedom not only of the slaves, who then were one-fifth of the population, but, ultimately, of all American citizens. (Bell, 1989, p. 50)

Another concept Bell (1979) addressed is *the price of racial remedies* that parallels interest convergence. Whereas interest convergence contended that Whites are only willing to advance something that is in the interest of people of color when it also advances their own interests, the price of racial remedies focused on the costs, metaphorically, Whites might have to pay for racial rem-edies. In other words, Whites might espouse support for remedies to amend racial injustices until there are actually costs to themselves.

To illustrate, Bell used the *Regents of the University of California v. Bakke* case. In this case, UC Davis Medical School twice denied admission of Alan Bakke, a White California man, who charged that his grades and test scores exceeded those of the minority students who had been accepted into the school. The Medical School had a quota system that reserved 16 percent of its seats for minority applicants. Bakke further claimed that his denied admittance was reverse discrimination related to race and cited the Civil Rights Act of 1964. The case made it to the U.S. Supreme Court, where the justices were divided. The result was the Court ruled that the use of quotas was unconstitutional but that race could be used as a criterion for admissions (Britannica, n.d.).

The price of racial remedies is seen in other historical issues as well, such as school desegregation:

> When the school desegregation efforts moved North, the attitude toward the South changed from condemnation to complicity with Northerners rallying to preserve neighborhood assignment patterns, avoid busing, and maintain the "educational integrity" of white schools . . . whites do not oppose desegregation in the abstract. What they resist is the price of desegregation. They fear that *their* [emphasis added] children will be required to scuffle for an education in schools that for decades have been good enough only for blacks. (Bell, 1979, p. 11)

Other examples of the price of racial remedies include (a) suburban zoning designed to keep out low-income housing—in other words, the "not in my backyard" mentality and (b) proportionate racial representation in high school extracurricular activities, such as student councils, cheerleading squads, and any activity where there is a limited number of spaces and the presumption of entitlement. The price of racial remedies reminds us that society may concede "its guilt, but denies its liability" and resists "any policy that appears to require that whites pay or even risk paying for racial wrongs that they did not themselves commit" but for which they reap the benefits (Bell, 1979, p. 12).

Richard Delgado

Concepts:

> counterstory/counternarrative
> revisionist history
> structural determinism

Another legal scholar who is a forerunner of CRT is Richard Delgado. He began his career in the mid-1970s at the University of California, Los Angeles (UCLA), where he was advised by senior faculty to do mainstream legal scholarship and not to involve himself in civil rights or other "ethic studies" (Delgado, 1984/1995, p. 46). He followed this advice until he earned tenure and then turned to "civil rights law and scholarship" (p. 46). What he discovered was that most of the publications on civil rights were written by White, male professors, although there were many professors of color writing on these subjects. However, they were not getting published in the premier journals nor being cited by the White scholars; their voices were silenced from the field. In 1984 Delgado wrote "The Imperial Scholar: Reflections on a Review of Civil Rights Literature," a controversial piece that exposed the marginalizing of scholars of color. Ten years later he returned to this issue in "The Imperial Scholar Revisited: How to Marginalize Outsider Writing, Ten Years Later." In this article he discussed the changes in the civil rights literature and sought to answer the question, "What happens when a group of insurgent scholars gains admission, gets inside the door, earns the credibility and credentials that warrant consideration by mainstream scholars?" (1992, p. 1350). Here the outsiders he focused on were critical race theorists and radical feminists, two groups that were only emerging at the time of the original article.

In "Imperial Scholar Revisited," he first examined whether the original imperial scholars changed their citation practices that left out the scholars of color and then whether "the two insurgent groups [were] cited by mainstream scholars generally" (Delgado, 1992, p. 1352). He concluded that

> although critical, feminist, and minority writers are increasingly appearing in the pages of our top journals, they are still not being integrated fully or easily into the colloquies, exchanges, and dialogues of legal scholarship. Some of the resistance may be intentional, but I believe most of it results from quite ordinary forces: preference for the familiar, discomfort with impending change, and a near-universal disdain for an account or "story" that deviates too much from one upon which we have been relying to construct and order our social world. (p. 1372)

These deviation stories appear to draw from his concept of *counterstory*, or what is now usually called *counternarrative*, which he introduced in two previous articles: "When a Story Is Just a Story: Does Voice Really Matter?" (1990) and "Storytelling for Oppositionists and Others: A Plea for Narrative" (1989). According to Delgado (1989), "the stories or narratives told by the ingroup [the dominant group] remind it of its identity in relation to outgroups [the marginalized group], and provide it with a form of shared reality in which its own superior position is seen as natural" (p. 2412). These narratives endorse a mindset that the world is as it should be, with White males at the top and everyone else beneath them. Counternarratives are the stories the marginalized group uses to subvert the dominant group's reality. The importance of counternarratives for the marginalized group is that they create "bonds, represent cohesion, shared understandings, and meanings" (p. 2412).

Delgado advanced other concepts as well. In *Critical Race Theory: An Introduction,* Delgado and his coauthor, Jean Stefancic, (2001), discussed *revisionist history* and *structural determinism*, as well as concepts we have introduced previously. They defined revisionist history as a view of history that contests the mainstream one; specifically, in CRT it is a challenge to the White interpretation of history to reflect the perspective of people of color. Structural determinism is the "concept that a mode of thought or a widely shared practice determines significant social outcomes [often ones that are unjust], usually without our conscious knowledge" (Delgado & Stefancic, 2001, p. 185), and because we are unconscious of these injustices, we are ill-equipped to redress them.

Delgado and Stefancic (2001) provided examples to illustrate. First, a child given three crayons—red, blue, and yellow—believes these are the only colors available for doing art and that none others exist. The child is not conscious of any other alternative colors. Second, and more to the point here, is what they call "tools of thought and the dilemma of law reform" (p. 26). Legal research relies on previous case law, and these cases are found through legal indexing tools. However, what happens when a case requires innovation, "not the application of some preexisting rule or principle" (p. 26)? The law replicates itself with each case dependent on the ruling of previous cases, much like DNA. New and innovative ways of looking at legal issues may exist, like intersectionality (see the DeGraffenreid case in the next section), but these concepts may not be available in the legal indexing. These tools are not in the toolbox, just like the purple crayon was not available to the child who was a budding artist. "The official vocabulary of the law, the structure of the law, determines what can be *seen* or considered" (p. 27).

Kimberlé Crenshaw

Concept:

  intersectionality

Next, we move to Kimberlé Crenshaw, who currently is the most famous legal scholar associated with the critical race theory movement. She is Professor of Law at UCLA and Columbia Law School and is most noted for her involvement in the genesis of CRT and her concept of intersectionality. She is a public intellectual and is often sought out for interviews and media appearances, particularly now in a time of contentious debate over what CRT *is* and what its place should or should not be in current society, particularly schools. In an interview with the progressive weekly magazine *The Nation*, Crenshaw was asked, "What is Critical Race Theory? And why is this happening now?" (Wiener, 2021, para. 1). She responded by referring to her first article on CRT, "Race, Reform, and Retrenchment," that she wrote in 1988[1]:

> The basic point of that article was that wherever there is race reform, there's inevitably retrenchment, and sometimes the retrenchment can be more powerful than the reform itself. And some of what we are experiencing right now is exactly that. (para. 2)

When the reporter responded with "The warriors against CRT think the idea is that, 'By your race alone, you will be judged.' They don't seem to know about intersectionality" (para. 5). Crenshaw replied, not only do they not know about it, they don't want to know about it. They don't care about what the ideas are. They can take the name, fill it with meaning, and create this hysteria, and that can be a winning issue when they really don't have any other agendas to push. Obviously, they don't get that one of the main points of Critical Race Theory is that to understand racism in our history only as a matter of prejudice or bias—as a matter of individuals who are morally bankrupt—is not to understand the history of race in America. The whole point of Critical Race Theory was to repudiate the idea that we can talk about racism only as a quality of individuals rather than as a structured reality that's embedded in institutions. (Weiner, 2021, para. 6)

Not only is CRT being intentionally or unintentionally misinterpreted, so is the concept *intersectionality* that is associated with CRT. Crenshaw told Vox news that the definition of intersectionality, a concept she coined, is also misrepresented. "This is what happens when an idea travels beyond the context and the content" (Vox, 2019, para. 10). Intersectionality, like CRT, emerged from legal debate. However, the concept entered the mainstream when it was published in the *Oxford English Dictionary* in 2015 (Vox, 2019). Crenshaw, laughing, told Vox "the thing that's kind of ironic about intersectionality is that it had to leave town—the world of the law—in order to get famous" (para. 25). The interviewer noted that

she [Crenshaw] compared the experience of seeing other people talking about intersectionality to an "out-of-body experience . . . sometimes I've read things that say 'intersectionality, blah, blah, blah,' and then I'd wonder, 'Oh, I wonder whose intersectionality that is,' and then I'd see me cited, and I was like, 'I've never written that. I've never said that. That is just not how I think about intersectionality' . . . . What was puzzling is that usually with ideas that people take seriously, they actually try to master them, or at least try to read the sources that they are citing for the proposition. Often, that doesn't happen with intersectionality [or CRT], and there are any number of theories as to why that's the case, but what many people have heard or know about intersectionality comes more from what people say than what they've actually encountered themselves." (para. 25–27)

We turn now to two of Crenshaw's works on intersectionality: her 1989 article "Demarginalizing the Intersection of Race and Sex: A Black Feminist Critique of Antidiscrimination Doctrine, Feminist Theory and Antiracist Politics," where she introduced the concept of intersectionality, and her 1991 article "Mapping the Margins: Intersectionality, Identity Politics, and Violence Against Women of Color," where she critiqued both feminism and antiracism for ignoring the intersection of race and gender that marginalized Black women.

In "Demarginalizing the Intersection of Race and Sex," Crenshaw (1989) argued that Black women's experiences are analyzed through a single axis, either gender or race, but not both. Thus, Black women are "theoretically erased," because they stand at the intersection of gender and race.

Because the intersectional experience is greater than the sum of racism and sexism, an analysis that does not take intersectionality into account cannot sufficiently address the particular manner in which Black women are subordinated. Thus, for Feminist Theory and antiracist policy discourse to embrace the experiences and concerns of Black women, the entire framework that has been used as a basis for translating "women's experience" or "the Black experience" into concrete policy demands must be rethought and recast. (p. 140)

Crenshaw (1989) demonstrated this thesis through three cases: *DeGraffenreid v. General Motors, Moore v. Hughes Helicopter, Inc*, and *Payne v. Travenol*. In the 1976 DeGraffenreid case, five Black women sued General Motors for perpetuating "the effects of past discrimination against Black women" (p. 141). Prior to the Civil Rights Act of 1964, the company had not hired Black women. In 1970, due to a recession, the company invoked its seniority-based layoff policy. Since the Black women were the last hired, they were the first to go— all of them. The court denied the suit because it was not brought on behalf of women in general or Blacks in general. It was specific to Black women. The court said the plaintiffs, the Black women, could not

combine statutory remedies to create a new "super-remedy" which would give them relief beyond what the drafters of the relevant statutes intended. Thus, this lawsuit must be examined to see if it states a cause of action for race discrimination, sex discrimination, or alternately either, but not a combination of both. (as cited in Crenshaw, 1989, p. 141)

However, the discrimination was not just because the Black women were women or just because they were Black. It was specifically because they were both women and Black. They were at the intersection.

In "Mapping the Margins," Crenshaw (1991) further developed her critique of feminist and antiracist discourses that have failed to recognize the intersectional identities of women of color. She studied male violence again women, specifically battery and rape, that are the result of *both* racism and sexism. "Because of their intersectional identity as both women *and* of color within discourses that are shaped to respond to one *or* the other, women of color are marginalized within both" (p. 1244).

She discussed three categories of intersectionality: structural, political, and representational. Structural is "the ways in which the location of women of color at the intersection of race and gender makes [their] actual experience of domestic violence, rape, and remedial reform qualitatively different than that of white women" (Crenshaw, 1991, p. 1245). Political is the ways in which "feminist and antiracist politics have, paradoxically, often helped to marginalize the issue of violence against women of color" (p. 1245). And representational, or the "cultural construction of women of color," is the ways in which women of color are represented in popular culture that can "elide the particular location of women of color, and thus become yet another source of intersectional disempowerment" (p. 1245). Each of the categories of intersectionality has sub-categories, and Crenshaw provided an in-depth discussion of each with examples. Herein we provide one example of structural intersectionality as it relates to the subcategory of battering.

Having visited a battered women's shelter in Los Angeles, Crenshaw (1991) found that the assault that led most women to the shelter was just the most urgent "manifestation of the subordination they experience" (p. 1245). They had no means of financial self-support. They were unemployed or underemployed, lacked job skills, and had child care responsibilities, all of which were "largely the consequence of gender and class oppression" (p. 1246). Women of color, however, experienced this gender and class oppression *and* "racially discriminatory employment and housing practices . . . [including] disproportionately high unemployment among people of color that makes battered women of color less able to depend on the support of friends and relatives for temporary shelter" (p. 1246). Thus, battered women of color experience the trifecta of race, gender, and class domination, and strategies that may be successful in meeting the needs of women "who do not share the same class or race backgrounds will be of limited help to women who because of race and class face different obstacles" (p. 1246).

DEFINING ELEMENTS OF CRITICAL RACE THEORY

Having discussed the concepts advanced by three of the prominent scholars of CRT, we conclude this chapter with a summary of the defining elements of critical race theory. In our review of the literature, we found nearly a dozen lists of defining elements of CRT in general and even more specific to education. Most include the same elements with some variation in language. Staying consistent with the historical time frame we have used for this chapter and drawing from the seminal authors of that time period, we have chosen the list from Matsuda, Lawrence, Delgado, and Crenshaw (1993). What follows is their list in its entirety:

1. Critical race theory recognizes that racism is endemic to American life. Thus, the question for us is not so much whether or how racial discrimination can be eliminated while maintaining the integrity of other interests implicated in the status quo such as federalism, privacy, traditional values, or established property interests. Instead, we ask how these traditional interests and values serve as vessels of racial subordination.

2. Critical race theory expresses skepticism toward dominant legal claims of neutrality, objectivity, color blindness, and meritocracy. These claims are central to an ideology of equal opportunity that presents race as an immutable characteristic devoid of social meaning and tells an ahistorical, abstracted story of racial inequality as a series of randomly occurring, intentional, and individualized acts.

3. Critical race theory challenges ahistoricism and insists on a contextual/historical analysis of the law. Current inequalities and social/institutional practices

are linked to earlier periods in which the intent and cultural meaning practices were clear. More important, as critical race theorists we adopt a that presumes that racism has contributed to all contemporary manifestation of group advantage and disadvantage along racial lines, including differences in income, imprisonment, health, housing, education, political representation, and military service. Our history calls for this presumption.

4. Critical race theory insists on recognition of the experiential knowledge of people of color and our communities of origin in analyzing law and society. This knowledge is gained from critical reflection on the lived experience of racism and from critical reflection upon active political practice toward the elimination of racism.

5. Critical race theory is interdisciplinary and eclectic. It borrows from several traditions, including liberalism, law and society, feminism, Marxism, poststructuralism, critical legal theory, pragmatism, and nationalism. This eclecticism allows critical race theory to examine and incorporate those aspects of a methodology or theory that effectively enable our voice and advance the cause of racial justice even as we maintain a critical posture.

6. Critical race theory works toward the end of eliminating racial oppression as part of the broader goal of ending all forms of oppression. Racial oppression is experienced by many in tandem with oppression on grounds of gender, class, or sexual orientation. Critical race theory measures progress by a yardstick that looks to fundamental social transformation. The interests of all people of color necessarily require not just adjustments within the established hierarchies, but a challenge to hierarchy itself. This recognition of intersecting forms of subordination requires multiple consciousness and political practices that address the varied ways in which people experience subordination. (pp. 6–7)

CONCLUSION

In this chapter we introduced critical race theory. We traced its emergence in the 1980s out of a critique of the ways in which the U.S. legal system and society at large addressed race and racial power. Additionally, although there was respect for the civil rights movement, CRT critiqued the movement's liberal ideology. We followed with a discussion of three of the prominent CRT theorists—Derrick Bell, Richard Delgado, and Kimberlé Crenshaw—the concepts they introduced, and a brief description of their major works. We closed the chapter with the six defining elements of CRT.

ce Theory in Education

In 1993 Gloria Ladson-Billings and William Tate presented a paper at the American Educational Research Association (AERA) conference titled "Toward a Critical Race Theory of Education." Two years later the article was published in *Teachers College Record* and to date has been cited over 7,000 times. The article introduced critical race theory into the field of education. Since that time critical race theory has been incorporated into Latinx critical research, disability studies, Indigenous/Tribal critical research, critical feminist research, LGBTQ+ studies, critical policy studies, and other approaches in education. We will discuss many of these in the upcoming chapters. For this chapter, we focus on selected works of Ladson-Billings and Tate that directly address CRT in education. We begin with a discussion of their pioneering work "Toward a Critical Race Theory of Education" and then discuss each author's individual contributions.

LADSON-BILLINGS AND TATE: "TOWARD A CRITICAL RACE THEORY OF EDUCATION"

Ladson-Billings and Tate (1995) proposed that education needed a theory that addressed social inequity, and thus school inequity, and was based on three propositions: "(1) race continues to be a significant factor in determining inequity in the United States; (2) U.S. society is based on property rights rather than human rights; and (3) the intersection of race and property creates an analytical tool through which we can understand social (and, consequently, school) inequity" (p. 47–48).

Problematizing Race

With regard to the first proposition, they acknowledged the problems associated with race in that race as an ideological construct "denies the reality of a racialized society and its impact on 'raced' people" and their lived experiences (Ladson-Billings & Tate, 1995, p. 48), whereas accepting race as real and not a social or ideological construct ignores the complexity of intersectionality and the ways in which groups are categorized. Race is thus conflated with social class, ethnicity, and nationality.

They further posited that in schools, looking at class or economic status alone does not account for the inequality experienced by students of color. In other words, race matters. As an example, we only need to look at school discipline data to see the disproportionate suspension rates and severity of disciplinary actions experienced by students of color compared to their White counterparts, even when social economic status is factored in.

Property Rights Over Human Rights

Ladson-Billings and Tate's (1995) second proposition contended that U.S. society is based on property rights rather than human rights:

> The grand narrative of U.S. history is replete with tensions and struggles over property—in its various forms. From the removal of Indians (and later Japanese Americans) from the land, to military conquest of the Mexicans, to the construction of Africans as property [slaves], the ability to define, possess, and own property has been a central feature of power in America. (p. 53)

This manifests in schools in tangible ways like property taxes and intangible ways like curriculum as intellectual property. Regarding property taxes, where one lives determines the quality of the schools. As Ladson-Billings and Tate say, the "better" the property, the "better" the schools. Akin to this is the "better" the property, the richer the school curriculum that requires more tangible property like science and computer labs, a well-sourced library, and so forth. It also means advanced classes like physics, Latin, and calculus that are rarely found in schools in low-income areas. These "property rights" provide more opportunities to learn and earn.

Critical Race Theory and Educational Inequity

From the discussion above we can see that the authors made the case for their third proposition that "the intersection of race and property creates an analytical tool through which we can understand social (and, consequently, school) inequity" (Ladson-Billings & Tate, 1995, p. 48). By using the "notion of property rights as a defining feature of the society" (p. 55), they proceeded to apply critical race theory and the concepts associated with it to educational inequity.

Interest Convergence

Ladson-Billings and Tate (1995) began the discussion of their third proposition with Derrick Bell's CRT concept of interest convergence that Whites only advance racial equity when it benefits them. They offered examples related to desegregation. The first was a school district in California in which there were five high schools, with one located in a predominantly Black community. To incentivize White students to attend the school, free camping and ski trips were offered. However, the only students who attended these trips were the White students who already owned the expensive camping and skiing equipment that was required. Ultimately, this strategy failed; enrollment declined, the school was closed, and the Black students were bused out of their neighborhoods to the remaining White high schools.

The second example was a "model" desegregation program implemented by the Buffalo, New York school district. In *The New York Times* article (1985) "School Integration In Buffalo Is Hailed As A Model For U.S.," it was reported that

> school officials sold integration in Buffalo, which is about 40 percent black, by promising a better school waiting for children at the end of the bus ride. They spent tens of millions of dollars creating 43 full-day prekindergarten programs that hooked many parents on public schools early. And they set up magnet schools reflecting virtually every philosophy in education, from the progressive to the traditional. (Winerip, para. 6–7)

Although the desegregation plan achieved racial diversity in the schools, the achievement of the Black students and Latinx students was low, yet their dropout, expulsion, and suspension rates were high. Ladson-Billings and Tate (1995) asked, "What, then, made Buffalo a model school desegregation program?" and concluded,

> in short, the benefits that whites derived from school desegregation and their seeming support of the district's desegregation program. Thus, a model desegregation program becomes defined as one that ensures that whites are happy (and do not leave the system altogether) regardless of whether African-American and other students of color achieve or remain. (p. 56)

Therefore, White parents and community members' support of the desegregation plans was not based on the benefits afforded African-American and other students of color but rather the benefits to their White children. In other words, the support was dependent on the convergence of the Whites' interests ostensibly with the interests of communities of color.

Counternarratives

The third example had to do with Delgado's CRT concept of voice or counternarratives. Mirroring Delgado's critique of the omission of the voices of scholars of color in the legal literature of the 1970s and 1980s, Ladson-Billings and Tate (1995) pointed to the omission of the voices of community members, school leaders, teachers, parents, and students in educational issues. "Without authentic voices of people of color . . . it is doubtful that we can say or know anything useful about education in their communities" (p. 59).

Whiteness as Property

For the final example, they returned to race and property and discussed Cheryl Harris's concept of Whiteness as property. A full discussion of this concept is beyond the scope of this chapter, so we refer you to Harris's 1993 article "Whiteness as Property." Whereas slavery created Blacks as property, Whiteness and the privilege afforded to Whites became a property right:

> The set of assumptions, privileges, and benefits that accompany the status of being white have become a valuable asset that whites sought to protect . . . Whites have come to expect and rely on these benefits, and over time these expectations have been affirmed, legitimated, and protected by the law. (Harris, 1993, p. 1713)

Harris (1993) proposed "property functions of whiteness" (p. 1731). These are rights of disposition, rights to use and enjoyment, reputation and status as property, and the absolute right to exclude. Ladson-Billings and Tate (1995) applied these rights to education.

Rights of Disposition. Historically Whites established the acceptable culture or norms in the United States and therefore in schools. "When students are rewarded only for conformity to perceived 'white norms' or sanctioned for cultural practices (e.g., dress, speech patterns, unauthorized conceptions of knowledge), white property is being rendered alienable [in other words, transferable]" (Ladson-Billings & Tate, 1995, p. 59). That is, Whiteness as a property is given, disposed, to the students.

Rights to Use and Enjoyment. Whites use and enjoy the privilege of Whiteness. Two examples of this in schools are material school property, such as well-maintained buildings and classrooms that are not overcrowded, and the curriculum. For example, schools serving predominantly White students emphasize higher-order skills like evaluation and synthesis, in contrast to lower-order skills like remembering and understanding.

Reputation and Status as Property. In law, cases of libel or slander demonstrate reputation and status as property. If someone's reputation and thus status is damaged, it constitutes damage to the individual's personal property. "In the case of race, to call a white person 'black' is to defame him or her. In the case of schooling, to identify a school or program as nonwhite in any way is to diminish its reputation or status" (Ladson-Billings & Tate, 1995, p. 60).

The Absolute Right to Exclude. "Whiteness is constructed in this society as the absence of the 'contaminating' influence of blackness" (Ladson-Billings & Tate, 1995, p. 60). Historically in education, the right to exclude, to keep out the "contaminating" influence of Blackness, was accomplished by denying

Blacks education, by allowing them education but in separate schools that were not equal, and now by de facto segregation accomplished through neighborhood schools, private schools, and in-school tracking.

Limitations of the Multicultural Paradigm

Lastly, Ladson-Billings and Tate (1995) discussed the limitations of the multicultural paradigm, wherein they included both multicultural education and multiculturalism. In doing, they drew parallels between critical race legal theory and its critique of civil rights law, and critical race theory in education and its critique of multicultural education and multiculturalism—both of which advance incremental rather than revolutionary change.

Historically, multicultural education was a reform movement focused on bringing about equality in schools and all educational institutions. According to Ladson-Billings and Tate (1995), its roots, however, resembled "the intergroup education movement of the 1950s, which was designed to help African Americans and other 'unmeltable' ethnics become a part of America's melting pot" (p. 61). The strategy was to reduce prejudice and to further assimilation.

Following the civil rights movement, the goal of assimilation was "supplanted by the reclamation of an 'authentic black personality' that did not rely on the acceptance by or standards of white America" (p. 61). Black studies and later ethnic studies were incorporated into the university curriculum. In many K–12 schools in the 1990s and even some today, the multicultural education of James Banks, Carl Grant, Christine Sleeter, Geneva Gay, and others has been reduced to a tourism approach with, for example, cultural fairs that highlight the food, clothing, and customs of "others," rather than focusing on culturally relevant and critical pedagogies.

Multiculturalism, as distinct from multicultural education, "is a political philosophy of 'many cultures' existing together in an atmosphere of respect and tolerance" and is often interchangeable with diversity of all kinds—racial, ethnic, gender, sexual orientation, linguistic, ability, etc. (p. 61). However, as Ladson-Billings and Tate pointed out, there are "growing tensions that exist between and among various groups that gather under the umbrella of multiculturalism—that is, the interests of groups can be competing or their perspectives can be at odds" (p. 61). However, these tensions are "rarely interrogated, presuming a 'unity of difference'—that is, that all difference is both analogous and equivalent" (p. 62).

Regarding the comparison of the critiques of critical race legal theory to critical race education theory, Ladson-Billings and Tate (1995) argued

> that the current multicultural paradigm [the one at the time of their writing, 1995] functions in a manner similar to civil rights law. Instead of creating radically new paradigms that ensure justice, multicultural reforms are routinely "sucked back into the system" and just as traditional civil rights law is based on a foundation of

human rights [rather than property rights], the current multicultural paradigm is mired in liberal ideology that offers no radical change in the current order. Thus, critical race theory in education, like its antecedent in legal scholarship, is a radical critique of both the status quo and the purported reforms. . . . As critical race theory scholars we unabashedly reject a paradigm that attempts to be everything to everyone and consequently becomes nothing for anyone, allowing the status quo to prevail. (p. 62)

Having discussed the seminal collaborative work by Ladson-Billings and Tate that introduced CRT into education, we will briefly address some of the individual contributions of each author related specifically to CRT in education.

NOTABLE CRITICAL RACE THEORISTS IN EDUCATION AND THEIR CONCEPTS

Gloria Ladson-Billings

Concepts:

   critical race theory in education
   culturally relevant pedagogy

Ladson-Billings began writing about CRT in the 1990s, first with Tate in the above-discussed article written in 1995. That same year she wrote "Toward a Theory of Culturally Relevant Pedagogy," where, drawing from "eight exemplary teachers of African-American students," she developed the concept of *culturally relevant pedagogy* (Ladson-Billings, 1995, p. 465). She determined that for teaching to be culturally relevant it must meet the following criteria: "an ability to develop students academically, a willingness to nurture and support cultural competence, and the development of a sociopolitical or critical consciousness" (p. 483).

She followed with her 1997 article, "I Know Why This Doesn't Feel Empowering: A Critical *Race* Analysis of Critical Pedagogy." This article was a subjoin to the conversation started by Ellsworth whereby Ellsworth critiqued critical pedagogy, writing that, as it was conceptualized at the time, it promoted repressive myths that marginalized those whom it was intended to support (see Chapter 3). Ladson-Billings advanced Ellsworth's argument and centered it specifically on race, discussing the ways the "discourse about race is denied and muted in analysis of educational and social inequality" (Ladson-Billings, 1997, p. 127) and asked, "in what ways might our understandings of critical theory and pedagogy be informed by our understandings of race? What are the potentials for struggling together around issues that are empowering, not alienating?" (p. 137). This is when she began threading CRT to culturally relevant pedagogy. She saw teacher preparation as the locus of this struggle. She concluded the article by suggesting that critical race theory could be used as a rubric for culturally relevant pedagogy.

Furthering this line of thought, in "Preparing Teachers for Diverse Student Populations: A Critical Race Theory Perspective" (1999) she used CRT to examine teacher preparation programs and found that (a) teacher educators are often working with "like-minded prospective teachers or resistant, often hostile prospective teachers" (p. 240); (b) programs often see addressing diversity as a "necessary evil imposed by the state and /or accrediting agency" and therefore comply by offering "a" course or module (p. 240); (c) although "CRT can be a way to explain and understand preparing teachers for diversity that moves beyond both superficial, essentialized treatments of various cultural groups and liberal guilt and angst." It also exposes "the way that theory works in such programs. Unfortunately, too many teacher education programs have no basis in theory" (p. 241); and (d) CRT ferrets out the way culturally relevant programs for "preparing teachers for diverse student populations challenge generic models of teaching and teacher education. Rather than submit to the discourse of PSWBW [Public School Way Back When], such programs and teacher educators establish themselves in opposition to the hegemony of an idealized past" (p. 241).

In between the two previous articles that linked CRT, culturally relevant pedagogy, and teacher preparation, Ladson-Billings published the article "Just What Is Critical Race Theory and What's It Doing in a Nice Field Like Education?" (1998), which addressed CRT and its place in education in general. She began this work with a history of CRT and then through a CRT lens examined curriculum, instruction, assessment, school funding, and desegregation. In the conclusion of the article, Ladson-Billings was prescient, warning of the dangers of embracing CRT as the new fad in education without having an understanding of its legal underpinnings. "CRT in education is likely to become the 'darling' of the radical left, continue to generate scholarly papers and debate, and never penetrate the classrooms and daily experiences of students of color" (Ladson-Billings, 1998, p. 22). Moreover, 2 decades on, CRT has become the spark that ignited a firestorm with the intersection of race, history, and education at its core. As Ladson-Billings (1998) predicted,

> adopting and adapting CRT as a framework for educational equity means that we will have to expose racism in education *and* propose radical solutions for addressing it. We will have to take bold and sometimes unpopular positions. We may be pilloried figuratively or, at least, vilified for these stands. (p. 22)

Ladson-Billings continues to advance the discussion of CRT in education in general and specifically in areas such as educational scholarship, social studies, Black identity, and her discipline of teacher preparation.

William Tate

Concepts:

> critical race theory in education
> voice
> Whiteness

Currently William Tate is the president of Louisiana State University, having served in leadership positions at several universities for the past 2 decades as well as serving as president of the American Educational Research Association (AERA) from 2007 to 2008. He continues to be a prolific researcher and writer. Currently his focus is on the (a) "social determinants of mathematics, engineering, technology, and science attainment"; (b) "geospatial and epidemiological modeling of health and human development"; (c) "political economy of urban metropolitan regions"; and (d) "leadership in public-private learning alliances and research collaborations" (LinkedIn, n.d.)

Prior to his collaboration with Ladson-Billings in 1995 that introduced CRT to education, he was already writing about CRT, drawing from the work of the legal scholars who conceptualized it. In 1994 Tate wrote "From Inner City to Ivory Tower: Does My Voice Matter in the Academy?" This work addressed one of the issues that Delgado raised in "The Imperial Scholar" and "The Imperial Scholar Revisited": the marginalization of the voices of academics of color.

In addition to the CRT concept of *voice*, Tate used centric and conflict theories to demonstrate how his personal experiences as a student in an urban Catholic elementary school and later as a public high school student, along with his experiences as a math scholar, were advanced and stymied. To illustrate the power of voice, Tate told a personal and compelling story of his elementary and high school experiences and the ways these experiences influenced his career path and theories regarding math education.

He grew up on the South Side of Chicago, attended Holy Angels Catholic Elementary School, and later attended a public high school. Holy Angels, led by a Black activist priest, used an Africentric perspective that "locate[d] students within the context of their own cultural references . . . [providing] students the opportunity to study the world from an African worldview" (Tate, 1994, p. 254). Tate told two stories about Holy Angels. The first demonstrated the Africentric approach the school embraced and the ways that personally affected him. He recounted an exchange with his White 5th-grade teacher, who explained in a spelling lesson that "coon" was a term that was used for raccoon. Tate raised his hand and explained that coon had two meanings and that the other was a pejorative used to described African Americans. The teacher was offended and told him to apologize to the class. He did not and was sent to the "office." The priest heard his story and said it was appropriate that he explained the dual meaning. The teacher did not return to that school the next year.

Years later when Tate went to the school to visit the priest, he asked why the teacher did not return, and the priest smiled and told him they had "philosophical differences." Tate (1994) said,

> I will speculate on the nature of these philosophical differences. I contend that the inability of my teacher to either recognize or discuss the interrelationship between his school knowledge, my home experiences, and my experiences in the community as an African American resulted in a tension between the school's Africentric philosophy and his color-blind approach to education. (p. 256)

Tate also learned at Holy Angel about conflict and social action. For a service to honor Martin Luther King Jr. (MLK), the portrait of a saint was replaced with a portrait of MLK. The archdiocese objected, and the priest was told to remove the portrait, as failure to remove it would result in suspension from the archdiocese and the loss of funding. The priest sought counsel from the school community, and they decided to stand on principle and refused to remove the picture, resulting in parents and students having to raise funds to support the school. Tate (1994) said he learned from this experience that

> there was a price to pay for my rights . . . but that the price was small in comparison to the denial of basic freedoms . . . Holy Angels provide[d] an example of how to empower children with a knowledge of self and a combative spirit of social reform. The result is a student who understands his or her importance to society. (p. 258)

This proved important to Tate as he entered public high school. There, a school administrator and counselor attempted to remove Tate and several other African American students from a senior physics class. No White students were to be removed. Several reasons were given as to why the students should not be in the class, all of which were unfounded. In fact, all the African American students being removed from the course had near-perfect science scores on the ACT test. The students presented their arguments as to why they were indeed prepared and capable to attend the course. The facts were clear, and the school administrator and counselor conceded. However, it took Tate "years to overcome the psychological scars associated with this degradation" (p. 247).

Tate's experiences at both Holy Angels and his high school influenced his trajectory into higher education and specifically math education. However, he expressed concern as to whether his voice mattered in the academy:

> My experience suggests African American students will be mathematically empowered in a school that seeks to build on their experiences, prepares them for societal conflicts, and provides them an opportunity to learn mathematics in multiple

contexts. This position is at odds with the traditional notion that mathematics is unconnected to human affairs. Thus I do not expect many of my colleagues to accept my analysis. Bell (1991) warns African American scholars that no amount of experience or expertise will validate their scholarship involving race; it will always be viewed as "special pleading." (p. 264)

He ends the article on a plea:

For those scholars of color dedicated to improving the experience of African American children in urban schools, there is no choice. We must continue the battle to have our experiences and voices heard in academic discourse. Our voices provide stories that help others think in different ways about complex, context-dependent domains like schools and communities. (p. 264)

Tate continues to use his voice to improve the experiences of African American children in urban schools and to advance CRT in education.

Two years after publishing the influential "Toward a Critical Race Theory of Education" with Ladson-Billings, Tate's "Critical Race Theory and Education: History, Theory, and Implications" (1997) appeared in *Review of Research in Education*. In this article, Tate extended the discussion of CRT in education. He began with a discussion of the similarities in the ways in which the legal structures and educational research both "contribute to existing belief systems and to legitimating social frameworks and policy that result in educational inequities for people of color" (p. 197). He then provided a history of CRT and focused on three of the key figures in the movement: Derrick Bell, Richard Delgado, and Kimberlé Crenshaw. Lastly, he explained the elements related to CRT, noting that CRT

1. recognizes that racism is endemic . . .
2. crosses epistemological boundaries . . .
3. reinterprets civil rights law in light of its limitations . . .
4. portrays dominant legal claims of neutrality, objectivity, color blindness, and meritocracy as camouflages for the self-interest of powerful entities of society . . .
5. [and] challenges ahistoricism and insists on a contextual/historical examination of the law and a recognition of the experiential knowledge of peoples of color in analyzing the law and society. (p. 235)

Furthermore, in his continual efforts to theorize race in educational research, in 2003 he wrote "The 'Race' to Theorize Education: Who Is My Neighbor?" Here Tate (2003) theorized *Whiteness*, a concept that was just emerging in the field:

The predominant viewpoint in the social sciences has been that people of color lack many of the characteristics associated with being white, thus the focus on scholarship has been on documenting these differences or examining interventions designed to remedy these so-called deficiencies (Padilla & Lindholm, 1995). Thus, whiteness has often been part of a binary comparison that attributes specific positive traits to whites and seeks to determine the presence or absence of these traits in another racial group. (p.122)

In theorizing Whiteness, Tate drew from biblical text, Thomas Jefferson, and the *Dred Scott v. Sandford* legal case. From Luke 10:25–29, he referenced a discussion Jesus had with a lawyer where Jesus says you should "love your neighbor as yourself," and the lawyer replies, "who is my neighbor?" (Amplified Bible, as cited in Tate, 2003, p. 123). Tate said of Jefferson that he stated "that the African, when freed from slavery, must be 'removed beyond the reach of mixture'" (Jefferson, 1974/1954, p. 143, as cited in Tate, 2003, p. 124). And from *Dred Scott* the decision demonstrated that the Jeffersonian opinion about Whiteness was maintained for over a hundred years in the legal system.

According to Tate (2003), "to understand whiteness and how it operates requires an understanding of the word neighbor" (p. 124). Thus, he answered the question "Who is my neighbor?" by quoting from the *American Dictionary of the English Language* that a neighbor is "one of the human race; any one that needs our help, or to whom we have an opportunity of doing good" (p. 124). He held that the United States is like a neighborhood but that slaves, African Americans, were not allowed into the neighborhood nor seen as neighbors; the courts upheld this for years, and it became the basis for our segregated society. "The human race was white and did not include blacks. Thus, by definition it was not possible to include blacks as a part of the 'neighborhood'" (p. 124).

According to Tate (2003), if we understand Whiteness as the definition of what it is to be human and Blackness as its binary and thus nonhuman and therefore should be out of the mix—that is, out of the neighborhood—then this allows us to understand the segregation of schools, residential housing, and so forth. He then connected the notion of neighborhood to Bell's concept of interest convergence, saying that "interest convergence represents how whites attempt to protect the neighborhood" and, specific to education, to protect "funding structures, assessment practices, admission policies, and course taking opportunities" (p. 125).

In 2005, Tate wrote "Ethics, Engineering and the Challenge of Racial Reform in Education," where he continued to discuss ways to advance CRT in education and offered cautions as well:

It is important to understand that the rapid proliferation of writings and articles associated with CRT including critiques of the movement are partly a function of media access. I have found the reaction to CRT to be largely bifurcated. The negative response to CRT provides important lessons [for scholars]. (p. 123)

In addressing his first concept, *ethics*, Tate returned to the metaphor of the "neighborhood" and the biblical charge to "love your neighbor as yourself." He did so through a discussion of the 2004 Alabama election to approve a constitutional amendment that would "repeal portions of the constitution that mandated racial segregation in schools and levied a poll tax for the right to vote" (Ballotpedia, 2021). The amendment was defeated. Opposition leaders such as Alabama judge Roy Moore and the Alabama Christian Coalition (ACC) claimed it was an economic issue, not a racial issue, contending it was a "stand against more education spending and for protecting parochial and home-school facilities" (Flono, 2004, as cited in Tate). Tate (2005) called out Moore and the ACC, saying they had "transparent links to theological positions that stand on principles of moral absolutism. Yet, in the face of social policy, relativism appears to guide their thinking and is linked to self-interest, rather than the greater good [the neighborhood]" (p. 125).

In discussion of the second concept, *engineering positive change in school achievement for underserved racial groups*, Tate (2005) contended that we must look at intergenerational effects such as family resources and education levels, as well as educational opportunity over generations, such as attending good schools. He concluded that

> CRT and other forms of race-based scholarship must examine carefully theoretical tenets that position their moral reasoning as part of a relativism project. In a world driven by slogans and media, some may be confusing basic notions derived from the sociology of knowledge which recognize the influence of cultural heritage, world view and societal values upon all perceptions of reality. This is not a call for moral relativism [the notion that truth depends on your standpoint]. Sound moral reasoning should not be divorced from matters of race and racism. (p. 126)

RESEARCH COMPONENTS OF EXAMPLE ARTICLE

Just as in critical theory, there are a limited number of empirical research articles employing CRT; most are theoretical, opinion, or essay. Furthermore, as we mentioned previously, many fall into categories that are derivatives of CRT, such as LatCrit and TribalCrit. To discuss the research components of CRT, we have chosen Felicia Moore Mensah's 2019 article "Finding Voice and Passion: Critical Race Theory Methodology in Science Teacher Education," published in the *American Educational Research Journal*. Dr. Mensah is associate dean and professor of science education in the Department of Mathematics, Science and Technology at Teachers College, Columbia University and identifies as an "educated African American woman, from a working-class background, who grew up in the rural south" (Mensah, 2019, p. 1418).

Mensah conducted a longitudinal case study of Michele (a pseudonym), an African American female teacher education student in a predominantly White teacher education program. Michele had been a student in Dr. Mensah's "graduate-level preservice elementary science methods course" (p. 1418). The study looked at Michele's "educational history first as a young child and then how she navigates a contested, racialized predominantly White teacher education program, grows and develops in science education, and secures her first full-time teaching appointment as an elementary teacher" (p. 1412).

Statement of the Problem, Purpose, and Research Question

CRT scholars contend that race is undertheorized in education in general, and then there are those, such as Christine Sleeter, Daniel Solorzano, Tara Yosso, and Rich Milner, who argue that it is also undertheorized in teacher education specifically. Since the integration of schools, there has been a decline in the number of Black teachers and a decline in Black college students choosing education as a major. This is problematic in that teachers of color serve as role models for all students and bring cultural awareness, allowing them to better understand students from diverse backgrounds. Moreover, teachers of color may bring critical pedagogies that challenge the status quo and better serve the needs of students of color. "Building a future pool of Black teachers comes from the preparation of preservice teachers of color. Therefore, their experiences in teacher education represents an area of growing importance as well" (Mensah, 2019, p. 1415). Mensah identified her statement of the problem by addressing Lincoln and Guba's question "Why is it important to do this?" (1985, p. 222), stating that

> science education is a marginalized content area in elementary school settings (Berg & Mensah, 2014; Gunning & Mensah, 2010; Mensah, 2010), and this is compounded by a limited number of science teachers of color in the teaching pool (Mensah & Jackson, 2018); consequently, the preparation of elementary science teachers of color is a topic needing attention. (p. 1416)

Her purpose was to address the gap in the literature by conducting a case study of Michele, a Black teacher education student interested in science education—her teacher education and beginning teacher experiences. Her research questions were:

> Research Question 1: In what ways did Michele understand race and racism in her educational narratives, and how did these experiences affect her preparation as a teacher of color?
> Research Question 2: What were Michele's experiences as a teacher of color in a White teacher education program?
> Research Question 3: What experiences shaped her development as a teacher of color desiring to teach science? (Mensah, 2019, p. 1414)

Theoretical Framework

Mensah's (2019) theoretical frame was CRT, into which she incorporated the concepts of counternarrative and intersectionality: "The notion of counternarrative is not to treat the narratives of people of color as less than or subordinate to the dominant narrative but to empower the telling of stories from the unique histories of people of color" (p. 1413). Additionally, Mensah expanded the traditional definition of counternarrative:

> Having an African American female science teacher educator is critical in Michele's retelling of her experiences in teacher education and science. She is provided the educational and emotional support she needs as a Black female science teacher.
>
> Hence, I am her counter-narrative to previous views of teacher education faculty, and the science methods course becomes the counter-narrative to previous views of science, teacher education courses, and who teaches these courses in teacher education programs. (p. 1447)

She also extended the definition of intersectionality beyond the ways race and racism "intersect with gender and class, and other social markers" (p. 1448) by introducing the concept of disciplinary intersectionality. "The notion of disciplinary intersectionality, such as a female teacher of color in science education, broadens and adds to this complexity in understanding race, racism, and science in teacher education" (p. 1414).

Methodology and Methods

Mensah (2019) considered CRT as both her methodology and her theoretical frame and coupled it with a longitudinal case study. "Case studies are differentiated from other types of qualitative research in that they are intensive descriptions and analyses of a single unit . . . such as an individual" (Merriam, 2001, p. 19), and in longitudinal case studies the data collection occurs over time, providing a deeper understanding of the event or person studied. Mensah also utilized counterstories, also called counternarratives, and theoretical sensitivity. Theoretical sensitivity, according to Strauss and Corbin (1990, as cited in Mensah), is "the attribute of having insight, the ability to give meaning to data, the capacity to understand, and capability to separate the pertinent from that which isn't" (pp. 1418–1419).

Positionality, the social, cultural, and political stance of the research, was also important to Mensah. She described herself as "an educated African American woman, from a working-class background, who grew up in the rural south" and is a science education professor at a "predominantly White elite graduate institution" (p. 1418). This allowed her to "better understand Michele's experiences as an African American female in her teacher education program but also to better position [herself] to tell and offer insights into the narratives Michele share[d] as a woman teacher candidate of color from a rural working-class background" (p. 1418). The context of the study was the science education class and the years following, including Michele's student teaching and her first few years of full-time teaching. The data sources included interviews, conversations, and artifacts from Michele's academic experiences, as well as her student teaching and first year of teaching.

Analysis and Results/Findings

Employing CRT, intersectionality, and "constructivist grounded theory" (Mensah, 2019, p. 1423) in her analysis, Mensah identified four "racial narrative themes":

(a) situating early childhood and school experiences in a racial context,
(b) loss of voice in teacher education and finding voice in science education,
(c) defending an approach to science teaching as an educated Black woman scientist, and
(d) planning and teaching science as self. (p. 1425)

The themes are discussed in detail in the following section.

Discussion and Recommendations

Mensah (2019) applied components of CRT in discussing her analysis of the data—the endemic nature of racism in the United States, the impact of race and racism, hegemony, and intersectionality. She appeared to be answering Ladson-Billings's call to use CRT as a rubric for culturally relevant pedagogy, although in higher education. Mensah's first theme, "situating early childhood and school experiences in a racial context" (p. 1425), addressed the endemic nature of racism in the United States. In Michele's early childhood experiences, she learned that "race meant a difference in 'skin tone'" (p. 1426) and that a lighter skin tone was seen as more attractive. This was significant on a personal level for Michele, as she is dark-skinned. She also experienced marginalization and racism when she was the only Black student in her suburban school, where she was judged not by her abilities but by her race and was seen as deficit.

The second theme, "loss of voice in teacher education and finding voice in science education" (p. 1425), spoke to the impact of race and racism, the marginalization of voice, and the normalization of Whiteness. "In [Michele's] teacher education program, the emotional impact of race and racism [was] that Michele 'struggle[d] and [fought]' to have a voice and to shape her identity as a female teacher of color at an elite, predominantly White institution" where there was "an overwhelming presence of whiteness" (p. 1430).

Regarding the third theme, "defending an approach to science teaching as an educated Black woman scientist" (p. 1434), Mensah focused on Michele's experience with the teacher education curriculum that maintained hegemony by teaching as though all preservice teachers were White, which implicitly and explicitly required the students of color to accept and maintain the White narrative.

In the last theme, "planning and teaching science as self" (p. 1437), Mensah addressed intersectionality, explaining that the science course she taught, and which Michele attended, presented a counternarrative of "who can do science, who can teach science, who is a scientist, who is a science teacher, and what is considered science knowledge to be taught and taught to whom" (p. 1449).

Mensah's recommendation was to create a culturally relevant teacher education program. She suggested that although there needs to be an increase in the representation of teacher education candidates of color, this is not enough: "There also must be a simultaneous commitment to the practices and curriculum that will meet the individual and collective needs of teachers of color once they are admitted" (p. 1449). This would include "ongoing support from recruitment to graduation without marginalizing teachers of color and making them 'fight and struggle' to be heard and seen in their teacher education programs" (p. 1450). She concluded, as several of the previous scholars have, that

> the usefulness of CRT's counter-narrative to foreground race and racism may not go far enough if the counter-narrative only supports the telling and not the theorizing of narratives shared within a broader context of teacher education curriculum, practice, and content. (p.1450)

CONCLUSION

Here we have expanded our discussion of CRT into the field of education and highlighted the work of the two trailblazers—Ladson-Billings and Tate. Furthermore, we discussed the research components—statement of the problem, purpose, and research question; theoretical frame; methodology and methods; analysis and findings; discussion and recommendations—using the article "Finding Voice and Passion: Critical Race Theory Methodology in Science Teacher Education" by Felicia Moore Mensah that employed CRT in higher education. The article addressed the educational history of Michele, a Black teacher education student in a predominantly White teacher education program, and her experiences as a beginning teacher.

CHAPTER 6

Critical Feminist Research in Education

Feminism is an often contested and highly emotion-laden term, especially in U.S. education circles (hooks, 2000; Olesen, 2018). As bell hooks (2000) put it, "Mostly [people] think feminism is a bunch of angry women who want to be like men" (p. xi). This is so much the case that readers might have been tempted to skip reading this chapter just to avoid being drawn into the fray. We hope you have not made that choice and are still reading, because critical feminist theory research in education has much to offer the field and provides highly useful lenses and research tools to help address enduring problems and inequities in schools, universities, and educational settings of all kinds. We begin this chapter with the background of critical feminist research.

BACKGROUND OF CRITICAL FEMINIST RESEARCH

Critical feminist research in education, in the United States and internationally, is situated at the intersection of several sociological structures and movements as well as academic fields of study. Among these are education, traditional critical theory, feminist social movements, and feminist scholarship in fields such as psychology, biology, history, sociology, and philosophy (Henry, 2011). To help us in the discussion of this busy intersection, key terms are defined next.

Terminology

In this chapter, and the following chapters in Part II, we rely heavily on guidance from the *Publication Manual of the American Psychological Association* (7th ed.) *(APA)*, as well as other sources in defining the terminology appropriate for each chapter.

Gender and Sex

"*Gender* refers to the attitudes, feelings, and behaviors that a given culture associates with a person's biological sex (APA, 2012b). Gender is a social construct and a social identity . . . *Sex* refers to biological sex assignment" (APA, 2020,

p. 138). The *APA Manual* offers more extensive guidance on these terms in addition to other terminology, including gender identity, reporting of gender, transgender and nonconforming people, sex assignment, gender and noun usage, gender and pronoun usage, and terms that imply binaries, which we will discuss in the next chapter.

Feminism

Given the countless definitions of feminism available, we like bell hooks's (2000) elegantly simple one: "Feminism is a movement to end sexism, sexist exploitation, and oppression" (p. xii). It is important to note what hooks's definition of feminism does *not* include. It is not limited to any particular race, class, background, nationality, religion, sex, or any category of individual people. Thus, this definition does not require that one identify as female to claim feminist ideology. Nor is this definition structured against men. Instead, it is *for* ending societal structures, beliefs, and practices that hold back and harm individual women and women as a group. "[Feminism is] about women gaining equal rights" (p. xii).

For educational research, this means that critical feminist research is not ideologically neutral (Olesen, 2018). Though the methods of scientific research may be employed in the service of feminist research aims, the overall research design for this type of work does not seek to discover or verify that sexism, sexual exploitation, and oppression of women exist in schools and other educational institutions. Such work begins with those issues taken as givens and seeks to uncover the ways in which such discriminations, biases, and oppressions operate and to formulate solutions to address them.

Types of Feminism

For educational researchers designing a feminist study, especially a critical feminist study, it is highly important to consider which version of feminism—that is, which set of political viewpoints and constructs—would be the most appropriate ones to guide the study and/or which type of feminism is consistent with the researcher's convictions and aims in doing this research (Olesen, 1994). It is not sufficient for the research to be *about* women or to have aims of advancing women and girls' interests (Freeman, 2019). Critical feminist research is more complex than that. The following definitions of types of feminism may be useful in untangling some of that complexity (Moghadam, 2022).

Liberal. Liberal feminism's primary goals are gender equality and equal access. It seeks to level the playing field and to allow women to compete on equal footing with men in all areas of society. Sarah Grimké's (1838/2015) often-repeated quote is an excellent illustration of the aims of liberal feminism: "But I ask no favors for my sex. I surrender not our claim to equality. All I ask of our brethren is, that they will take their feet from off our necks, and permit us to stand upright on that ground which God designed us to occupy" (Letter 2).

Radical. Radical feminism, in contrast to liberal feminism, seeks to go beyond equality within existing societal structures and to reorder society in ways that would eliminate patriarchy altogether. It views oppression of women as a biological class as the foundational societal oppression that cuts across all other identity categories. Radical feminism seeks revolutionary societal change. This was the primary form of feminism in the United States in the 1960s and 1970s (hooks, 2000).

Marxist. Marxist feminism is a variant of feminism that incorporates and expands upon Marxist political theory. It argues that women's oppression is linked to the gendered structures of capitalism. That is, productive labor in Marxism terms means the type of labor typically done by men, and reproductive labor is what is typically done by women. Thus, the more powerful, remunerated, and valued societal work is men's work (Olesen, 1994).

Cultural. Cultural feminism ascribes to the viewpoint that there is a *female essence* or *female nature* linked to biologically determined femaleness, and it seeks to redefine and revalue such characteristics. Further, in the view of cultural feminists, the distinct female ways are often superior to men's ways. Out of cultural feminist thought emerged such ideas as the *ethics of care* that women bring to the knowledge they construct and the work that they do (Noddings, 1993).

Eco. Ecofeminism is focused on the interactions and relationships between human females and the natural world. The term was coined by the French writer Françoise d'Eaubonne in her book *Le Féminisme ou la Mort* (1974). Ecofeminism is an ideology that sees climate change, gender equality, and social justice more broadly and as more intertwined than do other forms of feminist thought (B. T. Gates, 1996).

Waves of Feminist Movement

In addition to taking different forms or types, feminist thought, political theory, and activism are commonly described in research literature, and in popular culture, as having arisen in *waves*. "The metaphor of 'waves' representing the various surges of feminism began in 1968 when Martha Weinman Lear published an article in the *New York Times* called 'The Second Feminist Wave' [that differentiated] the suffrage movement of the 19th century with the women's movements during the 1960s" and redefined feminism (National Women's History Museum, 2021, The "Waves" of Feminism section). The first-wave feminists were influenced by women involved in other activist movements. "In particular, feminists drew strategic and tactical insight from women participating in the French Revolution, the Temperance Movement, and the Abolitionist Movement" (National Women's History Museum, 2021, The

"Waves" of Feminism section). This first wave of feminism is generally regarded as having ended in 1920, with the passage of the 19th Amendment to the U.S. Constitution that granted women the right to vote.

The second wave is usually defined as occurring from the 1960s to the early 1980s and is sometimes referred to as the time of the *women's liberation movement*. The Equal Rights Amendment was passed by the U.S. Congress during this time period, but the amendment was not passed by a sufficient number of states to achieve ratification.

In the 1990s, third-wave feminism in the United States focused on issues such as sexual harassment in the workplace and on women expressing their individuality and sexuality. The fourth-wave feminist movement is identified as the feminist political movement of the present day, though some argue that this activism is simply a continuation of the third wave and not a separate, distinct wave. All waves of the feminist movement in the United States and in the West have been heavily critiqued for their outsized focus on White women and issues that affect women of the middle and upper classes (Cannella & Manuelito, 2008; Collins, 1990; hooks, 2000).

Feminist research in education has intersected with these waves of feminist social movement, and influential works, including ones related to education, emerged in each of the different time periods. For example, the *Ain't I a Woman?* speech that was given by Sojourner Truth in 1851 is a shining example of first-wave U.S. feminist thought. Winona Branch Sawyer's *What Becomes of Girl Graduates?* in 1895 and *Female Teaching* by Catherine Booth in 1861 are other examples of writing that emerged from first-wave feminism.

A few standout pieces during the second wave included *The Feminine Mystique* (1963), by Betty Friedan; "After Black Power, Women's Liberation" (in *New York* magazine, 1969), by Gloria Steinem; *For the Equal Rights Amendment* (speech to the U.S. House of Representatives, 1970), by Shirley Chisholm; and "How Can a Little Girl Like You Teach a Big Class of Men?" (in *Working It Out*, 1977), by Naomi Weisstein.

Following along in the third wave of U.S. feminism, numerous standout publications emerged, including *The Beauty Myth*, by Naomi Wolf (1991); *The Mismeasure of Woman: Why Women Are Not the Better Sex, the Opposite Sex, or the Inferior Sex*, by Carol Tavris (1992); and *Gender Play: Girls and Boys in School*, by Barrie Thorne (1993). In the fourth wave, influential publications have included *Men Explain Things to Me* (2014), by Rebecca Solnit; *Everyday Sexism* (2016), by Laura Bates; and Abi Duré's coming-of-age novel *The Girl with the Louding Voice: A Novel*.

NOTABLE CRITICAL FEMINIST THEORISTS AND RESEARCHERS

To further assist in demystifying critical feminism for educational researchers, several influential researchers are included in the following list. The individuals are not necessarily all educational researchers, but their work is consistently found in the theoretical frameworks that guide critical feminist research in education.

Gloria Anzaldúa

Gloria Anzaldúa was a U.S. scholar of Chicana social theory, feminism, and queer theory, best known for her work on border, marginalized, and hybrid cultures. Her book *Borderlands/La Frontera: The New Mestiza* is in its 5th edition and continues to be highly influential for critical feminist researchers in education.

Jill Blackmore

Jill Blackmore is Alfred Deakin Professor and Professor of Education at Deakin University in Australia. She is known for her work on gender in educational administration and policy. Her book *Troubling Women: Gender, Leadership, and Educational Change* influenced a generation of scholars doing critical feminist educational research, particularly those interested in poststructural and postmodern modes of inquiry.

Judith Butler

Judith Butler is a Berkeley philosophy professor best known for their work on conceptualizing gender as performativity—that is, something that is iteratively performed by individuals according to powerful societal norms. They are the prolific and highly influential author of numerous books and articles, including their 1990 first edition and 1999 second edition of *Gender Trouble: Feminism and the Subversion of Identity*, that influence theoretical frameworks for critical feminist research studies in education.

Patricia Hill Collins

Patricia Hill Collins is a distinguished university professor of sociology emerita at the University of Maryland, College Park. She is best known for her work on race, class, and gender, and particularly on the ways gender operates within the African American community. Her book *Black Feminist Thought* was and is highly influential in critical feminist work in education.

Cynthia Dillard

Cynthia Dillard is a professor of teacher education known for her work on the spiritual lives of Black women teachers. She is dean at Seattle University's School of Education, and her most recent book is *The Spirit of Our Work: Black Women Teachers (Re)member* (Beacon, 2021), which "highlights the intersectional identities of Black women teachers and how they matter in a teaching life" (Cynthia B. Dillard, n.d.).

bell hooks

bell hooks was a U.S. author and activist best known for her work on the intersectionality of gender, race, social class, and capitalism. Her critiques of White women's feminism and exploration of various forms of cultural intersectionality continue to influence critical feminist researchers in education up to the present day; see her book *Feminist Theory: From Margin to Center*.

Patti Lather

Patti Lather is professor emerita in Educational Studies at The Ohio State University. She taught qualitative research methodology and gender in education courses there for over 30 years. Her four books (especially 1991's *Getting Smart*) and numerous articles continue to be highly influential for feminist educational researchers, particularly those interested in postmodern and poststructural philosophy and methods.

Nel Noddings

Nel Noddings was a Stanford philosophy professor best known for her highly influential work on feminist ethics of care; see *Caring: A Relational Approach to Ethics and Moral Education*. Noddings's books and journal articles are among the best-known cultural feminist works in education fields.

Sadker and Sadker

Myra and David Sadker wrote the highly influential book *Failing at Fairness: How Our Schools Cheat Girls*. Their masterful use of data provides great clarity for educators and the public to understand the ways in which educational disparities between girls and boys originate and grow during the K–12 school years. Both were professors at American University, where David currently holds the title professor emeritus. Myra passed away in 1995.

Charol Shakeshaft

Charol Shakeshaft is a professor of educational administration at Virginia Commonwealth University and AERA Fellow. She is known for her research on women in educational leadership and on sexual abuse and sexual misconduct in schools. Her 1986 book *Women in Educational Leadership* was among the very first to challenge the baked-in sexism of the foundational theories used in educational administration and leadership preparation.

RESEARCH COMPONENTS OF EXAMPLE ARTICLE

Building on the foundation laid by the work of these researchers and theorists and numerous others, critical feminist researchers in education continue to produce new scholarship that challenges the male-dominated status quo in education. To illustrate how such critical feminist educational research can be designed and conducted, we've selected the article "Exploring the Intergenerational Responsibility of Musical Mothering and Morality" by Sally Savage, a lecturer in the School of Early Childhood and Inclusive Education at Queensland University of Technology (Australia), which was published in *The International Journal of Community Music* in 2019. This article was selected based on its fit for our criteria of (a) serving as a clear example of the type of critical educational research that is the focus of the chapter, and (b) our desire to include diversity of authors, journals, and educational specialty areas. Savage's article fits the definition of critical feminist research in that it explicitly focuses on a feminist area of concern (mothering), is on an education topic (music education in this case), and uses critical feminist theory as part of its theoretical underpinning. Introducing her research, Savage (2019) said

> Responsibility for musical development in children is largely directed at mothers who are generally the primary caregivers of children in western societies. Middle-class mothers find ways to legitimate their mothering practices as morally good; child-rearing becomes "a self-conscious moral enterprise" (Hay 1993: 32) where mothers work hard to gain acceptance in society and with other mothers (Sayers 2005). Children's participation in music is seen to develop children of value who have the skills to succeed in later life, providing them with educational advantages, opportunities, social contacts and emotional capabilities. . . . By investing in their children, middle-class mothers are investing in themselves as "good" mothers using concerted cultivation and intensive mothering practice. (p. 112)

Statement of the Problem, Purpose, and Research Question

Savage (2019) clearly espoused the statement of the problem: "there is a scarcity of research that looks closely at the diversity of women's experiences of mothering, particularly through the lens of music as a social practice" (p. 111). Therefore, her purpose was "to expand music education research by analyzing the intersection of music, motherhood, gender, class and generation" (p. 111). The research question that guided the study was not directly reported in the article. However, the author stated that she investigated "the connection between musical mothering and morality, where involvement in musical practices provides middle-class women opportunities to validate their mothering" (p. 111).

Theoretical Framework

Savage (2019) employed two theoretical frames in her research: one was Bourdieusian, pertaining to Pierre Bourdieu; the other was feminist theory, or what we call critical feminist theory. She drew from Bourdieu's social reproduction and symbolic power theories and his concepts of habitus and capital—economic, cultural, social, and symbolic. However, she found that although Bourdieu's social reproduction theory was "useful in identifying structural constraints and how the musical habitus develops and is nurtured, there are limitations in his theory when considering the diversity of women's experiences, particularly in everyday life" (p. 116). Therefore, she turned to feminist theory: "Feminist theory is appropriate for exploring concepts of mothering and the work involved in creating and developing musical selves and children, primarily because it is usually women who do this work" (p. 116).

Methodology and Methods

In this research, Savage (2019) used what she called an experience-centered narrative methodology:

> This article draws on a small-scale research study into musical mothering and uses an experience-centred narrative methodology to share the mothers' stories of the role of music in family life. Narrative methods show how people see themselves within the social spaces they live in and the cultures they inhabit. (p. 116)

The method the author used to gather data from which to construct the narratives of "musical mothering" was "semi-structured interviews of approximately one-hour Durations [sic] . . . with individuals at a mutually agreed time and place to accommodate work and childcare arrangements" (p. 117). As this was intergenerational research, she interviewed mothers and their mothers (whom she labeled grandmothers) about "the ways in which they produce musical children and musical selves" (p. 111).

Analysis and Results/Findings

Savage (2019) presented the findings under the heading "Being the good mother through music" (p. 115). She thematized her data and described the ways in which the mothers and grandmothers enacted motherhood through music education for their children. These descriptions were not universally happy or positive tales. The participants revealed mixed feelings, conflicts, uncertainty, and pressures in their narratives of musical mothering.

For example, under the theme "The messiness of musical mothering," one participant, Susan, described the messiness of supporting her child's music education as a single working mother:

I was a piano teacher, so I was working ridiculous hours—all the prime times when you should have been spending time with your kids. I was working, and none of my friends were. They all had stable marriages and families where I was only one parent. I was often isolated because of that. (p. 118)

Study findings such as these reveal the complexity, and inequity, of commonly used concepts in education such as *parental involvement*. In other words, a different type of educational research, such as a positivist survey, could have captured this woman in the *parental involvement in child's music education* category as a yes, she was involved—but the reality is much messier than the yes/no binary such research might be set up to measure.

Discussion and Recommendations

Savage (2019) concluded that "mothers' experiences of music and morality are varied and often paradoxical, thus complicating the issue of middle-class motherhood and the roles that music plays in their practices" (p. 124). The importance of such findings is that they argue against Bourdieu's view that "all action is an investment for profit" (p. 124). The narratives by mothers in Savage's study demonstrate, instead, that music "can provide an opportunity to move beyond competitiveness to embrace difference, highlighting the unifying potential that music has" (p. 124). Thus, the author's findings challenge a dominant narrative and add research-based knowledge about how one form of inequity women face in dealing with schools (lopsided, incomplete, and sexist expectations of mothering) continues to operate. Savage did not offer any recommendations.

CONCLUSION

We began this chapter with the background of critical feminist research that included the necessary terminology, the types of feminisms, and the waves of the feminist movements beginning in the 19th century and taking us up to the present. Notable feminist researchers and their works were offered as a resource for those wanting to pursue critical feminist research. We concluded by examining the article "Exploring the Intergenerational Responsibility of Musical Mothering and Morality" from the field of music education to illustrate what the component parts of critical feminist research in education may look like.

CHAPTER 7

LGBTQ Studies and Queer Theory in Education

We begin this chapter with an explanation of the terms that are often conflated when discussing gender and sex. We follow with a brief history of the gay rights movement, providing context for our discussion of LGBTQ studies, queer theory, and queer studies. Next, we explain and contrast LGBTQ studies, queer theory, and queer studies and provide the historical and current influencers in these areas. Lastly, we offer an example of an LGBTQ study and review its research components.

TERMINOLOGY

In Chapter 6, "Critical Feminism Research in Education," we defined gender and sex as they applied to feminist theories and research. Here again we turn to the APA manual and extend our discussion of these terms and others that are necessary for our understanding of and use of LGBTQ+ theories.

Gender vs. Sex

Gender refers to the attitudes, feelings, and behaviors that a given culture associate with a person's biological sex (APA, 2012b). Gender is a social construct and a social identity. Use the term "gender" when referring to people as social groups. For example, when reporting the genders of participants in the Method section, write something like this: "Approximately 60% of participants identified as cisgender [assigned sex at birth that corresponds to one's gender identity] women, 35% as cisgender men, 3% as transgender women, 1% as transgender men, and 1% as nonbinary." *Sex* refers to biological sex assignment; use the term "sex" when the biological distinction of sex assignment (e.g., sex assigned at birth) is predominant. (APA, 2020, p. 138)

Gender Identity

Gender identity is a component of gender that describes a person's psychological sense of their gender. Many people describe gender identity as a deeply felt, inherent sense of being a boy, a man, or male; a girl, a women, or female; or a nonbinary gender (e.g., genderqueer, gender-nonconforming, gender-neutral, agender, gender-fluid) that may or may not correspond to a person's sex assigned at birth, presumed gender based on sex assignment, or primary or secondary sex characteristics (APA, 2015a). Gender identity applies to all individuals . . . and is distinct from sexual orientation . . . thus, the two must not be conflated. (APA, 2020, p. 138)

Transgender and Gender-Nonconforming People

Transgender is used as an adjective to refer to persons whose gender identity, expression, and/or role does not conform to what is culturally associated with their sex assigned at birth. Some transgender people hold a binary gender, such as man or woman, but other have a gender outside of this binary, such as gender-fluid or nonbinary. Individuals whose gender varies from presumptions based on their sex assigned at birth may use terms other than "transgender" to describe their gender, including "gender-nonconforming," "genderqueer," "gender-nonbinary," "gender-creative," "agender," or "two-spirit," to name a few. (APA, 2020, pp. 138–139)

Reporting of Gender

Authors are strongly encouraged to explicitly designate information about the gender identities of the participants making up their sample (e.g., whether participants are transgender, cisgender, or other gender identities) rather than assuming cisgender identities . . . Cisgenderism or cissexism refers to the belief that being cisgender is normative, as indicated by the assumption that individuals are cisgender unless otherwise specified . . . [and] the belief that there are only two genders. (APA, 2020, p. 138)

APA also emphasizes that people should be referred to by the name of their choosing, which may not be their legal name. Furthermore, when reporting research, "do not refer to the pronouns that transgender and gender-nonconforming people use as 'preferred pronouns' because this implies a choice about one's gender" (APA, 2020, p. 140). Rather, use the pronoun a person identifies with; for example, a transgender man may indicate the use of "he," "him," or "his." And a gender-nonconforming person may use the nonbinary pronoun "they."

BRIEF HISTORY OF THE GAY RIGHTS MOVEMENT

In 1913 Henry Gerber, a German immigrant, came to the United States. A few years later, he was institutionalized in a mental hospital for being homosexual. When the United States entered World War I, declaring war on Germany, Gerber was given the option of joining the army, where his German language would be useful, or being imprisoned in the United States as an enemy alien. He joined the army. During his military tenure in Germany, he became involved with the

Bund für Menschenrechte (the League for Human Rights), which focused specifically on the rights of "sexual minorities." After the war, he returned to the United States and in 1924 formed the Society for Human Rights in Chicago, the first recorded gay rights organization in the United States. Gerber is considered the "grandfather of the American gay movement" (Kepner et al., 2002, p. 24).

Then in 1950 Harry Hay founded the Mattachine Foundation, another gay rights group. It has a complicated history that is dependent on the telling. Initially the Foundation was a "small group of homosexuals, influenced by communist ideology, [who] came together to organize homosexuals in defense of their rights as citizens" (Meeker, 2001, p. 79). In 1953, due to conflict among the founding leaders, a group splintered off and was reformed as the Mattachine Society. The society was considered by some as far more conservative than its predecessor, embracing "conservative politics advocating that homosexuals adjust to life in a homophobic society adopting heterosexual social and cultural mores" (Meeker, 2001, p. 79). However, according to Meeker this "retreat to respectability" (a term used by D'Emilio in *Sexual Politics, Sexual Communities*) was just a ruse that allowed the organization to "speak simultaneously to homosexuals and homophobic heterosexuals" while communicating very different messages. "This practice of dissimulation disarmed some of the antigay sentiment in American society while it also enabled the homophiles to defend and nurture the gay world" (Meeker, 2001, p. 81).[1]

The late 1950s and 1960s led to advancements in understanding gender and sexuality as well as gay rights. In 1955 George Jorgensen Jr. was the first well-known U.S. person to undergo sex reassignment in Denmark, becoming Christine Jorgensen. There had, however, been others. The most famous was Lile Elbe, the Danish painter who in 1930 began a series of reassignment surgeries in Denmark (Blumberg, n.d.). In 1965, Dr. John Oliven coined the term "transgenderism" (Oliven, 1965, p. 514). The term later evolved to "transgender." Then in 1969 there were the Stonewall Riots, a turning point in the gay rights movement. The Stonewall Inn was a Mafia-run gay club on Christopher Street in New York City that was raided by the police, leading to 6 days of protests and riots. A year later, in 1970, the first gay parade was held—the Christopher Street Liberation Day.

The 1970s brought about openly gay elected officials like Harvey Milk, who was elected in November 1977 and sworn in January 1978 as a member of the San Francisco Board of Supervisors. He was assassinated in November of that same year. During that time Milk commissioned Gilbert Baker, an artist friend, to design a symbol for gay pride. Baker designed the rainbow flag that continues to represent gay pride (Black & Prince, 2019-present). Sadly, the 1980s brought the AIDS epidemic that disproportionately affected gay men. As of 2019 "an estimated 1,189,700 people aged 13 and older had HIV in the United States" (Centers for Disease Control and Prevention, n.d., section HIV Prevalence Estimate).

The 1990s and early 2000s were a mixed bag of progress and setbacks. In 1993 during President Clinton's term in office, when he was unable to get a ban against lesbian, gay, and bisexual persons in the military lifted, Clinton enacted the Don't Ask, Don't Tell policy. It required that "lesbians, gay men, and bisexuals (LGB) must remain silent about their sexual orientation and behavior if they are to serve in the military. In turn, the military [was] restricted from asking personnel about their sexual orientation" (G. Gates, 2007, para. 2). It was repealed in 2011 during the Obama presidency. The Clinton administration also brought about the Defense of Marriage Act (DOMA) that denied federal benefits to same-sex couples. However, the 2015 ruling by the Supreme Court in the *Obergefell v. Hodges* case that "the Fourteenth Amendment requires a State to license a marriage between two people of the same sex and to recognize a marriage between two people of the same sex when their marriage was lawfully licensed and performed out-of-State" (*Obergefell v. Hodges*, p. 1) effectively made DOMA unenforceable and same-sex marriage legal.

In 2009, the first hate crime legislation in the United States, the Matthew Shepard and James Byrd Jr. Hate Crime Prevention Act, was passed. And with regard to transgender rights, there is a complicated history. For example, in 2016 when Eric Fanning became the first openly gay U.S. secretary of the Army, or any military branch, the transgender ban was removed from the military. In 2018 President Trump reinstated the ban with limited exceptions, like complete gender transition. But then within the first month of President Biden's presidency, he revoked the ban entirely.

LGBTQ STUDIES, QUEER THEORY, AND QUEER STUDIES

The first undergraduate course in the United States on LGBTQ studies was taught in 1970 at the University of California, Berkeley (McNaron, 1997). Several other universities followed suit that same year. In a recent search of major university catalogs related to the topic at hand, we found departments, majors, or certification programs titled Gay and Lesbian Studies; Queer and Sexuality Studies; LGBT Studies; Queer Studies; Gender and Sexuality Studies; LGBTQI Studies; and Women's, Gender, and Sexuality Studies. This was only a sampling, and there certainly may be others. However, it demonstrates the diversity of names that the study of issues and theories related to gender, sexuality, and identity fall into. Perhaps this is due to the evolving attitudes and politics related to these issue at the various universities.

The history of lesbian and gay studies, LGBT, LGBTQ, and queer studies is problematic and difficult to trace. Some questions we asked were: Did LGBT studies emerge at the same time as lesbian and gay studies? When was "Q" added to the LGBT initialism? Does the "Q" stand for questioning or queer in LGBTQ? Our research revealed contradictions in the answers to all of these questions and more. We even found queer studies and queer theory used interchangeably. In an effort to get clarity, we did an exhaustive review of the literature regarding these topics in general and education specifically. The articles were thorough, but not necessarily pedagogical, and contradictory, which might be expected. However, the best description we found that addressed many of our questions and would not require us to offer a tome, for which we do not have space, was a 2017 university course syllabus, *Introduction to Queer Theory*, by Dr. J. Jeanine Ruhsam at the University of Massachusetts. We particularly appreciated the contrast she offers between LGBT or LGBTQ studies and queer theory. We have inserted further explanatory comments:

> Queer Theory critically examines the way power works to institutionalize and legitimate certain forms and expressions of sexuality and gender [seen as heterosexual, "normal," normative] while stigmatizing others [seen as abnormal, "other," queer]. Queer Theory [in the early 1990s] followed the emergence and popularity of Gay and Lesbian (now, LGBT or Queer) Studies in the academy. Whereas LGBT Studies seeks to analyze LGBT people as stable identities [seeing oneself as always basically the same person—past, present, and future], Queer Theory problematizes and challenges rigid identity categories, norms of sexuality and gender and the oppression and violence that such hegemonic norms justify. Often considered the "deconstruction" of LGBT studies, Queer Theory destabilizes sexual and gender identities allowing and encouraging multiple, unfettered interpretations of cultural phenomena. It predicates that all sexual behaviors and gender expressions, all concepts linking such to prescribed, associated identities, and their categorization into "normal" or "deviant" sexualities or gender, are constructed socially [created and accepted by society] and generate modes of social meaning. Queer theory follows and expands upon Feminist Theory [poststructural Feminist Theory] by refusing the belief that sexuality and gender identity are essentialist categories [have a true nature] determined by biology that can thus be empirically judged by fixed standards of morality and "truth." (Ruhsam, 2017, p. 1)

Whereas Ruhsam compares LGBT studies and queer theory, she does not address both queer theory and queer studies. Most of the universities we researched preferred the course title Queer Theory to Queer Studies. However, one example of a course on queer studies was Johnathan Katz at the University of Pennsylvania. His *Intro to Queer Studies* (n.d.) course states that

> this course will introduce students to the historical and intellectual forces that led to the emergence of queer theory as a distinct field, as well as to recent and ongoing debates about gender, sexuality, embodiment, race, privacy, global power, and social norms. We will begin by tracing queer theory's conceptual heritage and prehistory in psychoanalysis, deconstruction and poststructuralism, the history of sexuality, gay and lesbian studies, woman-of-color feminism, the feminist sex wars, and the AIDS crisis. (para. 1)

The difference between these two sample syllabi appears to be that the queer theory syllabus focuses on queer theory as an analytical approach, whereas the queer studies syllabus mainly addresses the historical and intellectual development of the theory.

NOTABLE LGBTQ AND QUEER THEORISTS AND RESEARCHERS

Unlike some of the previous chapters, there is no consensus on the pioneering scholars who introduced LGBTQ and/or queer theory into education. There is, however, agreement on the historical influences. These include, but are not limited to, Michel Foucault, Judith Butler, Eve Kosofsky Sedgwick, Gloria Anzaldúa, and Audre Lorde. Selected current scholars within various fields of education include the following:

Kevin Kumashiro

Kevin Kumashiro is the former dean of the School of Education at the University of San Francisco and was previously professor of Asian American Studies and Education at the University of Illinois at Chicago. He is a past president of the National Association for Multicultural Education. His research interests include educational policy, teacher preparation, school reform, and educational equity and social justice. One of his most cited works is "Toward a Theory of Anti-Oppressive Education."

Catherine Lugg

Catherine Lugg is professor emerita of education at the Graduate School of Education at Rutgers University. "She is recognized for her pioneering research surrounding LGBT issues and the politics of education" (Rutgers, n.d.), as well as educational history and policy, the influences of media on policymaking, and social history. One of her most significant works is "Sissies, Faggots, Lezzies, and Dykes: Gender, Sexual Orientation, and a New Politics of Education."

Cris Mayo

Cris Mayo is a professor in the Department of Education and director of the Interdisciplinary Studies master's degree program at the University of Vermont. She has written extensively on issues related to gender and sexuality and is currently the editor-in-chief of the *Oxford Encyclopedia on Gender and Sexuality in Education*. Two of her books received the American Educational Studies Association (AESA) Critic's Choice Book Award: *Disputing the Subject of Sex: Sexuality and Public School Controversies* in 2008 and *LGBTQ Youth and Education: Policy and Practices* in 2014.

Shameka Powell

Shameka Powell is an emerging professor of prominence. They won the American Educational Research Association (AERA) Division G: Social Context of Education Distinguished Dissertation Award in 2016. Powell is an assistant professor at Tufts University in Educational Studies focusing on educational opportunity and the intersectionality of race, class, and gender in schools. "Specifically, they interrogate how institutional agents create, exacerbate, and alleviate stratification patterns within schools [and] situate their research within Critical Race Theory and Queer of Color Theories" (Tufts University, n.d.). One of their recent publications is "Toward a BlackQueerEducator Politic and Praxis."

James T. Sears

James Sears is a former professor at the University of South Carolina, Trinity University, Harvard University, and Penn State. In 2006 he won the AERA's Queer Studies SIG Body of Work Award. His 1997 book, *Lonely Hunters: An Oral History of Lesbian and Gay Southern Life, 1948–1968*, received acclaim and aroused controversy.

RESEARCH COMPONENTS OF EXAMPLE STUDY

In choosing an article as an example for LGBTQ studies or queer theory, again we looked for an empirical article. And again, most of the articles, particularly related to queer theory, are theoretical, not empirical. Moreover, as we addressed above, there are contradictions as to what the Q stands for in LGBTQ. Some say *queer* and some say *questioning*. This may not seem important, but it is, since LGBT are set identities and queer is definitely not. As Ruhsam (2017) explained, LGBT studies assume stable identities, whereas queer studies "problematize and challenge rigid identity categories" (p. 1).

The article we chose is "Refusing Relevance: School Administrator Resistance to Offering Professional Development Addressing LGBTQ Issues in Schools" by Elizabethe Payne and Melissa Smith. It was published in *Educational Administration Quarterly* in 2018. It needs to be noted that the authors state that the Q is LGBTQ stands for both queer and questioning. We do not agree with this categorization for the reasons mentioned above. However, the article provides a good example to illustrate the research components of LGBTQ studies, with Q standing for questioning, but not queer studies or queer theory. For an in-depth discussion of queer theory, see the aforementioned scholars.

Statement of the Problem, Purpose, and Research Question

The statement of the problem, according to the authors, was that "little empirical research specifically addresses school administrator's efforts to create more inclusive school environments for LGBTQ students" (Payne & Smith, 2018, p. 184). Most of the research focused on school leaders' attitudes toward LGBTQ students and their responsibilities in meeting the students' needs:

> What the field lacks is empirical data about principals who are grappling with the work of addressing gender and sexual diversity in their schools. Given that students

and teachers have reported that "they consider school administrators to be a key barrier to LGBT visibility in schools" (Grace, 2007, p. 4), it is imperative that educational research begin asking school principals and other administrators questions about LGBTQ safety and inclusion. (p. 189)

Therefore, the purpose of Payne and Smith's study was to address this gap in the literature.

Payne is the director of the Queering Education Research Institute (QuERI), and Smith is an assistant director of research there. Both are also professors, Payne at City University of New York and Smith at the University of Central Arkansas. In their work at QuERI, they developed and offered to schools no-cost professional development, the Reduction of Stigma in Schools program (RSIS), and focused on meeting the needs of LGBTQ families and students. Educators attending the professional development were their research participants. Their research question was "What are participants' perceptions of their administrators' support for their efforts to support LGBTQ students?" (p. 195).

Theoretical Framework

A critical lens incorporating the concepts of social reproduction, systemic oppression, and heteronormativity informed this work. Schools have often been characterized as institutions that reproduce the existing social structure—that is, social reproduction. This includes reproducing racism, sexism, and anti-LGBTQ attitudes. This contributes to systemic or institutional oppression that is built into the structure, in this case schools and education, itself. It is often invisible to those within the structure who only see individual acts as racist or homophobic, but not the system itself. Heteronormativity is the belief that heterosexuality is the normal, the acceptable, sexual orientation. This positions those who are not heterosexual as deviant, as not normal.

Methodology and Methods

The methodology the authors employed was an LGBTQ case study drawn from a larger evaluation study of "educators' responses to the RSIS professional development program" that focused on "creating more affirming school environment for LGBTQ students and families" (Payne & Smith, 2018, p. 194). The evaluation study included

> semistructured interviews with 11 educators who had attended RSIS workshops, 322 written evaluations completed at the end of each workshop, follow-up questionnaires completed by 11 key participants, thick descriptive field notes recounting all introductory meetings with school personnel for 3 years, phone and email exchange records for all school contacts, the content delivered for each RSIS presentation, and an in-depth interview with the first RSIS graduate student intern responsible for delivering the program. (p. 195)

In analyzing the evaluation data, it became apparent that

> administrators' support for or attitudes toward LGBTQ students emerged as a re-curring issue shaping their [program participants] efforts to (a) bring LGBTQ-focused professional development into their schools and (b) . . . implement content and strategies they learned during RSIS professional development. (p. 195)

Based on this finding, the researchers extended their study to address the "[program] participants' perceptions of their administrators' support for their efforts to support LGBTQ students" (p. 195). The methods included semi-structured individual interviews with 19 program participants, including social workers, teachers, counselors, principals, and psychologists.

Analysis and Results/Findings

Data from the original evaluation research were analyzed using emergent coding—that is, codes that are not preset but that emerge from the data. Carspecken's critical approach was used to determine key themes (see Carspecken, 2013). These were "barriers to LGBT-focused professional development and barriers to implement LGBT-inclusive practice" (Payne & Smith, 2018, p. 195).

The authors focused solely on the first theme: barriers to LGBT-focused professional development. Several subthemes were identified. The first, "reject-ing relevance and refusing risk," can be seen in the statements and attitudes of the school administrators. Their "language ranged from total denial that 'those kinds of kids' or 'those kinds of families' were part of the school com-munity, to surprise that LGBTQ students *are* present [in the schools]" (p. 199). Furthermore, the administrators did not want to risk bringing an "inappropri-ate" topic into the school. .

The second subtheme was "innocence and taboo in middle school" (p. 202). In interviewing middle school principals, the researchers found they "were ad-amant that their students were too young for LGBTQ-focused professional development to be relevant to their school" (p. 202) and indicated that the students were nonsexual so teachers did not need to hear about LGBTQ issues. The third subtheme was "passing the buck: teacher interest, school board ap-proval, and fear of community response" (p. 203). Summarizing one princi-pal's response to the training, the researcher stated that

> he was pretty much adamant that the teachers were not going to have any [interest in attending], and the parents [would object], so that they would have to bring [the possibility] of the RSIS workshop to the school board for approval and that never really [happened]. (p. 204; brackets original to the text)

The final, and fourth, subtheme was "the safety of 'safety'" (p. 206). Here the administrators understood that because risk factors were associated with *not* providing LGBTQ training to their teachers and staff, they needed to be more amenable to the training. This, however, was problematic. The authors found that

> administrator desire and concern to reduce the risk experienced by LGBTQ students and enhance safety is a welcome response, and we have certainly used the safety framework to start conversations with school leaders who claimed a lack of previous knowledge or expressed high levels of discomfort around the topic of LGBTQ students. However, the pitfalls of the safety discourse cannot be ignored: Framing the inclusion of LGBTQ issues in this way defines LGBTQ youth as victims and educators as protectors rather than affirming the position that LGBTQ identities should become a visible, valued part of the school culture. Additionally, the use of "safety" as the institutional goal—rather than inclusion of sexual and gender difference—maintains existing institutional values rather than challenging or expanding them. (p. 207)

Discussion and Recommendations

The resistance to offering professional development on LGBTQ issues in schools was predicated on several issues: (a) sexual and gender diversity was not seen as relevant to teaching and learning and was presumed to affect only a few students, if any; (b) administrators' beliefs that professional development on issues related to LGBTQ students was not relevant; thus, if training was considered it was typically scheduled as a concurrent session that allowed teachers to pick and choose which training to attend, or it was only mandated for "guidance counselors and other specific student support professionals positioned to address student 'risk'" (Payne & Smith, 2018, p. 208); (c) a lack of understanding about gender and sexual identity may have caused administrators to assume "that raising the issue of LGBTQ students means raising the issue of student sexual activity. This concern [was] particularly prevalent in middle and elementary schools, where students [were] perceived to be 'too young' to be aware of sexuality" (p. 208); (d) because administrators did not "see" LGBTQ families and students in their school, they believed there was no problem to be addressed; and (e) "supporting LGBTQ students and families was seen by many administrators to be a politically charged act—rather than a professional obligation—and one in opposition to the values of the larger community" (p. 208).

In determining what would need to happen for administrators to see the relevance of and be open to professional development related to understanding and serving LGBTQ students and families, the authors concluded that the first step was to increase administrators' knowledge level related to sexual and gender diversity. They referred to the research of Greytak, Kosciw, and Boesen (2013), who, according to Payne and Smith (2018) "found that administrators are 'less aware of anti-LGBT bullying, harassment, name-calling, and biased language (pp. 87–88), but professional development significantly increased school administrators' awareness of the school experiences of LGBTQ students'" (p. 209).

Payne and Smith (2018) recommended that this training should be specifically designed for school administrators, not in conjunction with teachers and staff, and address the administrators' possible "biases, sexism, homophobia, and transphobia and consider what supportive instructional methods and climate look like for LGBTQ students if all students are to be academically successful" (p. 209). Additionally, the training should provide administrators with "opportunities to learn about and recognize the need for a continuous process of interrupting the systematic exclusion and stigmatization of LGBTQ students in all arenas of school life: curriculum, social culture, policy, extracurricular activities, school ceremonies, and rituals," and it is their "obligation to support the academic achievement of every child" (p. 209). Once administrators have acquired the needed knowledge and understanding of the "relationship between social stigma and academic outcomes," they need a more complicated understanding of schools as social systems that reproduce and are complicit in "the problem of LGBTQ bullying and [should be introduced] to the concepts of heteronormativity, heterosexism, and how these work . . . [and] are often reinforced and reproduced through curriculum, school rituals, traditions, and awards that privilege heterosexuality and gender conformity" (p. 210). The authors concluded that

> finally—and possibly more important—professional development must help administrators stop assuming all students and parents are straight simply because educators cannot physically observe their queerness. When school administrators can dismantle this assumption about their students and the families they serve, they are more able to understand LGBTQ students' needs and experiences as relevant to their daily decision-making. *THIS* is the relevance we need to convey to school leaders (p. 211).

CONCLUSION

In this chapter we began by explaining the terms that are necessary in any discussion of gender and sex. To provide context, we followed with a brief discussion of the history of the gay rights movement. In the next section, LGBTQ studies, queer theory, and queer studies were contrasted, which was followed by notable researchers and theorists in these areas. Lastly, we concluded by using Payne and Smith's article, "Refusing Relevance: School Administrator Resistance to Offering Professional Development Addressing LGBTQ Issues in Schools," to illustrate the research components indicative of LGBTQ studies.

CHAPTER 8

Indigenous/Tribal Critical Research in Education

This is yet another chapter that required careful consideration of terminology for use in the chapter title and throughout the text. The terms used to refer to the people and groups whose lives are affected by this type of research are many and varied, as are the names of the critical theories used to guide the research. We have chosen *Indigenous/Tribal Critical Research*.

We start our discussion by noting the problematic nature of *all* of the terms we need to use in our explanation of how to conceptualize and conduct research using Indigenous/Tribal Critical theories. As Denzin and Lincoln (2008) pointed out (quoting Smith): "'The term *research* is inextricably linked to European imperialism and colonialism. (L.T. Smith, 1999, p. 1). L.T. Smith (1999) contends that 'the word itself is probably one of the dirtiest words in the indigenous world's vocabulary'" (p. 4). So many ills and abuses have been inflicted on Indigenous Peoples and cultures around the world in the name of research that it casts a shadow on the process itself.

Given that history, in thinking about research conducted with and for Indigenous Peoples, it is especially important to be mindful of language. *Indigenous* means simply the people who originally lived in a place. This covers a wide and diverse group of people worldwide. In the United States, some might immediately think of Native Americans who lived in what is now the United States for centuries before European colonists arrived. Around the globe, however, many groups would qualify as being the Indigenous People of that area. The *Publication Manual of the American Psychological Association* (2020) provides the following guidance:

> When writing about Indigenous Peoples, use the names that they call themselves. In general, refer to an Indigenous group as a "people" or "nation" rather than as a "tribe."

> - In North America, the collective terms "Native American" and "Native North American" are acceptable (and may be preferred to "American Indian"). "Indian" usually refers to people from India. Specify the nation or people if possible (e.g., Cherokee, Navajo, Sioux).
> - Hawaiian Natives may identify as "Native American," "Hawaiian Native," "Indigenous Peoples of the Hawaiian Islands," and/or "Pacific Islander."

- In Canada, refer to the Indigenous Peoples collectively as "Indigenous Peoples" or "Aboriginal Peoples" (*International Journal of Indigenous Health*, n.d.); specify the nation or people if possible (e.g., People of the First Nations of Canada, People of the First Nations, or First Nations People; Métis; Inuit).
- In Alaska, the Indigenous People may identify as "Alaska Natives." The Indigenous Peoples in Alaska, Canada, Siberia, and Greenland may identify as a specific nation (e.g., Inuit, Iñupiat). Avoid the term "Eskimo" because it may be considered pejorative.
- In Latin America and the Caribbean, refer to the Indigenous Peoples collectively as "Indigenous Peoples" and by name if possible (e.g., Quechua, Aymara, Taíno, Nahuatl).
- In Australia, the Indigenous Peoples may identify as "Aboriginal People" or "Aboriginal Australians" and "Torres Strait Islander People" or "Torres Strait Island Australians." Refer to specific groups when people use these terms to refer to themselves (e.g., Anangu Pitjantjatjara, Arrernte).
- In New Zealand, the Indigenous People may identify as "Māori" or the "Māori people" (the proper spelling includes the diacritical macron over the "a"). (2020, p. 144)

In this chapter we focus on the Indigenous People of the United States. We use the suggested terminology of APA, Native American, but also the terminology used by the authors we quote that were dependent on the time and context of their writing.

BACKGROUND OF INDIGENOUS/TRIBAL RESEARCH

Brayboy (2013) points to the 1916 work of Arthur C. Parker as one of the earliest printed examples of what would become Indigenous/Tribal Critical theory:

> In 1916 Parker presented a list of grievances or "charges" against the U.S. as a result of the spiritual, physical, and intellectual dislocation experienced by Indigenous peoples at the hands of forcibly imposed Western colonial notions of jurisprudence and religious civilizing missions. (p. 89)

Though, of course, such grievances against colonialism and resistance among Indigenous Peoples had been around for centuries, much of it was found in oral history and song, so Parker's written work represents an important milestone.

Almost 50 years later, critical and postcolonial research about Native and Indigenous topics began to appear in U.S. educational research journals. The *Journal of American Indian Education (JAIE)* was established in 1961 by Robert Roessel Jr., who was editor and director for the Center for Indian Education (CIE) at Arizona State University (ASU). It has been published continuously since. In 1976, John Tippeconnic III became the CIE center director. For more than 40 years, his research, scholarly publications, and policy advocacy have influenced others involved in critical Tribal and Indigenous research.

In the 1990s, researchers such as Teresa L. McCarty, who studies American Indian languages and schooling, and K. Tsianina Lomawaima, who studies American Indian policy history and Indigenous knowledge systems, began to have work published in major journals and books by established presses. Then, around the turn of the century, Tiffany S. Lee joined the ranks of those studying and publishing on Native American language and identity, particularly for Native youth.

In the mid-2000s, current CIE director and JAIE coeditor Bryan Brayboy was among the first to articulate the principles of an Indigenous/Tribal Critical theory (TribalCrit) for education (see below). Briefly, it arose from CRT and postulates that colonialism and racism are deeply engrained and almost invisible in education. Indeed, the history of the education of Native Americans is malicious. Starting in 1869 and continuing into the 1960s, Native American children were taken from their families to boarding schools run by the federal government and churches (National Native American Boarding School Coalition, n.d.). The goal of the "Indian" boarding schools, according to Captain Richard Henry Pratt (1892), was to "kill the Indian in him and save the man" (p. 46), a phrase he used in an 1892 speech at the National Conference of Charities and Correction in Denver. Pratt was known as the founder of the first off-reservation boarding school, where Indian children were taken off the reservation, removed from their families, and placed in these schools with the goal of educational assimilation. "It was not until the 1978 Indian Child Welfare Act was implemented that Native American parents gained the legal right to refuse to oblige with the placement of their children in off-reservation schools" (Ellington, 2021, pp. 9–10).

Today, non–Native American teachers, who may lack the necessary cultural competence, continue to teach Native American students. This makes the need for culturally responsive schooling (CRS) that incorporates social and cultural tenets into the curricula critical (Castagno & Brayboy, 2008). The need is not new:

> The first officially recognized call for CRS came in 1928 with the publication of the *Meriam Report* . . . [which] called for more Indigenous teachers, early childhood programs, and the incorporation of tribal languages and cultures in schools . . . little change occurred until more than 30 years later. (Castagno & Brayboy, 2008, pp. 944–945)

Beginning in the 1970s, a series of federal reports and legislation addressed Indigenous education. They "offered data on the academic performance of Indigenous youth and the lack of curriculum that supported tribal languages and cultures in schools," provided "funding for creating tribal culture and language programs for schools," supported "increasing the number of Native educators," and facilitated "the development of schools and educational programs that were tribally controlled" (p. 945).

This was followed by the widespread embrace of CRS by the educational establishment in the 1980s and 1990s, which made it easier to incorporate CRS principles into curricula at schools:

> In 1998, President Clinton issued Executive Order 13096 on AI/AN [American Indian/Alaskan Native] education, which included recognition of the "special historic responsibility for the education of American Indian and Alaska Native students," a commitment to "improving the academic performance and reducing the dropout rate" of Indigenous students, and a nationwide effort among tribal leaders and Indian education scholars to develop a "research agenda" guided by the goals of self-determination and the preservation of tribal cultures and languages ("American Indian and Alaska Native Education," 1998). (Castagno & Brayboy, 2008, pp. 945–946)

However, despite the best of intentions, many schools that serve Native American students fall short on cultural responsiveness, and Native American student educational achievement lags and offers a ripe area for critical research.

TERMINOLOGY

Colonialism

Colonialism is the domination of a people or of an area by a foreign state or nation for the purpose of extending power and exploitation of people and resources.

Postcolonialism

Postcolonial is the historical period or state of affairs after Western colonization ended. Postcolonialism as a theory is interested in the cultural, political, and economic legacy left by colonialism and imperialism. It also refers to new thought, new theory, resistance, and resiliency that arose during and after the Western colonial period.

TribalCrit

Tribal Critical Theory (TribalCrit) is a political theory that builds on critical race theory's (CRT) well-established tenets by adapting it specifically to the challenges faced by Indigenous Peoples. Brayboy (2006) explains,

> while these theories [LatCrit and AsianCrit] have developed to meet the specific needs of Latinos/as and Asian Americans, they largely maintain the basic premise

of CRT that racism is endemic in society. In contrast, the basic tenet of TribalCrit emphasizes that colonization is endemic to society. (p. 429)

Thus, the societal oppressions wrought by colonialism on Indigenous Peoples around the world are the central focus of TribalCrit rather than racism, which is the central focus of CRT.

NOTABLE INDIGENOUS/TRIBAL THEORISTS AND RESEARCHERS

Maenette Ah nee-Benham

Maenette Ah nee-Benham is chancellor at the University of Hawaii, West Oahu. She is a *kānaka maoli* (Native Hawaiian) scholar and teacher. Her research focuses on alternative and Indigenous forms of school leadership. See, for example, the book she coauthored with R. H. Heck, *Culture and Educational Policy in Hawaii: The Silencing of Native Voices.*

Bryan Brayboy

Bryan Brayboy (Lumbee) is President's Professor and Borderlands Professor of Indigenous Education and Justice, School of Social Transformation at Arizona State University, and director of the Center for Indian Education. (Arizona State University, n.d.). He is a prolific researcher and author. His elaboration of the concept of tribal critical race theory, which he called TribalCrit in "Toward a Tribal Critical Race Theory in Education" (2006), was and continues to be highly influential among scholars conducting critical Indigenous research in education.

Susan Faircloth

Susan Faircloth (Coharie) is professor and director of the School of Education at Colorado State University. A former Fulbright Scholar, her research focuses on Indigenous education, education of culturally and linguistically diverse students with special needs, and ethical issues in educational leadership. The article "Exploring Methodological and Ethical Opportunities and Challenges When Researching with Indigenous Youth on Issues of Identity and Culture," coauthored with A. Hynds and M. Webber, is an example of her work.

Frances Rains

Frances Rains (Choctaw/Cherokee and Japanese) is professor emerita at Evergreen State College. Her work focuses on social justice/White privilege and American Indian history and education issues. Her chapter "Is the Benign Really Harmless? Deconstructing Some 'Benign' Manifestations of Operationalized

White Privilege" in the book *White Reign: Deploying Whiteness in America* was used by both of us for years in our *Systems of Human Inquiry* course, as it is a piece that speaks to the reader and clearly explains concepts so that our students would have a "now I get it moment."

Rebecca Tsosie

Rebecca Tsosie (Yaqui descent) is Regents Professor at the James E. Rogers College of Law at the University of Arizona. She has published widely on issues of sovereignty, self-determination, cultural pluralism, environmental policy, and cultural rights. One of her most notable works is her 2012 publication "Indigenous Peoples and Epistemic Injustice: Science, Ethics, and Human Rights" in the *Washington Law Review*.

Linda Tuhiwai Smith

Linda Tuhiwai Smith (Māori—Ngāti Awa and Ngāti Porou) is a professor of Indigenous education at the University of Waikato in New Zealand. Her critical work on Western scholarly research conducted on Indigenous Peoples has been highly influential in education research circles, especially her 1999 book *Decolonizing Methodologies*.

RESEARCH COMPONENTS OF EXAMPLE ARTICLE

We have chosen as our example study for Indigenous/Tribal Critical Research in education the 2020 article "Understanding Cultural Differences: White Teachers' Perceptions and Values in American Indian Schools" by Rikkilynn Archibeque and Irina Okhremtchouk, published in the *Journal of American Indian Education*. Archibeque is a history teacher at Estrella Foothills High School in Goodyear, Arizona and Okhremtchouk is associate professor of educational administration and coordinator of educational administration programs in the Graduate College of Education at San Francisco State University.

Statement of the Problem, Purpose, and Research Question

Regarding the statement of the problem, the authors (2020) did not address the paucity of research on their topic, but we can attest, after an exhaustive review of the literature, that there is limited empirical research on American Indian education. The most recent research we found on this topic was in students' dissertations, so hopefully published peer-reviewed articles derived from these dissertations will be forthcoming. Therefore, the statement of the problem was that there is limited research on "White teachers' experiences of perceived cultural differences in their classrooms while working with American Indian students" (p. 75). The purpose, then, was to add to this research. The authors' research question was: "What are White teachers' perceptions and values of the cultural and classroom exchanges they experience while working with American Indian students?" (p. 81).

Theoretical Frame

TribalCrit was the theoretical lens Archibeque and Okhremtchouk (2020) used for this work. They described the rationale for using this lens:

> TribalCrit provides alternative ways of thinking about culture, knowledge, and power and illuminates various forms of colonization that affect American Indian students. The theory rejects the idea of educational assimilation for American Indian students and, instead, centers the idea that schools should maintain the cultural integrity of Indigenous students by increasing academic knowledge alongside cultural knowledge, rather than in place of it. (p. 77)

Methodology and Methods

The authors' methodology was a "multiple case study" (p. 81) of the experiences, values, and perceptions of five White teachers, three women and two men, who taught in a junior high school on "an Indian Reservation in Northeastern Arizona" (p. 75). The teaching experience of the participants ranged from 4 to 35 years. All the women teachers had previously taught in non-reservation schools. The men had only taught on reservations. The methods for the study were "semistructured interviews following a researcher-developed protocol" that was informed by a "teacher readiness conceptual model" constructed by the authors (p. 81). This model addressed the knowledge and skills teachers needed to successfully teach American Indian students. The topics were: "Historical Understanding of American Indian Education [;] Understanding of Community Values and Belief Systems [;] Relationships with Students, Families, and Community [;] Adaption of Curriculum for Culturally Relevant Resources [;] and Culturally Responsive Teaching" (p. 80). These are consistent with the tenets of TribalCrit the authors discussed above.

Analysis and Results/Findings

The analysis strategies Archibeque and Okhremtchouk (2020) employed were "constant comparative analysis with theoretical memo writing" (p. 81). In the first cycle of analysis they created "five parent codes" (pp. 81–82) and from these child codes or subcodes. In the second cycle they used axial coding "to rename, drop, and/or regroup codes into meaningful categories, resulting in 25 child codes" (p. 82). This resulted in the recoding of "the entire dataset using the final axial coding categories" (p. 82).

Five themes emerged from their data analysis: "(1) social dynamics, (2) pedagogical dynamics, (3) classroom practices, (4) personal belief systems, and (5) on-the-job-learning" (p. 83). To provide just a couple of examples from the themes, one aspect of social dynamics was building relationships. For the most part, the teachers understood the importance of relationship-building. "However, the teachers generally spoke of relationship building from a Eurocentric perspective that relied heavily on their own value system they brought to [the] reservation as compared to that of the student's/community's where they work and live" (p. 83). Another example from the on-the-job-learning theme was the teachers overwhelming lack of "readiness to work with American Indians students" (p. 90). One teacher stated,

> the only professional development I remember from the district was where they took us around. We got on the bus, we rode around on [the] bus and they told us the names of the different communities . . . and . . . not to you know . . . about looking in the eye. They won't, you know, that's disrespectful to look someone in the eye and so forth. [pause] And . . . then they had like an Indian taco with frybread [pause]; that's not enough [sounds frustrated]. That is not enough for any new person coming into the reservation. . . . There is no way . . . that that . . . you know, helped—that really didn't help me at all. (p. 91)

The authors, speaking to the lack of authentic training for teachers, said, "All of this adds to the clear lack of investment in students and their school and life trajectories" (p. 91).

Discussion and Recommendations

Achibeque and Okhtemtchouk (2020) concluded that their study showed "teachers' perceptions and classroom experiences are nested within their personal value systems, which often align with hegemonic, mainstream frameworks of education rather than local Indigenous knowledge systems" (p. 75). Applying their conceptual model of teacher competencies indicating readiness to teach American Indian students, they found that based on their findings, "there is a profound disconnect between what the extant literature deems best [the readiness competencies] and the reality [the teachers' attitudes and practices]." (p. 92). The teachers "relied on their own value system as a default mechanism to fall back on and imposed these values on their professional practice and students" (p. 94).

Therefore, they recommended that what is "best for Native American students and their academic as well as social development is Native American teachers. . . . The second best option is to require involved and ongoing professional development starting with historical understanding and knowledge of community values" (p. 94). The authors contended that historical knowledge must be the first step because without that understanding, "the jump to culturally responsive ways of teaching would be superficial and, arguably, meaningless" (p. 94).

CONCLUSION

In this chapter we covered how critical research in education can be designed and conducted using Indigenous/Tribal perspectives. We discussed the background of such research, defined key terms, and identified several influential authors who work with critical Indigenous research in education and TribalCrit. We also analyzed an example article from the *Journal of American Indian Education*, "Understanding Cultural Differences: White Teachers' Perceptions and Values in American Indian Schools." Educational researchers who design and conduct critical Indigenous/Tribal studies need to heed the "call for a collaborative social science research model that makes the researcher responsible" that directs them "to take up moral projects that respect and reclaim indigenous cultural practices" (Denzin & Lincoln, 2008, p. 15).

CHAPTER 9

Latinx Critical Research in Education

The terms researchers and others use to name people and groups in whose interest this type of research is done are highly varied, change frequently, and are loaded with political history. We've chosen *Latinx Critical Research in Education* as our chapter title and as our way to refer to research done in educational settings that seeks to advance the lives and experiences of people who identify as Latina, Latino, Latinx, Chicano, Chicana, Hispanic, Mexican American, or other related identifications. We recognize that this choice is not unproblematic, but the use of *Latinx* seemed the most inclusive choice. Following the guidance provided in the *Publication Manual of the American Psychological Association* (7th ed.),

> when writing about people who identify as Hispanic, Latino (or Latinx, etc.), Chicano, or another related designation, authors should consult with their participants to determine the appropriate choice. Note that "Hispanic" is not necessarily an all-encompassing term, and the labels "Hispanic" and "Latino" have different connotations. The term "Latino" (and its related forms) might be preferred by those originating from Latin America, including Brazil. Some use the word "Hispanic" to refer to those who speak Spanish; however, not every group in Latin America speaks Spanish (e.g., in Brazil, the official language is Portuguese). The word "Latino" is gendered (i.e., "Latino" is masculine and "Latina" is feminine); the use of the word "Latin@" to mean both Latino and Latina is now widely accepted. "Latinx" can also be used as a gender-neutral or nonbinary term inclusive of all genders. There are compelling reasons to use any of the terms "Latino," "Latina," "Latino/a," "Latin@," and/or "Latinx" (see de Onís, 2017), and various groups advocate for the use of different forms. Use the term(s) your participants or population uses; if you are not working directly with this population but it is a focus of your research, it may be helpful to explain why you chose the term you used or to choose a more inclusive term like "Latinx." In general, naming a nation or region of origin is preferred (e.g., Bolivian, Salvadoran, or Costa Rican is more specific than Latino, Latinx, Latin American, or Hispanic). (APA, 2020, pp. 144–145)

Though this guidance is helpful, we acknowledge that it was set out in 2020 and that world circumstances and language usage continue to evolve. Thus, it might not meet the preference of some of our readers.

With that language choice in mind, this is the chapter in which we discuss educational scholarship guided by Latinx critical theories. We begin with a brief background, then identify influential theorists and scholars, and, finally, offer an example of such scholarship based on a published journal article.

BACKGROUND OF LATINX RESEARCH

According to Stefancic (1997),

> Latino/a critical scholarship, though largely ignored, has been around for a long time. One might say that its progenitor was Rodolfo Acuña, whose book *Occupied America,* originally published in 1972, is now in its third edition. Acuña was the first scholar to reformulate American history to take account of U.S. colonization of land formerly held by Mexico and how this colonization affected Mexicans living in those territories. His thesis has proven as powerful for Latinos as the potent theories of Derrick Bell have been in understanding the dynamics of race for blacks. (p. 423)

Thus, Latinx critical research has existed in the United States for at least 50 years.

In the legal field, Latina/Latino Critical Theory (LatCrit) emerged around 1995 when a group of legal scholars coalesced to develop principles and to fight gross injustice in the law and court systems (Valdés & Bender, 2021), much like the emergence of critical race theory (CRT). Delgado Bernal, in her 2002 article "Critical Race Theory, Latino Critical Theory, and Critical Raced-Gendered Epistemologies: Recognizing Students of Color as Holders and Creators of Knowledge," argued for employing both CRT and LatCrit in educational research.

> For too long, the histories, experiences, cultures, and languages of students of color have been devalued, misinterpreted, or omitted within formal educational settings. . . . LatCrit is similar to CRT. However, LatCrit is concerned with a progressive sense of a coalitional Latina/Latino pan-ethnicity (Valdés, 1996), and it addresses issues often ignored by critical race theorists. I see LatCrit theory adding important dimensions to a critical race analysis. For example, LatCrit theorizes issues such as *language, immigration, ethnicity, culture, identity, phenotype, and sexuality* [emphasis added]. (p. 108)

Thus, LatCrit in education both employs and expands on topics, tactics, and tools brought forth by CRT to challenge dominant narratives about people of color and to include these same people as valuable producers and holders of knowledge in schools, universities, and other educational settings.

Solórzano and Yosso (2001) further elaborate about what such research work *looks like* by providing a deeper description of what is accomplished by one of the tools used in LatCrit and CRT scholarship—counterstories, also called counternarratives (see our definition of counterstory in Chapter 4). According to Solórzano and Yosso (2001),

> counter-stories can serve at least four theoretical, methodological, and pedagogical functions: (1) they can build community among those at the margins of society by putting a human and familiar face to educational theory and practice; (2) they can challenge the perceived wisdom of those at society's center by providing a context to understand and transform established belief systems; (3) they can open new windows into the reality of those at the margins of society by showing the possibilities beyond the ones they live and demonstrating that they are not alone in their position; and (4) they can teach others that by combining elements from both the story and the current reality, one can construct another world that is richer than either the story or the reality alone. (p. 475)

Counter-storytelling and other LatCrit tools can thus be employed to design and conduct research in schools and other educational settings that challenges the status quo and creates a knowledge base that better serves to improve schooling for Latinx students.

NOTABLE LATINX THEORISTS AND RESEARCHERS

Dolores Delgado Bernal

Dolores Delgado Bernal is a professor at California State University Los Angeles. She was one of the early researchers adopting and refining LatCrit in education. See, for example, her 2002 article "Critical Race Theory, Latino Critical Theory, and Critical Raced-Gendered Epistemologies: Recognizing Students of Color as Holders and Creators of Knowledge." Her research focuses on Latinx educational pathways.

Kris Gutiérrez

Kris Gutiérrez is a professor of language, literacy, and culture at the University of California, Berkeley. She is a past president of the American Educational Research Association, and her work on designed learning environments, hybrid spaces, and teaching STEM for learners in nondominant communities has been highly influential and widely published. Her most cited empirical article to date, cowritten with Patricia Baquedano-López and Carlos Tejeda (1999), is "Rethinking Diversity: Hybridity and Hybrid Language Practices in the Third Space."

Luis Moll

Luis Moll is professor emeritus in language and literacy at the University of Arizona. A member of the National Academy of Education, he is best known for his work on funds of knowledge, an assets-oriented theory of the bodies of knowledge immigrant and other Latinx children bring with them to school. His 2005 book, coedited with Norma González and Cathy Amanti, *Funds of Knowledge: Theorizing Practices in Households, Communities, and Classrooms*, won the 2006 Critics' Choice Award of the American Educational Studies Association.

Cherríe Moraga

Cherríe Moraga is a poet, playwright, author, and professor of English at the University of California, Santa Barbara. She (along with Gloria Anzaldúa) edited the groundbreaking book *This Bridge Called My Back: Writings by Radical Women of Color* in 1981. This book and her subsequent work continue to be highly influential for critical Latinx scholars.

Daniel Solórzano

Daniel Solórzano is a professor in the Graduate School of Education at UCLA. He is known for his work on CRT and racial microaggressions. His most cited work to date is "Critical Race Methodology: Counter-storytelling as an Analytical Framework for Education Research," which he coauthored with Tara Yosso. He is a member of the National Academy of Education.

Enrique Trueba

Enrique Trueba was, as Foley (2005) phrased it, "a Latino critical ethnographer for the ages" (p. 354). His long career as a scholar was devoted to advocacy for those most in need in educational systems and supporting talent development among immigrant populations. One of his most influential works is the 1989 book *Raising Silent Voices: Educating the Linguistic Minorities for the 21st Century*.

Francisco Valdés

Francisco Valdés is a professor at the University of Miami School of Law. He is considered the "father" of LatCrit in legal studies and has written extensively on the topic. See his 2021 book (along with Steven Bender) *LatCrit: From Critical Legal Theory to Academic Activism*, which according to the publisher is considered "part roadmap, part historical record, and part a path forward" (Valdés & Bender, 2021, backcover).

Richard Valencia

Richard Valencia is professor emeritus at The University of Texas at Austin in the Center for Mexican American Studies. His scholarly work focuses on underserved students in public schools, particularly issues related to Mexican Americans. His 1997 edited book *The Evolution of Deficit Thinking: Educational Thought and Practice* is widely cited. The book's description provided by the publisher explains why this work is so powerful:

> Deficit thinking refers to the notion that students, particularly low-income minority students, fail in school because they and their families experience deficiencies that obstruct the leaning process (e.g., limited intelligence, lack of motivation, inadequate home socialization). Tracing the evolution of deficit thinking, the authors debunk the pseudo-science and offer more plausible explanations of why students fail. (back cover)

The book remains highly influential for scholars who study Latinx issues in education.

Tara Yosso

Tara Yosso is a professor in the Graduate School of Education at the University of California, Riverside. Her research focuses on cultural capital among Latinx students, resistance to media microaggressions, and counter-storytelling. In merely 20 years, she has become a prominent scholar in critical race studies. In 2017 the Critical Race Studies in Education Association honored her with the Derrick Bell Legacy Award. Her 2006 article, "Whose Culture Has Capital? A Critical Race Theory Discussion of Community Cultural Wealth," has been cited nearly 10,000 times.

RESEARCH COMPONENTS OF EXAMPLE ARTICLE

Our example study for LatCrit is a 2018 article published in the journal *Educational Studies* by Luis Fernando Macías, a professor of Chicano and Latin American Studies at California State University, Fresno. His article, "The Scheme Game: How DACA Recipients Navigate Barriers to Higher Education," focused on the ways a group of college-going immigrant students in Ohio navigated political and structural impediments to their education. According to the author, "these barriers often include a complicated process for in-state tuition consideration, as well as exclusion from the majority of educational subsidies [like federal aid]" (p. 609).

Statement of the Problem, Purpose, and Research Question

Macías (2018) described the problem being addressed, but does not directly answer the "Why is it important to do this?" question (see Chapter 2), nor does he directly state the purpose of the research or research question. We can, however, discern them from his description of his research. He stated, college-bound recipients of DACA—a 2012 US administrative policy officially ti-tled Consideration for Deferred Action for Childhood Arrivals—face a series of ad-ministrative and financial barriers in pursuing postsecondary education. . . . This research sheds *new light* [emphasis added] on DACA students' own understanding of their financial exclusions and the often-ingenious methods they use to finance higher education. (p. 609)

Based on Macías's comment that his research "sheds new light," we can assume that there is little research on the experiences of DACA students and the finan-cial issues they have to deal with—the statement of the problem. Therefore, the purpose of the research was to garner an understanding of the administrative and financial barriers DACA students experience pursuing postsecondary edu-cation and the ways they attempt to ameliorate them. The research question, which was not directly stated, was something like: What do the DACA students who were participants understand about the administrative and financial bar-riers to pursuing their higher education goals, and how have they attempted to overcome them?

This type of research would also fall under the category of policy imple-mentation research. Education in the United States is heavy on laws and poli-cies but light on systematic research on the implementation or effects of these laws and policies, particularly for historically marginalized individuals and groups. There is limited research that includes the perspectives of the intended recipients (or targets) of the policy. This is what makes LatCrit suitable for this study—its design addresses an issue of concern for the Latinx community in education, and its methods are carried out in ways that are consistent with the inclusive and respectful expectations of LatCrit research.

Theoretical Framework

The author (2018) identified four components in his theoretical framework—CRT, LatCrit, scheme game, and marginalization and navigation in hip-hop. Regarding CRT, Macías focused on

CRT's challenge of meritocracy as a dominant ideology. CRT scholars challenge notions of meritocracy that posits educational and professional success as deter-mined solely by a person's hard work and intellect. These meritocratic notions fuel deficit views and treatment of non-White students by neglecting the racial struc-tural inequalities inherent across institutions. (p. 612)

Discussing his use of LatCrit, he said,

a LatCrit framework in education examines how culture, phenotype, language, and immigration status are used to classify some students as foreign and thus justify their exclusion from equal opportunities and resources. (p. 612)

The scheme game, according to Macías, is an epistemological perspective

> which outlines how foreign-born youth of Color, raised in the United States, con-
> ceptualize their persistence through a complicated college admissions process and
> exclusion from educational funding. Participants' perspectives are rooted in hip-
> hop practices and reflected in hip-hop vernacular. This perspective is telling because
> it demonstrates that participants understand their experiences with racist, nativist
> forms of marginalization and take corresponding action through a quintessentially
> American epistemology: hip-hop. (p. 611)

And, describing the marginalization and navigation in hip-hop, Macías said,

> hip-hop texts commonly outline motifs of hard work, financial independence, mon-
> etary gain, and the importance of being quick-witted in the face of limited oppor-
> tunities and multiple institutional obstacles . . . [rappers] use terms like *grindin'*,
> *hustlin'*, and *schemin'* to identify their attempts at financial gain by outmaneuvering
> the various forms of racialized, institutional economic oppression they experience.
> (pp. 613–614)

Macías cautioned, though, that

> there is an important distinction in how hip-hop texts use grind, scheme, and hus-
> tle and how they are understood in this study. In the context of this work, these
> terms specifically refer to how DACA recipients of Color navigate the policies that
> hinder their participation in higher education and how they mitigate the financial
> burdens. The hip-hop ethos of street smarts, from which these terms are derived,
> remain intact but participants do not resort to any sort of illicit or unethical activ-
> ity to achieve their goals. (p. 614)

LatCrit, interwoven with the three other theoretical perspectives, provided the
appropriate theoretical lens for Macías's study of how DACA students navigate higher education.

Methodology and Methods

In addressing his methodology and methods, Macías (2018) stated

> a critical race grounded methodology informs this qualitative work's data col-
> lection and analysis. This methodology situates grounded theory's systematic
> approach to the development of theory, which emerges from the data, within
> a CRT framework that positions [People of Color's] POC's lived experiences
> of [sic] as the foundational data (Malagon, Huber, & Vélez, 2009). Collab-
> oration with participants is embraced as part of the development of theory.
> (p. 614)

Thus, the methodology combined a CRT framework with a grounded theory approach to develop theory from the lived experiences of DACA students in higher education.

The author's methods included 28 individual and one group interview with five participants. Macías's positionality played an important role:

> I acknowledge my positionality as a first-generation US citizen. I connected with participants over our shared immigrant experiences such as learning English, culture shock, and even experiencing microaggressions in school. However, my experience differs from theirs because my US citizenship allows me to access educational resources in fundamentally different ways. (pp. 614–615)

Thus, the researcher and his participants shared some experiences but differed on the important dimension of U.S. citizenship.

Macías noted that participants were recruited through immigrant rights organizations, university student groups, and a mentorship program. Furthermore, "sampling only DACA recipients was done with the purpose of exploring the program's impact on access to higher education" (p. 615). The next step in the research process, data collection,

> consist[ed] of audio-recording participants' testimonios about their postsecondary pursuits throughout ongoing conversations. Testimonios are acts of emergency narrative that denounce injustices and document the experiences and acts of survival of oppressed groups (Solorzano & Bernal, 2001). As a methodology, testimonios democratize modes of data collection and analysis because they are more collaborative in nature and attentive to the various ways of knowing and learning in marginalized communities. (p. 615)

Data resulting from these testimonios were analyzed using conditional matrix coding.

Analysis and Results/Findings

Macías's (2018) findings were categorized in the context of the scheme game and included grindin', hustlin', and schemin'. Grindin' is work at traditional jobs. Most of the participants worked a full or part-time job to pay for their living expenses and tuition. Hustlin' is informal but legitimate work that students depended on to supplement their traditional jobs. They needed the additional money to cover their educational expenses. These jobs included, for example, "translation services and reselling tickets to university sporting events" (p. 618).

Schemin' in hip-hop culture is "shrewd planning to outsmart opponents or authorities. Schemin' in this context is the series of calculated approaches participants take . . . in last-resort attempts to side-step policies than hinder their educational pursuits" (p. 620). For example, one student who did not have the money to make a mid-semester tuition payment and had exhausted all options "made an online payment but changed the last digit in his payment information. He nervously waited and saw that the transaction went through. Weeks later, he received an email notifying him of an issue with his payment and that a 30-day grace period was allotted to resolve the issue" (p. 621). With the additional time allotment, he was able to finish the semester and pay the bill.

Discussion and Recommendations

Macías (2018) discussed the importance of what these stories add to the research literature that counters dominant narratives about DACA students:

> Based on testimonios from participants who engage in concurrent forms of funding endeavors, this work maintains that no amount of grindin', hustlin', or schemin' can approximate the financial support that educational subsidies provide. This assertion counters narratives that posit DACA as equal or comparable to funding opportunities available to US residents or citizens. (p. 622)

Moreover, the need for students to engage in the scheme game to finance their education can negatively affect their mental and emotional health, in turn affecting their personal and academic goals. Also, having to self-fund their education can delay degree completion and increase the probability of attrition. Macías recommended that universities

> rewrite administrative codes that ensure in-state tuition to all high school graduates of the state, regardless of immigration status. Additionally, individual institutions can establish and promote a scholarship application process informing undocumented students of non-federally funded scholarships at the university, college, and department level available to them. The promotional material, as well as the scholarship itself, should state "US citizenship or legal permanent residency not a requirement." (p. 626)

CONCLUSION

In this chapter on critical Latinx research in education, we first acknowledged and addressed the issue of terminology when referring to "people of Hispanic or Latinx ethnicity" (APA, 2020, p. 142). Next, we offered a brief background and then identified prominent theorists and researchers whose work has and continues to influence researchers working in this area of scholarly research in education. We concluded with an example study on DACA students in higher education to explain the research components appropriate for LatCrit research. Researchers looking to conceptualize and carry out critical Latinx studies in education should find useful explanations and resources here in this chapter.

CHAPTER 10

Critical Disability Studies in Education

In this chapter we discuss critical research in education conducted by, with, and for individuals who have disabilities. This is a very broad and diverse group of people, as human disabilities can be physical, mental, social, and/or emotional. We chose the term *critical disability studies,* and we use people-first language in this chapter.

> "People First Language" (PFL) puts the person before the disability, and describes what a person has, not who a person is. PFL uses phrases such as "person with a disability," "individuals with disabilities," and "children with disabilities," as opposed to phrases that identify people based solely on their disability, such as "the disabled." (DC.Gov, n.d., Usage Guidelines section)

We recognize that different groups within the disability community may prefer different terms and a different approach to identifiers. We have used guidance from the *Publication Manual of the American Psychological Association* (7th ed.), which appears below:

> Disability is a broad term that is defined in both legal and scientific ways and encompasses physical, psychological, intellectual, and socioemotional impairments (World Health Organization, 2001, 2011). The members of some groups of people with disabilities—effectively subcultures within the larger culture of disability—have particular ways of referring to themselves that they would prefer others to adopt. When you use the disability language choices made by groups of disabled individuals, you honor their preferences. For example, some Deaf individuals culturally prefer to be called "Deaf" (capitalized) rather than "people with hearing loss" or "people who are deaf" (Dunn & Andrews, 2015). Likewise, use the term "hard of hearing" rather than "hearing-impaired." Honoring the preference of the group is not only a sign of professional awareness and respect for any disability group but also a way to offer solidarity.

> The language to use where disability is concerned is evolving. The overall principle for using disability language is to maintain the integrity (worth and dignity) of all individuals as human beings. Authors who write about disability are encouraged to use terms and descriptions that both honor and explain person-first and identity-first perspectives. Language should be selected with the understanding that the

expressed preference of people with disabilities regarding identification supersedes matters of style. (APA, 2020, p. 136)

Thus, we carefully considered these suggestions before deciding to title this chapter *Critical Disability Studies in Education* and to use PFL. Next, we discuss the background of critical disability studies, define terms, and highlight the notable theorists and researchers in this area. We conclude by discussing the research components of a critical disabilities article.

BACKGROUND OF CRITICAL DISABILITY STUDIES

In this section, we turn to the history and background of critical disability studies in education and identify key concepts and researchers. Critical disability studies is a field that emerged in the United States and internationally in the 1970s as a product of the civil rights movement. According to Meekosha and Shuttleworth (2009), "The International Year of Disabled People in 1981 raised disability as a human rights issue in the global public discourse" (p. 48). In other words, critical disabilities studies rose in visibility and viability as an academic discourse, along with other societal inequities, during a time of global social movement on civil rights issues.

As a field of study, critical disability studies analyzes "disability as a cultural, historical, relative, social, and political phenomenon" (Hall, 2019, para. 1). Furthermore, the evolution of critical disability studies from traditional disabilities studies arose due to the limitation of psychological and medical models of disability in society that primarily focused on individuals and did not consider larger societal factors. Meekosha and Shuttleworth (2009) explained:

> The growing presence of disabled people in society, in particular their presence in the community following centuries of institutionalisation, has further contributed to an awareness of the responsibilities of educational institutions to disabled citizens. At the same time, the limitations of medical and individual pathology models in both explaining the situation of disabled people and enabling their full citizenship, have resulted in the flowering of new explanatory paradigms—particularly in the humanities and social sciences. (pp. 48–49)

Thus, since the early 1980s, there has been a growing volume of work in critical disability studies that is interdisciplinary and focused on full societal participation for individuals with disabilities.

Two established journals publish critical disabilities scholarship. *Disability Studies Quarterly* is in its 42nd year, published by the Society for Disabilities Studies (SDS). Additionally, *Disability and Society* has been published since 1987 (known previously as *Disability, Handicap, & Society,* 1987–1993) and "is an international disability studies journal providing a focus for debate about such issues as human rights, discrimination, definitions, policy and practices" (Taylor & Francis, 2020, para. 1).

Other forms of disability studies have emerged after critical disability studies. DisCrit, for example, combines the tenets of critical race theory (CRT) with those of critical disabilities studies to conduct research at the intersection of race and disability. Crip Theory focuses on another intersection—that between queer theory and critical disability studies. These types of critical disabilities research are discussed in greater detail below.

TERMINOLOGY

Traditional Disability Studies

According to Hall (2019), in contrast to *critical* disability studies, the topic of this chapter,

> traditional disability studies is an interdisciplinary field with origins in the promotion of the social model of disability. . . . Disability studies largely focuses on achieving political inclusion for disabled people. To that end, work done under the auspices of disability studies often uses the language of civil rights, minority politics, and liberal justice frameworks. (sec. 1.2)

In this definition, then, traditional disability studies is seen as more like liberal feminism, as opposed to critical feminism (see Chapter 6), in that its aims are aligned with liberal justice frameworks focused on equality and inclusion.

Critical Disability Theory or Studies

Critical disability theory, on the other hand, is a set of interdisciplinary theoretical approaches used to "analyze disability as a cultural, historical, relative, social, and political phenomenon" (Hall, 2019, sec. 1.1). Some like Meekosha and Shuttleworth (2009) and Vehmas and Watson (2014) prefer the term "critical disability studies" (CDS), as do we. CDS includes social theory, which has its roots in critical theory. Hall (2019), citing Meekosha and Shuttleworth (2009), identified four primary principles drawn from critical social theory that are foundational to critical disability theory:

> First, "critical social theory is irreducible to facts", meaning that the methods of such a theory outstrip quantitative analysis and reject reduction to the quantitative; further, such theory rejects "atheoretical, context-free science", claiming that such science is an inappropriate way to access phenomena under analysis (2009: 52; see also Samuels 2014). Second, "critical social theory links theory with praxis in the struggle for an autonomous and participatory society" (2009: 52).

This praxis involves viewing autonomy as "emancipation from hegemonic and hierarchical ideologies" rather than reducing autonomy to independence, as was common in disability theorizing in the 1970s–1990s (2009: 52–53). Third, "critical social theory is self-aware of its historicity", meaning that it sees its own work as embedded within a time and place, reflexively targeting itself with the historical analysis it applies to social structures and institutions (2009: 53–54). Fourth, "critical social theory engages in dialogue among cultures"; on this point, Meekosha and Shuttleworth "call for an explicit dialogue with human rights and emancipatory thinking from the diversity of cultures" and hope to avoid "projecting an international ideal" from Western to non-Western cultures (2009: 54). (sec. 1.1)

Thus, one can see stark differences between what is seen as key principles for critical disability theory or studies and those for traditional disability theory. For example, rather than pressing for simple inclusion of individuals with disabilities, as does traditional disability studies, critical disabilities theory or studies seeks emancipation from oppressive ideologies that created exclusionary practices to begin with.

DisCrit

It is important to note that *all* critical disabilities research in education and elsewhere does not fall under the category of critical disabilities studies. To illustrate this point, disability critical race theory (DisCrit) adds race to the focus for such research along with disability. Thus, DisCrit focuses on the dual marginalization experienced in schools and elsewhere by people of color who are also identified with a disability (Banks, 2015; Leonardo & Broderick, 2011). It builds on the traditions of CRT but expands and shapes the theory to form its own tenets. These are listed below.

(1) DisCrit focuses on ways that the forces of racism and ableism circulate interdependently, often in neutralized and invisible ways, to uphold notions of normalcy.
(2) DisCrit values multidimensional identities and troubles singular notions of identity such as race or dis/ability or class or gender or sexuality, and so on.
(3) DisCrit emphasizes the social constructions of race and ability and yet recognizes the material and psychological impacts of being labeled as raced or dis/abled, which sets one outside of the western cultural norms.
(4) DisCrit privileges voices of marginalized populations, traditionally not acknowledged within research.
(5) DisCrit considers legal and historical aspects of dis/ability and race and how both have been used separately and together to deny the rights of some citizens.

(6) DisCrit recognizes whiteness and Ability as Property and that gains for people labeled with dis/abilities have largely been made as the result of interest convergence of white, middle-class citizens.

(7) DisCrit requires activism and supports all forms of resistance. (Connor et al., 2021, p. 598)

DisCrit, then, provides another avenue for conducting critical disabilities research that also includes race as a co-focus.

Crip Theory

An additional form of critical disability studies that pushed traditional theoretical and research boundaries even further from older norms is Crip Theory. The name follows in the tradition of other social theory claimed by groups historically targeted for oppression (i.e., queer theory) in that it uses reverse discourse to repurpose a formerly pejorative term into a label of strength:

> Queer theory and critical disability theory productively collude under the umbrella of "crip theory", pushing understanding forward in both arenas and along new lines (McRuer 2003, 2004, and 2006a; Mollow 2017; Schalk 2013). Queer theory and disability theory have shared interests, including challenging medicalization. (Hall, 2019, sec. 2.1)

Crip theory, thus, views disability as an important identity variable that should be recognized and given value though intersectional theory and research.

NOTABLE CRITICAL DISABILITIES STUDIES
THEORISTS AND RESEARCHERS

The theories discussed in the preceding section are by scholars who have given them birth and are among many others, both inside and outside of education, who work in the area of critical disability studies. We have selected a few others whose work has influenced education to highlight in our discussion below. We do this not to provide an exhaustive list or a *correct* list, but simply to provide readers with starting places to do their own research and to dive into what is currently known about and from critical disability studies.

Alfredo Artiles

Alfredo Artiles is a professor in the Graduate School of Education at Stanford University. His scholarship focuses on the dual nature of disability as an object of protection and a tool of stratification. He is a member of the National Academy of Education and is the author of numerous highly influential articles and books, including his 2013 article "Untangling the Racialization of Disabilities: An Intersectionality Critique Across Disability Models."

Liat Ben-Moshe

Liat Ben-Moshe is a disability scholar and assistant professor at the University of Chicago. Her work focuses at the epistemological level on the construction of race, disability, and criminalization. She has written several influential works that contribute to knowledge and theory in the area of DisCrit, particularly "Disabling Incarceration: Connecting Disability to Divergent Confinements in the USA" (2013).

Colleen Capper

Colleen Capper is professor emerita at the University of Wisconsin. She was an early leader in advancing issues of equity for students with disabilities in school leadership development and in organizational theory. She is the author or coauthor of four best-selling books on these topics, including Capper and Elise Frattura's 2008 book *Meeting the Needs of Students of All Abilities: How Leaders Go Beyond Inclusion.*

Judith Heumann

Judith Heumann is a U.S. civil and disability rights activist. Among numerous honors and accomplishments, she helped author the Individuals with Disabilities Act and served as adviser for disabilities for the Clinton and Obama administrations as well as for the World Bank. Heumann was a Ford Foundation Fellow and is the author of *Being Heumann: An Unrepentant Memoir of a Disability Rights Activist* (2020).

Marcia Rioux

Marcia Rioux was a distinguished research professor and professor emerita in the School of Health Policy and Management in York University's Faculty of Health. Founder of York's Critical Disabilities Program, she was the author of more than 70 highly influential reports, articles, and chapters. In 2014, she was invested into the Order of Canada for her scholarship in the field of social justice and for her advancement of the rights of persons with disabilities. She was also known as a legal scholar. A representation of her legal work is the 2011 book *Critical Perspectives on Human Rights and Disability Law*, which she coedited with L. A. Basser and M. Jones.

George Theoharis

George Theoharis is a professor of Educational Leadership and Inclusive Elementary/Early Childhood Education in the Teaching and Leadership

Department at Syracuse University. His research focuses on advancing equity and inclusion, especially for students with disabilities, through socially just leadership. His writing in this area has been and continues to be very influential. His book *Leadership for Increasingly Diverse Schools*, coauthored with Martin Scanlan, is in its second edition.

RESEARCH COMPONENTS OF EXAMPLE ARTICLE

For the example article in this chapter, we use "Seeing the Unseen: Applying Intersectionality and Disability Critical Race Theory (DisCrit) Frameworks in Preservice Teacher Education" by Ebony Perouse-Harvey, an assistant professor of Special Education at Southern Connecticut State University. It was published in the journal *Teachers College Record* in 2022. In this article, Perouse-Harvey

> explores how intersectionality and DisCrit can be used as analytic tools to scaffold preservice teachers' ability to see the ways in which referrals to and services within special education reproduce inequities as a function of race and perceptions of ability that are rooted in White, middle-class, able-bodied norms. (p. 51)

Thus, the author used DisCrit to problematize both race and ability norms in the preparation of preservice teachers.

Statement of the Problem, Purpose, and Research Question

Perouse-Harvey (2022) addressed the problem and purpose of her study with a discussion of the educational double jeopardy that Black students identified with disabilities face in the U.S. educational system, which is historical and ongoing and which results in differential outcomes for these students compared to their peers in other demographic groups. She stated that "schools are White spaces" (p. 53) and, further, that "incorporating critical theoretical frameworks in teacher education coursework to help expand preservice teachers' knowledge base around the intersection of racism and ableism and their reflection on their interactions with Students of Color and/or Students Identified with (Dis)abilities is necessary" (pp. 53–54). Though not explicitly labeled as such, these statements represent the research problem—that not enough is known about preservice teachers' interaction with critical theoretical frameworks in education coursework.

This problem, then, leads to the purpose of the article—to learn how White preservice teachers, when exposed to critical frameworks, engage with the content and whether or not this experience impacts the preservice teachers' levels of critical consciousness. To fulfill this purpose, the author sought answers to two overarching research questions:

1. How do White preservice teachers engage with critical frameworks intended to unearth the impacts of racism and ableism on Black students?
2. What do their responses reveal about their level of critical consciousness? (p. 54)

Theoretical Framework

The theoretical framework for this study is contained in its own section and is quite robust. Perouse-Harvey (2022) discussed two broad areas. The first was "Partnering Intersectionality and DisCrit as Frameworks for Instruction" (p. 55), which was broken down into three smaller components. The first discussed Collins and Bilge's (2016) Domains of Power. The second applied the same concept to educational settings—Manifestations of Domains of Power in Schools. The tenets of DisCrit were the third component covered in this area.

The author's second broad area for her theoretical framework was "Applying the Continuum of Dysconsiousness/Critical Consciousness to Preservice Teacher Classroom Engagement" (p. 58). In this section she noted that "preservice teachers can range in their positions related to race and ability from dysconsciousness to critical consciousness . . . [L]earning and unlearning happen over time and conflicts between previously held beliefs and new ideas are inevitable" (p. 59).

Methodology and Methods

In describing the methodology, Perouse-Harvey (2022) stated, "This article reports on a qualitative case study of general education preservice teacher engagement with the critical frameworks of intersectionality and disability Critical Race Theory (DisCrit)" (p. 53). The participants were "preservice general education teachers in the last semester of coursework of an intensive 12-month master's program in secondary education at a large predominantly White Midwestern university" (p. 51). Four of the students self-identified as White and able-bodied (two women and two men), and one identified as a White, male, and (dis)abled. The author identified as a "Black able-bodied woman; a former special educator of Students of Color, predominantly Black children; and a current teacher educator" (p. 59). Data collection occurred throughout the entire course that the author taught and the students attended. These included "video recordings of whole group discussions and audio recordings of small group discussions" (p. 52) and Perouse-Harvey's practitioner memos. Data were analyzed using descriptive and in vivo coding.

Analysis and Results/Findings

From her data analysis, Perouse-Harvey (2022) identified four levels of engagement her students demonstrated in relation to the class content:

As I analyzed the class discussion data, patterns in preservice teachers' engagement with critical frameworks emerged. Preservice teachers engaged in discussion moves that demonstrated either resistance to or acceptance of the critical frameworks they learned in class. I observed four modes of engagement: *resistant deflection, resistant engagement, quiet adoption*, and *active adoption*. (p. 73)

According to the author,

Resistant deflection is when a preservice teacher would engage their colleagues in conversations that distracted from the group's discussions of the critical frameworks and /or discussions of racism/ableism. . . . *Resistant engagement* is when a preservice teacher engages in group discussion to present perspectives that are contrary to the critical frameworks presented and does not respond to the issues of racism/ableism that are being discussed. . . . *Quiet adoption* is when a preservice teacher does not participate as often as their peers in small and whole group discussions, but they appear to actively follow the trajectory of discussion . . . [and] *active adoption* is when a preservice teacher initiates discussion, consistently shares their perspectives, and/or invites members of their group into discussions about racial inequity and/or tends to monopolize discussions on issues of inequity. (pp. 73–74)

Discussion and Recommendations

In discussing her findings, Perouse-Harvey (2022) stated,

findings of my research reiterate the need for deliberate engagement with preservice teachers on issues of race and its intersection with other marginalized identities to provide them with the tools to articulate their thinking, question previously held assumptions, and develop practices to disrupt inequity as noted by various scholars that study racism and ableism in teacher education. (pp. 74–75)

She pointed out that her findings support the conclusions of earlier work in the field about developing practices with preservice teachers to disrupt inequities along race and disability lines, and then elaborated on four pedagogical practices in her classroom that seem to have the most productive effects. They are:

- Leveraging Small Group Discussion as an Assessment Tool
- Engaging Differing Orientations Toward Racism and Ableism
- Responding to Resistant Deflection and Engagement
- Participation Structures and Instructor Pedagogy (pp. 77–79)

Her recommendations were consistent with her choice of DisCrit as a framework, since action and activism along with research are important components of this approach.

CONCLUSION

In this chapter we explored critical disability research in education. We briefly discussed its background, addressed three forms it can take (in addition to traditional disability studies), and identified a few key theorists and researchers in the field whose work readers can use to springboard into the larger literature. Also, we explicated an example study that appeared in the journal *Teachers College Record*. This study, which used DisCrit as a framework, focused on classroom intervention with preservice teachers designed to raise their engagement with issues of race and disability in their future classrooms. Through these sections of our chapter, we have shown how research in educational settings can be designed and implemented using critical disability frameworks.

Part III

ADDITIONAL TYPES OF CRITICAL RESEARCH IN EDUCATION

Critical Policy Studies in Educat

A discussion of the background of critical policy studies[1] starts off this chapter. We begin with how it emerged and follow by differentiating between critical policy analysis and traditional policy analysis. We then specifically address critical policy studies in education. Next, we address the notable theorists and researchers in the field. The last section is an empirical research article that is an example of a critical policy study of the California Community College Student Equity Policy and the subsequent individual student equity plans of 28 California community colleges.

BACKGROUND OF CRITICAL POLICY STUDIES

The Emergence of Critical Policy Studies

Critical policy studies (CPS), often referred to as critical policy analysis (CPA), or critical policy scholarship, emerged from the work of Harold Lasswell, a scholar of political science and a polymath whose writings spanned the 1930s to 1970s. He is considered the founder of policy sciences (Braman, 2003). In his original thinking, he proposed that *"sciences are policy sciences when they clarify the process of policy making in society, or supply data needed for the making of rational judgments on policy questions"* (Lasswell, 1948/2009, p. 120). However, as he continued to contemplate on power and leadership and democracy, he envisioned a new approach—"policy sciences of democracy" (p. 118). He pressed for a "progressive democratization of society," stating that "if the policy sciences are to aid democracy, they must contribute to the continual reconstruction of whatever practices stand in the way of democratic personality and polity" (Lasswell, 1948/2009, p. 148). His framework "stress[ed] context . . . encourage[d] a multiplicity of methods, and [was] guided by a concern to address practical problems" (Torgerson, 2017, p. 340). Although policy sciences of democracy eventually led to CPA, this did not happen until the 1980s. Journals either dedicated specifically to CPA or that published much of the work came later; *The Journal for Critical Education Policy Studies* did not launch until 2003, and the journal *Critical Policy Studies* began in 2006. At that time, the journal was called *Critical Policy Analysis*. The name was changed in 2009.

ıs Critical Policy Analysis Different From Traditional Policy Analysis?

What makes CPA different from traditional policy analysis (TPA) is the approach it takes. TPA follows four tenets:

1. TPA focuses considerable energy on planning, adapting, implementing, examining, and/or evaluating policy-related educational changes or reforms. Change or reform is typically viewed as a deliberate process that can be planned and managed.
2. TPA frames research behavior as goal-driven, where rational individuals weigh the costs, benefits, and subsequent outcomes of a given action or strategy.
3. TPA takes for granted that researchers are capable of obtaining, accumulating, and understanding the knowledge necessary for identifying and deciding between policy solutions as well as planning for implementation and evaluation.
4. TPA assumes that researchers can evaluate policies, policy alternatives, and practices and express their evaluations to stakeholders in manners that can be used to identify and ameliorate problems. (Diem et al., 2019, p. 4)

In other words, TPA is "positivistic in its philosophical stance [indicated as the *paradigm* on Table 1] and instrumentalist in its purpose—it focuses on producing knowledge relevant for policy decisions" (Molla, 2021, p. 1).

Stephen Ball (2021), one of the most influential scholars in social theory and educational policy analysis, critiqued the early policy studies:

> All of these early studies were trying to make sense of how policy gets done rather than what policy does. That is, initially the focus was on who does policy and with what ideas. Latterly attention shifted, for some analysts [poststructuralists], to how policy forms the objects about which it speaks. That is, the attempt to understand how some issues are identified as policy problems, and others not, and how, following from that, some solutions are made obvious and necessary and others are ignored. (pp. 387–388)

One can see in this critique the influence poststructuralism and Foucault had on Ball's later thinking and work. A discussion of poststructural policy analysis is beyond the scope of this book. However, for an example of this work see James J. Scheurich's 1997 "Policy Archaeology: A New Policy Studies Methodology" in *Research Method in the Postmodern*.

Critical Policy Studies in Education

In the 1980s, "as power and control in education became increasingly consolidated and as the movement toward accountability and consolidation marched across the globe, a growing number of educational policy scholars, dissatisfied with traditional frameworks, began using critical frameworks in their analyses"

(Young & Diem, 2017, p. 3), thereby problematizing the "effects of market forces in education [with the rise] of neoliberalism" (Molla, 2021, p. 3). CPS draws from Stuart Hall's cultural theory, beginning in the 1950s; Michel Foucault's discourse analysis, from the 1970s; and Stephen Ball's policy sociology, from the 1980s; as well as others.

One of the most influential scholars in this field is Michael Apple. Speaking to the "politics of critical policy analysis," Apple (2019) contended that "critical policy analysis is grounded in the belief that it is absolutely crucial to understand the complex connections between education and the relations of dominance and subordination in the larger society—and the movements that are trying to interrupt these relations" (p. 276). To further this understanding, he posed what he calls "simple questions." Regarding critical policy studies in education, he said,

> rather than simply asking whether students have mastered a particular subject matter and have done well on our all too common tests, we should ask a different set of questions: Whose knowledge is this? How did it become "official"? What is the relationship between this knowledge and how it is organized and taught and who has cultural, social, and economic capital in this society? Who benefits from these definitions of legitimate knowledge and who does not? What are the overt and hidden effects of educational reforms on real people and real communities? What can we do as critical educators to challenge existing educational and social inequalities and to create policies, community relations, curricula, and teaching that are socially just? (p. 277)

Therefore, whereas TPA asks what is working and not working and then makes a plan, implements it, and monitors and evaluates it, CPS asks questions such as: What knowledge is privileged? Who gets a voice in making policy, who does not, and why? Who is affected by the policy? Does the policy advance social justice?

NOTABLE CRITICAL POLICY THEORISTS AND RESEARCHERS

Michael Apple

We previously introduced Michael Apple in our general discussion of critical theory in education. However, we would be remiss if we didn't also address his contribution to critical policy analysis and studies. He is the John Bascom Professor of Curriculum and Instruction and Educational Policy Studies at the University of Wisconsin, Madison and Professor of Educational Policy Studies at the Institute of Education, University of London (University of Wisconsin-Madison, n.d.). Over the years he and Stephen Ball, the two most prominent scholars of critical policy studies in education, had an ongoing academic conversation regarding critical work in general, as well as critical policy analysis/

studies in particular. In 2007, Ball signified his respect for Apple by publishing the article "Reading Michael Apple—The Sociological Imagination at Work" in *Theory and Research in Education*. To understand the trajectory of Apple's thinking over time, we recommend his 2013 book, *Knowledge, Power, and Education: The Selected Works of Michael W. Apple.*

Stephen Ball

Stephen Ball is professor emeritus of sociology of education at the University College London's Institute of Education. In 2013, Michael Apple reciprocated Ball's article about him and wrote "Between Traditions: Stephen Ball and the Critical Sociology of Education." In concluding the article, Apple stated,

> there is much more that can and should be said about Stephen Ball's continuing contributions. Having seen him teach, observed his dedicated mentorship of postgraduate students, and been present in the United Kingdom and many other nations when in seminars and before large academic and nonacademic audiences—including his influential lectures at the Havens Center at the University of Wisconsin—he has challenged dominant interpretations of educational realities and challenged his audiences to act against them, I also know the flame that burns underneath his usual calm exterior. This talented bricoleur deserves his place in the very top rank of critical sociologists of education. And, like many other critical scholar/activists, I shall certainly continue to learn from him. (pp. 214–215)

As we suggested with Michael Apple, to understand Stephen Ball's thinking over time, we recommend his book *Education Policy and Social Class: The Selected Works of Stephen J. Ball.*

Catherine Marshall

Catherine Marshall is the William Eaves Distinguished Professor Emerita of Educational Leadership and Policy at the University of North Carolina at Chapel Hill. Her teaching and research use an "interdisciplinary approach to analyze the cultures of schools, state policy cultures, gender issues, and social justice issues" (Sage Publishing, n.d., Catherine Marshall section, para. 1) Among Marshall's honors are

> the Campbell Award for Lifetime Intellectual Contributions to the Field, given by the Politics of Education Association (2009) . . . [and] a Ford Foundation grant for Social Justice Leadership (2002). In the American Educational [Research] Association [AERA], she was elected to head the Politics and Policy Division, and she also created an AERA Special Interest Group called Leadership for Social Justice. (Sage Publishing, n.d., Catherine Marshall section, para .2)

She is the author of *Feminist Critical Policy Analysis.*

RESEARCH COMPONENTS OF EXAMPLE ARTICLE

"Achieving Racial Equity From the Bottom-Up? The Student Equity Policy in the California Community Colleges" (Ching et al., 2020) is the article we chose as an example of critical policy studies, which the authors refer to as critical policy analysis (CPA). It was published in 2020 in the journal *Educational Policy* and addresses the equity policies designed to "foster success and close the outcome gaps experienced by racially minoritized students in community colleges" (Ching et al., 2020, p. 819). At the time of publication, Cheryl Ching was an assistant professor at the University of Massachusetts Boston; Eric Felix was a PhD candidate at the University of Southern California; Marlon Castro was a PhD candidate and research assistant at Pennsylvania State University; and Adrián Trinidad was a PhD student and research assistant at the University of Southern California.

Statement of the Problem, Purpose, and Research Question

College access, specifically targeted toward racially minoritized students, students from low-income communities, and/or students who are the first in their families to attend college, has been a federal and state policy priority for decades. Community colleges serve as the gateway to higher education and have become the focus of equity policies. The problem, however, is that this gateway

> is compromised by (a) low levels of completion, whether defined as earning a degree or certificate, or transferring to a 4-year institution (Bailey, Calcagno, Jenkins, Leinbach, & Kienzl, 2006; Bailey, Leinbach, & Jenkins, 2006) and (b) high placement rates in non-credit, developmental education courses, followed by circuitous progression through and /or exit from college. (Ching et al., 2020, p. 820)

The purpose, therefore, of Ching et al.'s research was to concentrate on one specific equity policy—the California Community Colleges' (CCC) Student Equity Policy (SEP)—that sought to eliminate inequitable outcomes at public 2-year institutions to answer their research question, "How do equity policies focus on improving [racially minoritized students'] success by closing the outcome gaps they experience?" (p. 821). This policy was chosen because (1) the California college system is the largest in the United States, "with over 100 campuses serving 2.1 million students, or roughly 20% of all community college students nationwide (CCC Chancellor's Office, 2016)" and enrolls "71% of college students attending public institutions"; (2) "the vast majority of California's college-going racially minoritized students, particularly African American and Latinx students, begin their higher education journeys in the CCC (Public Policy Institute of California, 2016)"; (3) "6-year completion rates for first-time college students who started at a CCC in 2010–2011 show[ed] a gap of 29 percentage point [sic] between Asians who have the highest, and African Americans who have the lowest, completion rates"; and (4) California made a nearly $480 million investment in the SEP "between 2014–2015 and 2017–2018 academic years" (p. 821).

The authors did not directly address the statement of the problem—that is, the gap in the literature—but they did state that although their work used CPA and added to empirical policy studies, they are the only ones to date who have incorporated CPA with "the concept of equity-mindedness" (p. 854).

Theoretical Framework

The theoretical frame that Ching and colleagues (2020) used to structure their research was CPA and equity-mindedness. We have already defined CPA, so we turn to equity-mindedness. This is a concept that was advanced by Estela Mara Bensimon. Ching et al. explained that

> to realize opportunities afforded by policies like the SEP to bring about racial equity, Bensimon (2005, 2007, 2012) argues that the problem of unequal outcomes must be reframed. She proposes that what is needed are "equity-minded" approaches that foreground race and the needs of racially minoritized students, and that situate inequitable outcomes as the responsibility of higher education institutions and practitioners. Equity-mindedness is not about remediating racially minoritized students who are perceived as deficient, but about respecting their aspirations and struggles, and changing existing policies, practices, and structures that are found to underserve them. With equity-mindedness, data showing the low achievement of racially minoritized students is seen less as an issue of their poor preparation, motivation, and engagement, and more as a matter of how race, class, ideology, history, and power structure educational opportunities and perpetuate inequality in the United States. Equity-mindedness thus requires an awareness of how policies, cultural norms, and practices that seem race-neutral may in fact disadvantage racially minoritized students and reproduce racial hierarchies. Recognizing that racial equity may demand the unequal treatment of students or distribution of resources, equity-minded colleges and practitioners willingly invest more resources, time, and effort on racially minoritized students, relative to other student groups. (p. 826)

Combining CPA with equity-mindedness allowed Ching et al. to combine the tenets of critical theory with a focus on equity in their analysis of the SEP.

Methodology and Methods

The methodology was a case study of both the SEP and the community college equity plans. It was a qualitative study employing document analysis. According to the authors (2020), their investigation proceeded in two phases. We started with an examination of the history and current design of the SEP, focusing in particular on the place of race and racial equity over time. We then conducted an analysis of campus equity plans to understand how a randomly selected subset of community colleges interpreted and used planning—the SEP's primary tool (Schneider & Ingram, 1990)—to address equity for racially minoritized students. (p. 827)

Consistent with CPA, in an attempt to understand the "potential effects and consequences" of the SEP policy, in phase one the authors examined the policy's "origins, the problems it was intended to tackle, its development over time, who it benefits and disadvantages, and its underlying values" (p. 827). Specifically, they looked at state legislation, historical documents, memos, and the template "for developing equity plans, guidelines on calculating inequities in outcomes, and presentation slides from related trainings" (pp. 827–828). They asked, "What discourse around (a) race, (b) racially minoritized students, and (c) racial equity is present or omitted?" (p. 828).

In phase two they acquired the 112 equity plans from all the community colleges in the California system at the time of the study. They limited their analysis to 28, which were selected using the "'randbetween' function in Microsoft Excel." The plans were "geographically dispersed across" California, and the majority were from minority-serving institutions (MSIs) (p. 831).

Analysis and Results/Findings

To direct their analysis, the authors (2020) developed a protocol based on CPA and equity-mindedness. The authors described the protocol as having

two sets of questions. The first set facilitated our analysis of plan content and enabled us to extract relevant sections for our subsequent interpretive analysis of how equity, race/ethnicity, students, practitioners, and institutional roles and responsibilities are conceived and discursively framed . . . For example, we asked, "Which student groups has the plan identified as the focus of plan activities?" and "Are the activities [targeted] for specific student groups?" Questions like these allowed us to see whether and how campuses tailored their proposed activities to groups experiencing inequities in outcomes. The second set of questions focused our "interpretation of interpretations." For example, drawing on the idea of equity-mindedness, we focused on how the "text" of the plans promoted who is responsible for the inequitable outcomes identified and thus where the arena of change should be situated to achieve equity (i.e., student, practitioner, or institution). Questions in this section of the protocol included the following: "How are students discursively framed in general? Racially minoritized students in particular?" and "How are practitioners' role in mitigating inequity discursively framed?" (pp. 831, 833)

A system was established to test the protocol and ensure consistent interpretations. After meeting to "resolve discrepancies in interpretation, identify emerging patterns, and develop a final set of questions to synthesize and move the analysis further" (p. 833), the authors settled on the following questions:

> How is equity and inequity framed and defined? Is inequity framed as a problem that needs to be fixed? For whose benefit? How are data and calculations of inequity used to frame and define equity? In what ways does the use of data and evidence advance or hinder efforts to close outcome gaps? How are inequitable outcomes addressed? What types of activities are suggested? (pp. 833–834)

The data were coded whereby the authors inductively looked for patterns of "how equity [was] defined, how inequity [was] measured and calculated, and what type and level of change [was] proposed" (p. 834). They also used an equity-minded lens to focus on "(a) race-conscious versus race-neutral approaches, (b) deficit- versus asset-based conceptions of racially minoritized students, and (c) student versus practitioner and/or institutional responsibility for equity" (p. 834).

They found that the Student Equity Policy was not race-neutral, as it continued to focus on racially minoritized students. However, the document's "language, initial goals, and current focus [at the time of this research] show[ed] how its text and framing evolved from more to less race-conscious over time" (p. 837). When analyzing the individual equity plans, the authors found that an emphasis on

> local efforts and latitude to pursue strategies conducive to campus needs, culture, and organizing structures created a "circumstance" (Ball 1997) in which plans varied in how they (a) calculated inequities; (b) understood who (e.g., students, practitioners) and what (e.g., policies, practices) to remediate; and (c) intended to achieve equity. (p. 838)

The 28 plans fell into four categories based on the approach they took: "(a) doing more of the same by expanding, modifying, and/or enhancing existing efforts [eleven plans]; (b) undertaking ad hoc, scattershot, or one-time activities [six plans]; (c) targeting inequities strategically [eight plans]; and—in the rarest of cases—(d) taking an equity-minded approach [three plans]" (p. 844).

Discussion and Recommendations

To reiterate, the authors (2020) had two main findings. The first was that the "SEP's policy language and framing shifted from being more to less explicit about race and racial equity over time" (p. 848). The policy emphasized all-student strategies without specifically referencing "students from racially minoritized (and other non-dominant) groups" (p. 849). This may have been a result of California Proposition 209, which states "the state shall not discriminate against, or grant preferential treatment to, any individual or group on the basis of race, sex, color, ethnicity, or national origin in the operation of public employment, public education, or public contracting" (California Proposition 209, 1996).

The second was that the equity plans in the sample differed "along three dimensions: how outcome gaps are calculated, who and what are the foci of change, and what strategies are proposed . . . Two thirds of the plans . . . identified how the students who are disproportionately impacted [were] not like 'prepared' students" (p. 850). The authors suggested

> that the overwhelming focus on what students lack—particularly if students are not afforded the opportunity to inform this focus—crowds out serious consideration of how campus climate, institutional policies, and practitioner beliefs and actions contribute to inequities, as well as to why, despite decades of extensive effort and significant resources devoted to improving the college access of racially minoritized students, inequities remain. (p. 849)

The authors concluded that although the California SEP in effect is a race-neutral policy, they still believed that it could be "a powerful policy response to mitigating outcome inequity, precisely because it assumes that organizational-level changes are needed to advance equity and asks colleges to engage in an improvement and transformation process" (p. 852).

Thus, their recommendations were that within any equity policy "race and racial equity" must be emphasized and proactive steps should be taken "against efforts that seek to diminish the framing of race in equity policies" (p. 853). The focus on racial equity should not just be included in the equity policy but "should be reflected in plan development guidelines and other supplementary documents," as the authors found that "college responses to the guidelines from the Chancellor's Office varied, resulting in plans that could be described as equity-minded on one end, and as doing more of the same on the other end" (p. 853). They also emphasized that they were not calling for usurping colleges' autonomy, which allows them to meet their specific needs, but did recommend that the guidelines "include stronger language and framing to keep practitioners focused on improving the outcomes of racially minoritized students" (p. 853). Lastly, they recommended that "practitioners use the SEP, including the money it affords and the planning process it requires, to conduct a more thorough study of disproportionate impact at their campuses" (p. 853), in that

> the Chancellor's office only requires a study based on disaggregated outcomes data. . . . Practitioners could undertake additional research to better understand the nature of racial inequities on their campus, for example, a campus racial climate study (Harper & Hurtado, 2007); focus groups and surveys with racially minoritized students (Community College Equity Assessment Lab [CCEAL], 2016); and a practitioner inquiry and research process (Bensimon, Polkinghorne, Bauman, & Vallejo, 2004). Importantly, the purpose of this research should be to expand

practitioner awareness about how racially minoritized students experience the college. (p. 853)

CONCLUSION

In this chapter we went through the emergence of critical policy studies, often called critical policy analysis, and provided an explanation of the difference between critical policy analysis and the traditional form of policy analysis. We then turned to education and discussed the move away from traditional to critical policy analysis in the 1980s as the accountability movement took hold. As with the other chapters, we called attention to notable researchers and theorists. We concluded with an example article to illustrate the research components appropriate for CPA.

CHAPTER 12

Critical Quantitative Studies in Education

Quantitative research methods in the social sciences may, initially, appear antithetical to the aims of critical studies in education, as quantitative methods come out of the philosophical paradigm of positivism that values objective knowledge, one truth free from context, values, and history (see Table 1.1). In other words, the world *is* as we see it and everyone would or "should" see it that same way. Critical studies, coming from critical theory, holds that there are multiple truths and that knowledge is dependent on lived experiences that are not the same for everyone, and the social structures that have developed over time which privilege some and marginalize others. The methods that critical studies embrace are not value-free but "subjectivist, formed between the research and researched, and aims for emancipation from oppression" (Lincoln & Guba, 2013).

Nonetheless, in education, some types of research questions and some study designs require the use of numeric data and statistics (Teranishi, 2007). The solution to this dilemma requires that the researcher be cognizant of the challenges involved with integrating ostensibly neutral methods within a critical research design and take steps to address those challenges (Gillborn et al., 2018). How this is done will be explored in this chapter.

We begin by discussing the background of critical quantitative research and its emergence in educational research. We then identify a set of influential theorists and researchers in this area. The final section of the chapter explicates an example of a critical quantitative research article.

BACKGROUND OF CRITICAL QUANTITATIVE STUDIES IN EDUCATION

In 2007, Frances K. Stage edited a special edition of the journal *New Directions for Institutional Research* that contained a collection of articles focused on the use of quantitative methods for critical research in education. In her introductory article for this special edition, she set out two tasks for critical quantitativists:

1) Use data to represent educational processes and outcomes on a large scale to reveal inequities and to identify social or institutional perpetuation of systematic inequities in such processes and outcomes. This work has become increasingly possible during the past two decades as a result of the proliferation of large representative databases, both national and institutional, broadened access to them, and the development of myriad analysis approaches.

2) Question the models, measures, and analytic practices of quantitative research in order to offer competing models, measures, and analytic practices that better describe experiences of those who have not been adequately represented. This task focuses on professional self-regulation and requires that quantitative researchers become less polite and more critical of themselves and their colleagues. It requires the development of inquiry focused on all aspects of quantitative research, questioning the status quo on approaches to problems and actively seeking to constantly improve the state of the art, including models, measures, and the application of analytic methods. (pp. 10–11)

These two tasks foreshadowed more specific calls by other researchers for conducting quantitative research in ways that attended to the effects of racial and other social biases at work in standard research practices.

Among other authors in this special journal issue was Robert Teranishi (2007). He argued that quantitative methods may be appropriate and useful in critical scholarship in education in his article "Race, Ethnicity, and Higher Education Policy: The Use of Critical Quantitative Research." It called for the use of quantitative methods in studies involving racial categories in higher education settings on the grounds that other methods might not be able to adequately account for the heterogeneity among racial and ethnic groups, particularly Asian Americans. For example, though Asian Americans together as a group may perform at the top of many measures of educational achievement and attainment, Southeast Asian groups, particularly Hmong, frequently score near the bottom of all groups. So, the finding that "Asian Americans did well on this assessment" may be only a partial truth that masks large inequities and makes it difficult to identify and to address educational challenges that face groups such as Hmong students (Teranishi, 2007). Teranishi further called for an integration of quantitative methods that could disaggregate data within groups according to the tenets of critical race theory (CRT) that acknowledge and foreground the effects of racism in society. In other words, decisions made at every step along the way of design and execution of quantitative research would be made with CRT tenets in mind.

In 2018 Gillborn et al. further examined the combination of CRT with quantitative methods and outlined initial principles of what they called QuantCrit. Gillborn and his colleagues asserted, "Contrary to popular belief, and the assertions of many quantitative researchers, numbers are neither objective nor color-blind" (p. 159). Thus, for critical quantitative research studies, research would best be integrated with CRT tenets. Gillborn et al. suggested that an analogous set of tenets for such research, which they termed QuantCrit, would be:

(1) the centrality of racism
(2) numbers are not neutral
(3) categories are neither "natural" nor given: for "race" read "racism"
(4) voice and insight: data cannot "speak for itself"
(5) using numbers for social justice. (p. 169)

For researchers designing and conducting QuantCrit, then, the processes and analyses would follow accepted quantitative and statistical social science research methods. These would be performed with the QuantCrit tenets, cited above, which are intentionally parallel with the CRT tenets.

To give examples of what "keeping the tenets in mind" means, Gillborn et al. (2018) provided extended discussion. Regarding Principle 2 (numbers are not neutral), they presented the instance of researchers advocating for the use of predicted performance rather than actual performance on student achievement tests:

> In this way, statisticians would redefine certain levels of achievement inequity as unproblematic; if Black students do as badly as they are predicted (based on previous cohorts) then they would no longer be "under-achieving" . . . [This] amounts to *the colonization of interpretation* i.e. by mobilizing statistics in these ways commentators (including governments and independent academics) act to redefine the facts of educational achievement and equity. By presenting numbers as a neutral technology (free from political interference and sentimentality) statisticians sometimes act to assert that their view is the only *true* or *legitimate* understanding of the world, a view where inequitable educational achievement by some minoritized groups is taken for granted, normalized and consequently erased from the agenda. (p. 171)

The important take-away with this example is that the numbers (of predicted achievement based on past performance by racial groups) tell one story, but the decisions about how the numbers would be generated and what would be released to the public were made by humans, and, furthermore, those humans likely had conscious or unconscious racial biases driving their decisions.

Following on the work of Gillborn et al., Sablan (2019) argued for the expansion of QuantCrit into a wider group of statistical techniques including measurement theory. She said,

> when taken with an appropriate lens (Padilla, 2004), measurement theory, including survey methodology and scale development, can adequately contribute to critical race dialogues. This is due to the possibility that counterstories can be incorporated into scale development, and validation techniques can refine asset-based theories. (p. 186)

Sablan and other researchers (Garcia et al., 2018; Strunk & Locke, 2019) consistently point out that, while the integration of statistical and quantitative techniques with CRT tenets into QuantCrit may be far from perfect at the present moment, this type of research is needed and has the potential to contribute to critical studies in ways that customary methods have not.

In the next section, we identify several notable theorists and researchers who work in critical quantitative studies. Some are in the field of education, and some are not. As we've pointed out in other chapters, this list is not intended to be rank-ordered or definitive in any way. It is, rather, a starting point for critical researchers in education who are interested in critical quantitative studies to begin their own literature reviews.

NOTABLE THEORISTS AND RESEARCHERS IN CRITICAL QUANTITATIVE STUDIES

Edward Fuller

Edward Fuller is an associate professor at Penn State University. His research focuses on "education evaluation and policy analysis; program evaluation; teacher and administrator quality, supply, demand, and turnover; school leadership; trust in schools; teacher and school leader working conditions; STEM education; and school accountability systems" (Penn State College of Education, n.d.). He has long used quantitative research methods to study these issues through a critical lens. See, for example, his 2011 article "Do Principal Preparation Programs Influence Student Achievement Through the Building of Teacher-Team Qualifications by the Principal: An Exploratory Analysis," coauthored with Michelle Young and Bruce Baker.

David Gillborn

David Gillborn is professor emeritus at the University of Birmingham in the United Kingdom. His research focuses on "race inequalities in education, especially the role of racism as a changing and complex characteristic of the system. He has written 6 books and more than 180 refereed articles, chapters and reports" (University of Birmingham, n.d.). Gillborn is a fellow of the British Academy and is the author of the 2008 book *Racism in Education: Coincidence or Conspiracy?*

Laura Perna

Laura Perna is professor and vice provost for faculty at the University of Pennsylvania. Her research focuses on college access, affordability, and success, especially for low-income, first-generation, and nontraditional students. She is a member of the National Academy of Education and the coauthor of

The State of College Access and Completion: Improving College Success for Students from Underrepresented Groups (2013).

Frances Stage

Frances Stage is a professor of Higher Education at New York University. She has authored over 150 publications, including 12 books. Her research focuses on college student access and success, the methods used to study them, and critical quantitative research. She is the coeditor of *Research in the College Context: Approaches and Methods* (2015).

Kamden Strunk

Kamden Strunk is an associate professor of educational research at Auburn University. His research interests include queer studies in education and critical approaches to quantitative methods. Among numerous influential publications, he is the coeditor of *Research Methods for Social Justice and Equity in Education* (2019).

Robert Teranishi

Robert Teranishi is a professor of social science and comparative education at the University of California, Los Angeles. He is the Morgan and Helen Chu Endowed Chair in Asian American Studies and codirector of the Institute for Immigration, Globalization and Education at UCLA. His research focuses on "race, ethnicity, and the stratification of college opportunity" (Institute for Immigration, Globalization and Education, n.d.). He is the author of *Asians in the Ivory Tower: Dilemmas of Racial Inequality in American Higher Education* (2010).

Tukufu Zuberi

Tukufu Zuberi is a professor of sociology and Africana studies and the Lasry Family Professor of Race Relations at the University of Pennsylvania. His research focuses on race and African and African Diaspora populations. In addition, he is a writer and producer of *African Independence*, an award-winning, feature-length documentary film, and the author of *Thicker Than Blood: How Racial Statistics Lie* (2001).

RESEARCH COMPONENTS OF EXAMPLE ARTICLE

Our example article is "More Than 'Papelitos': A QuantCrit Counterstory to Critique Latina/o Degree Value and Occupational Prestige" by Pérez Huber, Vélez, and Solórzano that appeared in the journal *Race and Ethnicity in Education* in 2018. Lindsay Pérez Huber is a professor at California State University, Long Beach; Verónica Vélez is an associate professor at Western Washington University; and Daniel Solórzano is a professor at the University of California, Los Angeles.

The article by Pérez Huber and colleagues (2018) was not written in the typical format of a social science research article. Therefore, our explanation of the article and the research components will divert somewhat from our previous chapters. The authors described their research process and the format of their article in this way:

> [W]e began this journey wondering whether we could engage an analysis of quantitative data that would tell a story of degree value in Communities of Color that was similar to the stories we have collected in our qualitative data. This study evolved from a series of questions we asked about degree value specifically and the use of quantitative data to measure that value. We present this article in the form of a counterstory that better reflects the iterative process we engaged, asking research questions and analyzing data to help us find answers, which developed further questions. (p. 209)

Here we need to explain the overall logic of their study. Pérez Huber et al.'s (2018) initial question was *"How do we use numbers to tell the stories of Communities of Color?"* (p. 210). This question arose from the authors' concern about a 2013 Pew research study that reported that Latinx students' enrollment in college had surpassed that of White students. The Pew research implied that Latinx educational attainment had also improved and was reaching the level of Whites. This was contrary to the 30 years of research the authors, collectively, had conducted. More importantly, the authors were concerned that the Pew's "misuse" of data could "lead to a reduction in concern and resources for remedying the educational inequities so many Latina/o students continue to encounter" (p. 210). The data did not consider the demographic shifts that showed that the Latinx population increasing as the White population was declining.

This led to their second question, "[H]ow do Latina/o students fare in postsecondary enrollment when we consider population growth particularly in states like California, Texas, and New Mexico where Latinas/os represent a majority of our elementary and secondary student population?" (p. 212). This question took the authors to the U.S. Census Bureau's Current Population Survey (CPS). They examined the "proportion of adult Latinas/os over 25 years of age in California who had attained a degree at the high school, baccalaureate, master's degree and doctorate degree levels . . . with the same data for whites" (p. 212). These data indicted that the Latinx population was "underrepresented at all levels of degree attainment, while whites were overrepresented" (p. 213).

The authors then came upon an article in the *Atlantic* titled "'Which College—and Which Major—Will Make You the Richest?'" that directed them to the question, *"What's the most valuable college education in the country?"*

(p. 213). In the *Atlantic* article was "a list of the top 10 college and universities that produced the 'most valuable college degrees' in the US" (p. 213). The authors responded,

> because we are educational researchers we knew that the highest ranked institutions on this list were predominantly and historically white. Because we are critical race theorists, we knew that the *Atlantic* article was suggesting something else. That was, the highest "quality" students attracted to these institutions were predominantly and historically white. (p. 213)

Their third question, then, was *How was "the concept of 'value'" determined?* (p. 213). According to Pérez Huber and colleagues,

> the concept of degree value brought us to the next phase of our research and the next step in our QuantCrit counterstory. If Latinas/os and other Students of Color are not significantly represented in those institutions that confer the most "valuable" college degrees, we asked [question 4], *what is the occupational payoff for Latinas/os with advanced degrees?* (p. 214)

They returned to the U.S. Census data and found that there was only a 1 in 6 likelihood that a Latinx college graduate with a bachelor's degree would be in what was defined as a professional occupation compared to 1 in 2 for Whites. This guided them to question 5, *"If Latinas/os are less likely to have 'valuable' college degrees, as defined by ROI* [return on investment] *measures, and those degrees may not translate to professional-level jobs, then what is the value of a postsecondary education for Latina/o students?"* (p. 215). This led the authors to discuss their own stories of what their degrees meant to them, their families, and their community. They also returned to the qualitative data they had collected over the years with Latinx parents regarding what higher education meant to these parents. These data "redefined the concept of 'value' from an economic-based meaning to what [the authors called] 'symbolic value'" (p. 216). This was articulated by one of their participants, a "Latina im/migrant activist mother" who spoke about the value of education:

> As courageous and revolutionary mothers, we understand why degrees are problematic and contradictory. Just because we don't have degrees doesn't mean we are any less intelligent. For us, the "papelito" [piece of paper] is a symbol of struggle—that we are here and we aren't leaving. For others, maybe for the rich and the whites, a degree means access to a better job or a better salary. It's an individual goal. But for many of our children, who are undocumented, it's much more. It's for all of us. It's for those that came before and those that will come after. (p. 215)

From this came their sixth question: *"Are there ways to quantitatively show which professional occupations are the most valued or prestigious in our communities?"* (p. 216). To answer this question they looked at the Duncan

Socioeconomic Index (SEI), which ranks the prestige of 700 occupations, al-though this measure is controversial. The "Duncan SEI reflects the correlation between education, income, and occupation, and serves as a proxy for 'pres-tige'" (p. 216). According to the Duncan SEI, the most prestigious jobs are "chief executive officers, engineers, surgeons, and computer systems scientists" (p. 217).

Again Pérez Huber and colleagues returned to the Census data, as they wanted to determine "to what extent college-educated Latinas/os, and other People of Color, landed in these most 'prestigious' positions relative to whites" (p. 217). What they found was that Latinx and African Americans are under-represented in both "baccalaureate attainment, but even more so when it comes to obtaining a 'prestigious' or 'valued' Duncan occupation" (p. 218).

From this they arrived at their final question:

> Are there other ways to measure occupational prestige in our communities? Is the Duncan SEI and other similar metrics, the only way to measure the value we place in our occupational decisions, and, by extension, the college degree we pursue to obtain those jobs? (p. 218)

To answer this, the authors returned to the Census data and disaggregated it for the topmost prestigious jobs, according to the Duncan SEI, by race and eth-nicity. They found that Latinas/os, African Americans, and Native Americans ranked K–12 teaching as number one. This was "based on the number of indi-viduals who identified professionally with that occupation," the same measure used by the Duncan SEI (p. 218). Also highly valued were postsecondary teach-ers, educational administrators, social workers, counselors, and nurses. Among Whites and Asian Americans, the work of lawyers and physicians were the most highly rated. The authors stated that they analyzed the rankings

> discussing what they revealed about the meaning of occupational value or worth for Communities of Color generally, and Latinas/os in particular. We noticed a pat-tern. Occupations associated [with] service, care for others, and social advance-ment were clustered among the top for Latinas/os, African Americans, and Native Americans (p. 219). . . . [In other words] professions more inclined to social ser-vices or social advancement . . . that encourage "giving back" to our communities. (p. 218)

Now that we have worked through the authors "wonderings," we will briefly address the research components, as we have in the previous chapters.

Statement of the Problem, Purpose, and Research Question

As we stated, this article did not follow the typical research format, so the authors (2018) did not directly state the statement of the problem, purpose, and research question/s. However, these were all revealed in the journey their wonderings took them on. The statement of the problem was that there is limited research that looks at degree value and occupational prestige from the lens of communities of color, and specifically for these authors' communities, Latinx communities. The purpose of their research, then, was to add this perspective to the literature. And their wonderings represented their research questions, with the overarching question being: "How do we use numbers to tell the stories of Communities of Color?" (p. 209).

Theoretical Framework

Pérez Huber and her colleagues (2018) did directly address their theoretical framework. They framed their inquiry both theoretically, using CRT, and epistemologically, employing Chicana Feminist Epistemology (CFE). CFE, according to the authors, "acknowledges the forms of knowledge Chicana/o researchers have gained from our personal, professional, and academic experiences" (p. 211). They referred to this as *cultural intuition*, a term associated with Bernal (1998).

> Our positionalities as Chicana/o researchers have provided us with particular perspectives gained from our academic, professional, and personal experiences to make meaning of data. Cultural intuition informed our critique of the dominant discourse on degree value in higher education. We drew explicitly from own experiences in the educational pipeline and those related to what our postsecondary degrees have meant to us, our families, and our communities. This is our personal knowledge. The academic and professional forms of knowledge we draw upon are grounded in our years of experience as researchers in the field of education, examining the educational experiences of Latina/os communities, and particularly related to this study, those concerning academic outcomes and degree attainment. (p. 211)

In addition to drawing on their own experiences and their cultural intuition, the authors employed another concept known as *groundtruthing*, drawn from Vélez and Solórzano (2017). Groundtruthing refers to deferring to community expertise—that is, getting the truth from the ground, the community. As Pérez Huber et al. explained,

> groundtruthing our data, analysis and findings requires that we insist each step of the research process is driven by community expertise, particularly when the research is attempting to understanding [sic] phenomena connected to race and racism. . . . we refuse to allow numbers to speak for themselves. (p. 212)

As our description of the authors' research journey shows, both cultural intuition and groundtruthing were key in their approach to QuantCrit. As the authors stated, "Informed by CRT and CFE, which frame *what* knowledge matters in our research process, groundtruthing emphasizes *who* is important as experts and data verifiers while cultural intuition underscores and details *how* they are important" (p. 212).

Methodology and Methods

There's not much more we can say about the authors' methodology and methods, as we have described them step by step above. Turning to the authors (2018), though, they stated,

> our counterstory shares our methodological journey of theorizing and applying a QuantCrit approach, an emerging methodology, that centers and extends the commitments of critical race scholarship to (re)imagine quantitative approaches and analyses in research, particularly when studying People of Color. (p. 209)

Analysis and Results/Findings

Here, too, there isn't much more we can say about the analysis and results that we haven't already stated. What is important to acknowledge is the reciprocal process the authors employed of looking at the data *as is* and then looking at the data through the lens of cultural intuition and groundtruthing, providing a counterstory. The result is that data do *not* speak for themselves.

Discussion and Recommendations

The discussion of the data and its meaning went on throughout the research process, as it does with all research. The authors (2018) concluded that "social responsibility and advocacy, or the desire to give back to one's community by helping others, must be considered in measurements of occupational prestige for Latinas/os and other Communities of Color" (p. 222). With this in mind, they developed the Critical Race Occupational Index (CROI), which pulls from CRT in education. The CROI is "a metric for exploring occupational outcomes for People of Color that challenges dominant narratives about occupational prestige and offers an approach for employing quantitative methods critically toward this end" (p. 221). The text of the CROI is included in the Pérez Huber et al. article, referred to herein.

The authors end by summarizing this current work and providing the direction in which they believe this work should go next. This should be useful for researchers, including doctoral students, who want to follow this line of study.

> We hope that our counterstory and the analysis that resulted from our journey with educational and occupational attainment data show that quantitative data is critical but not sufficient for telling the stories of People of Color. Quantitative data allows us to explore these stories and provides a snapshot of experiences that can lead to other research questions for further analysis to understand. This study has

lead [sic] us to ask other questions that future research should explore. Some of these questions are—What are other ways that we can measure the ROI of postsecondary degrees for People of Color? What would the CROI tell us about the educational and occupational outcomes of undocumented communities, or Women of Color, or between educational generations within Communities of Color? Is there a relationship between college choice and occupational choice for Students of Color? These questions show the iterative nature of QuantCrit, posing new research questions from current analyses to be explored in future research. (p. 223)

CONCLUSION

In this chapter we discussed Critical Quantitative Studies, or QuantCrit, in education. We began by pointing out that QuantCrit came about because of the need to do quantitative research in ways that recognized implicit biases. Integration of quantitative methods with CRT tenets provides a powerful methodology for contributions to critical studies. Next, we introduced some of the notable theorists and researchers in this area. Finally, we presented an example of a QuantCrit paper titled "More than 'Papelitos': A QuantCrit Counterstory to Critique Latina/o Degree Value and Occupational Prestige," by Pérez Huber, Vélez, and Solórzano, published in *Race and Ethnicity in Education* in 2018. The authors explored how educational statistics for people of color can be distorted and used cultural intuition and groundtruthing to tell a counterstory as a strategy for employing QuantCrit. This article is a good example for those researchers who wish to look at the real story behind the numbers.

CHAPTER 13

Critical Social Epidemiological Studies in Education

A relatively new field of inquiry in education, and one we believe is significant, is social epidemiology. The term "social" epidemiology, in contrast to epidemiology, did not appear in print until it was used by Alfred Yandauer in his 1950 article "The Relationship of Fetal and Infant Mortality to Residential Segregation: An Inquiry into Social Epidemiology," published in *American Sociological Review* (Krieger, 2001). Although in the 1990s there were epidemiologists doing social epidemiological work, the field and the term social epidemiology had not garnered recognition. The first textbook in the discipline, *Social Epidemiology*, was not published until 2000, and the Social Epidemiology office of the journal *Social Science and Medicine* was established the following year. Some contend, however, that W. E. B. DuBois's 1899 study, *The Philadelphia Negro*, marked the nascency of social epidemiology, albeit he did not use the term.

In this chapter we begin with definitions of epidemiology and social epidemiology, including a discussion of place and the social determinates of health. Next, we provide our rationale for why social epidemiological research fits within a book on critical theory in education. As with the other chapters, we conclude with a research example of social epidemiology in education and highlight the research components. We do not, however, include a section on Notable Researchers and Theorists in that the field is newly emerging. We do highlight the work of William Tate, who, along with his coauthors, have been forerunners in social epidemiology of education, and Kathryn Bell McKenzie and her coauthors, who recently published *Community Equity Audits: Communities and Schools Working Together to Eliminate the Opportunity Gap* (2nd ed.), which is an example of how to do social epidemiological work in communities in an effort to impact student success.

WHAT IS THE DIFFERENCE BETWEEN EPIDEMIOLOGY AND SOCIAL EPIDEMIOLOGY?

William Tate, whom we introduced in Chapter 5, along with Catherine Striley, coauthored "Epidemiology and Education Research: Dialoguing About

Disparities" in 2010. This was a discussion between Tate, an educator, and Striley, a psychiatric epidemiologist, arguing that "epidemiology and education research as fields should engage in greater dialogue about pressing matters involving social disparities" (Tate & Striley, 2010, p. 1). They contended that "health disparities and education disparities are interdependent" and defined epidemiology as "the study of the distribution and determinates of health related states in specific populations and the application of this evaluative process to efforts to control health problems" (p. 1), whereas Honjo (2004) defined *social* epidemiology as "a branch of epidemiology that focuses particularly on the effects of social-structural factors on states of health. Social epidemiology assumes that the distribution of advantages and disadvantages in a society reflects the distribution of health and disease" (p. 193) that can ultimately affect educational outcomes.

For example, where one lives, *place*, matters. Due to historical segregation patterns, neighborhoods only a few miles apart "occupy vastly different planes of community well-being—and few people are truly mobile between them" (Economic Innovation Group, 2016, p. 4). Individual and community well-being is determined by many things, including the social determinants of health that, according to the World Health Organization (2022),

> are the non-medical factors that influence health outcomes. They are the conditions in which people are born, grow, work, live, and age, and the wider set of forces and systems shaping the conditions of daily life. These forces and systems include economic policies and systems, development agendas, social norms, social policies and political systems. (p. 4)

We would add educational systems as well.

With regard to education, "most accountability models and research efforts only examine the status of academic achievement or attempt to attribute achievement to school-related factors (teachers, schools, or programs)" (Tate & Striley, 2010, p. 1), instead of addressing the social structural factors. To illustrate, two variables linked to academic success are time-on-task (the amount of time students spend on learning activities) and opportunity to learn (the circumstances that allow students to learn). Both are influenced by chronic illness such as asthma, which is "the leading cause of chronic disease-related school absenteeism" (p. 1). Children who miss school due to asthma are more likely to live below the poverty threshold and more likely to be Hispanic or Black (Hsu et al., 2016). These children's families may not have availability of health care due to lack of health insurance or may not have access to health care facilities due to lack of transportation (McKenzie et al., 2020).

Most of the research on the social determinants of health and distressed communities has been done by zip code (see, for example, Chetty & Hendren, 2018; Drewnowski et al., 2007; Economic Innovation Group, 2016). However, using zip codes for the analysis of epidemiological data is problematic in that zip codes lack "standardization and [are] highly dynamic in structure" (Grubesic & Matisziw, 2006, para. 1). McKenzie et al. (2020) conducted descriptive social epidemiological research using school attendance zones rather than zip codes. They compared the social determinants of health in two school communities in the same school district that were approximately 4 miles apart. To do so, they used census data and created an algorithm that allowed them to adjust for school attendance zones. They assessed five social determinants of health identified by the World Health Organization, the U.S. Department of Health and Human Services, and the United Health Foundation. These included socioeconomic status/poverty, availability of affordable and safe housing, exposure to crime and violence, availability of and access to health care, and availability of and access to community resources. They found that although the schools were in the same school district and only a few miles apart, the distribution of advantages and disadvantages between the two school communities was stark, and this most likely accounted for the significant differences between the achievement levels of the students at the two schools.

WHAT IS CRITICAL ABOUT SOCIAL EPIDEMIOLOGY?

Tate and Striley's (2010) call for a dialogue between educational researchers and social epidemiologists to address social disparities is consistent with the aims of critical theory to analyze social class and the economic and social conditions that create it. Returning to Anyon (2009), critical theory "points to holistic, rather than piecemeal, solutions to educational problems like low achievement. Holistic theory provides schema for action and social change that address the entire nexus of relevant issues or problems" (p. 15). However, most educational research aims the vision within the school walls when looking for causes and solutions to achievement issues (Tate & Striley, 2010). This is a piecemeal approach and disallows a critical analysis of the economic and social conditions that may create social disparities, as well as achievement disparities, and prevents systemic solutions.

RESEARCH COMPONENTS OF EXAMPLE ARTICLE

In choosing an article to represent social epidemiological research related to education, we followed the advice of Tate and Striley (2010) that the fields of epidemiology and education "should engage in greater dialogue about pressing matters involving social disparities" (p. 1). Gabriel Schwartz, Kathryn Leifheit, Jarvis Chen, Mariana Arcaya, and Lisa Berkman, the authors of our chosen article, "Childhood Eviction and Cognitive Development: Developmental Timing-Specific Associations in an Urban Birth Cohort," published in *Social Science & Medicine* in 2022, include social epidemiologists as well as an urban planner. The authors represent Harvard T. H. Chan School of Public Health (Schwartz), UCLA Philip R. Lee Institute for Health Policy Studies (Leifheit), Johns Hopkins Bloomberg School of Public Health (Chen), UCLA Fielding School of Public Health (Arcaya), and Massachusetts Institute of Technology Department of Urban Studies and Planning (Berkman). The intersection of their disciplines though the lens of critical social epidemiology provided insight into the challenges facing education.

Statement of the Problem, Purpose, and Research Question

Residential mobility is common in childhood. "Residential moves, however, are heterogeneous. Moves to better-resourced neighborhoods with more economic opportunity or social support could uplift children's learning and development, while sudden, forced displacement [viz., eviction] into more disadvantaged environments may have the opposite effect . . . undermining children's well-being" (Schwartz et al., 2022, p. 1). Moreover, poor housing quality can expose children to toxins such as lead paint, and

> eviction-related material deprivation is sufficiently extreme in the early childhood years that it is associated with a greater than two-fold increase in the prevalence of food insecurity. At the same time, housing instability is associated with a substantially higher prevalence of maternal depression. The fact that parental stress and poor mental health co-occur with housing instability and eviction's socioeconomic injuries may make them more damaging, as supportive relationships with trusted adults help children overcome life disruptions. A stressed parent handling the chaos of a sudden residential move may be less able to provide support. Eviction thus disrupts children's lives at multiple levels, or ecological systems, at once. Together, these characteristics make eviction an urgent area of study in child development for the estimated 1 in 7 children living in US cities who will be evicted at least once by the time they reach adolescence. (p. 2)

Above the authors described the social problem they addressed. However, the research problem, which is referred to in research and particularly in dissertations as the statement of the problem, is that, to the authors knowledge, "no published research has examined the effects of eviction on children's cognitive function" (p. 2). The purpose of their research, then, was to "bridge the gap between a growing public health and social science literature on eviction and child development research on residential mobility based in developmental psychology" (p. 2). Therefore, their research question asked "whether evictions, a particularly downwardly mobile and abrupt type of residential move, are associated with large or long-lasting impediments to cognitive skill development, and at which ages" (p. 2).

Theoretical Framework

There has been much discussion regarding theory in social epidemiology. Krieger (2014) noted that there is a range of theories in epidemiology writ large from dominant to alternative. The two dominant theories are biomedical and lifestyle. . . . [and] *focus* on individual-level biological characteristics, exposures, and behaviors . . . *emphasize* individually-oriented medical treatment and behavioral interventions . . . *ignore* sociodemographic and contextual variables or else treat them as "nuisance" variables whose effects can be controlled through statistical adjustments and . . . *conceptualize* [emphasis added] population rates as simply the aggregate manifestation of individual-level phenomena. Dominant metaphors [within these theories] portray the body as a machine and/or output of a genetic program, and "choice" as simply the taste of individual "consumers," independent of context or constraints. . . . Multiple causation is addressed through the invocation of a "web of causation," which in effect is "spiderless," and with the causal theory behind what and who appears in the web left unstated. (p. 46)

The alternative theories found within social epidemiology include *sociopolitical theories, psychosocial theories,* and *ecosocial theory* [emphasis added]. Sociopolitical theories analyze disease distribution "in relation to power, politics, economics, and rights: elucidating biological pathways is a secondary concern" (p. 46). The psychosocial theories emphasize "people's psychological perception of—and their health-damaging or health-enhancing responses to—social conditions, social interactions, and social status" (p. 48). Ecosocial theory engages "explicitly and literally with ecology (i.e. not ecology as metaphor)" and other theories

including eco-epidemiology . . . and critical epidemiology. . . . Ecosocial theory, in particular, pays heed to societal and ecologic context, to lifecourse and historical generation, to levels of analysis, and to interrelationships between diverse forms of social inequality, including racism, class, and gender. A central focus is on "embodiment," referring to how we literally embody, biologically, our lived experience, in societal and ecological context . . . another [focus] is on "accountability and agency," both for social inequalities in health and for ways they are—or are not—monitored, analyzed, and addressed. (p. 48)

Schwartz et al. (2022) did not state explicitly a theoretical frame for their work. However, it appeared to us that they were employing a critical lens and ecosocial theory. For example, when discussing the many ways that eviction may affect a child, from material deprivation—such as poor-quality housing and the health issues associated with it, like potential lead poisoning—to a "twofold increase in the prevalence of food insecurity" associated with "eviction-related material deprivation" and the subsequent stress experienced by parents that can impact their ability to provide the support a child will need to overcome the disruption to their life—the authors concluded that "eviction thus disrupts children's lives at multiple levels, or *ecological systems*, at once" [emphasis added] (p. 2). Moreover, when discussing the implications of their work they honed in on educational inequity, a focus of *critical theory*. "Our results suggest that eviction may be a driver of education inequity, most obviously by class but also by race" (p. 8). In summary, "evictions may exacerbate racialized educational injustice" (p. 8).

Methodology and Methods

As with the theoretical frame, the authors did not state a methodology. They did, however, explain their methods in great detail. From that description we surmised that their methodology is longitudinal cohort study. Longitudinal studies observe the same group of people over time, and a cohort is "a group of people born at about the same time, exposed to the same events" (Cozby, 1993, p. 71). Schwartz et al. (2022) studied "children evicted in infancy, early childhood, and middle childhood" to assess whether they exhibited "lower scores on four cognitive assessments (measuring executive function, mathematical reasoning, written language skills, and vocabulary skills) at age 9" (p. 1). Their data were drawn from the 2022 Fragile Families and Child Wellbeing Study:

> The Fragile Families and Child Wellbeing Study (FFCWS) is based on a stratified, multistage sample of **4898 children born in large U.S. cities (population over 200,000) between 1998 and 2000**, where **births to unmarried mothers were oversampled** by a ratio of 3 to 1. This sampling strategy resulted in the inclusion of a large number of Black, Hispanic, and low-income families. Mothers were interviewed shortly after birth and fathers were interviewed at the hospital or by phone. Follow-up interviews were conducted when children were approximately ages 1, 3, 5, 9, 15, and 22 (began late 2020). When weighted, the data are representative of births in large US cities. (para. 1)

Schwartz et al. (2022) did not include the follow-up interview data when the children reached 22.

Analysis and Results/Findings

The analysis included using "linear regression and selection weights [to analyze] longitudinal data from the "Fragile Families and Child Wellbeing Study" (Schwartz et al., 2022 p. 1). First the authors determined an eviction measure—whether families had "been evicted for lack of rent or mortgage payments any time in the past 12 months," and then they looked at "cognitive skills measures" (2022, p. 2–3). These included

> children's scores on four cognitive skills assessments at age 9: the WISC-IV Forward and Backwards Digit Span, two assessments from the Woodcock-Johnson III Tests of Achievement (the Applied Problems test and the Passage Comprehension test), and the Peabody Picture Vocabulary Test (PPVT), third edition. (p. 3)

Three analytic samples were created

> for fitting three sets of regressions. Each analytic sample was used to examine eviction at a specific developmental time. The first sample was constructed to estimate the association between eviction in the first year of life and cognitive skills at age nine. The second was constructed to estimate the association between eviction in early childhood—in the third or fifth year of life—and age nine cognitive skills, and the third was constructed to estimate the association between eviction in middle childhood (the year before the age nine wave) and age nine cognitive skills . . . [within each sample they ran] four multiple linear regressions, one for each cognitive skill assessment. . . . To construct each sample [the authors limited] the sample only to children living in rental housing (i.e., those who were at risk of rental eviction) immediately before a given eviction could have occurred. (p. 3)

Schwartz et al. found that children evicted in their 9th year—middle childhood—scored "a year of schooling" behind their counterparts (p. 1). There was not a statistical significance in cognitive skills between early childhood eviction (years 3–5) and children who had not been evicted during this time. However,

> eviction during infancy [first year of life] was . . . associated with large decrements in middle childhood executive functioning . . . mathematical reasoning . . . and symbolic learning/written language skills. Scores for these tests were a quarter of a standard deviation lower among evicted children eight years later, though p-values did not meet the 0.05 threshold typically used for determining statistical significance (i.e., 95% CIs crossed 0). This imprecision may be due to low statistical power: few children were evicted in any given wave. (p. 6)

Discussion and Recommendations

The authors (2022) indicated that there were limitations to their study. For example, the study was observational and, although it provided "fruitful ground for causal inference . . . caveats about causality in observational studies [applied] (i.e., [they assumed] no residual confounding, selection, or information bias; positivity; consistency; and no model misspecification)" (p. 7). However, their "longitudinal data and study design have real advantages, despite not being randomized. Future studies with more robust designs, larger samples of evicted people, and more detailed frequent follow-up are needed" (p. 7). They were, however, the first to "test whether eviction is associated with children's cognitive skills, net of an array of health, socioeconomic, demographic, and housing related confounders" (p. 5). They found that

> eviction in infancy and in middle childhood is a powerful predictor of future cognitive skill impairment, at least in communities similar to [their] sample. . . . The

associations [they observed] with eviction in infancy and middle childhood are substantive in light of the existing literature on educational and cognitive interventions. (p. 8)

Drawing from Chetty et al. (2014), the authors noted that "small improvements in educational or cognitive skills have long-lasting effects on lifetime earnings," but that according to Kraft (2018), "improving cognitive outcomes via intervention is difficult and expensive" (Schwartz et al. 2022, p. 8).

Thus, the authors recommended that schools should "consider soliciting students' housing instability histories and [provide] necessary supports to ensure evicted students' developmental needs are [met]" (p. 8), and because preventing evictions is "a cheaper and more effective way to safeguard children's cognitive skills than many other interventions," they encouraged further research to proceed with urgency. They concluded by speaking to "implications for educational inequity":

> Our results suggest that eviction may be a driver of educational inequity, most obviously by class but also by race . . . data from the National Assessment of Educational Progress show that the national Black-White achievement gap in fourth grade reading scores is 0.83 SDs. If our results for the PPVT are confirmed by a study with a stronger design for testing causal relationships, a single eviction in middle childhood could push children halfway across that gap. Evictions may exacerbate racialized educational injustice. (p. 8)

CONCLUSION

In this chapter we introduced a relatively new avenue of research for education: critical social epidemiology. We discussed the differences between epidemiology and social epidemiology and explained why we believe social epidemiological research can be critical research. Our example article, "Childhood Eviction and Cognitive Development: Developmental Timing-Specific Associations in an Urban Birth Cohort," was conducted by social epidemiologists and addressed whether residential evictions were "associated with large or long-lasting impediments to cognitive skill development [in children and young adults] and at which ages" (Schwartz et al., 2022, p. 2), and found that "eviction in infancy and in middle childhood is a powerful predictor of future cognitive skill impairment" (p. 8). They contended that evictions can be "a driver of educational inequality" (p. 8).

This article is different from most in this book in that it uses quantitative data and, as we discussed in Chapter 12, quantitative research can be critical. Moreover, we believe any researcher and/or practitioner interested in educational equity should also take an interest in the out-of-school factors that affect student health and well-being.

CHAPTER 14

The Future of Critical Research in Education

"We are a society that has been structured from top to bottom by race. You don't get beyond that by deciding not to talk about it anymore. It will always come back; it will always reassert itself over and over again" (Public Broadcasting System [PBS], 2005). We agree with this quote from a PBS interview with Kimberlé Crenshaw and would extend the sentiment to other societal inequities regarding gender, sexual orientation, language, wealth distribution, disability, Indigenous/Tribal status, and others relevant to critical research in education that are discussed in this book. Progress on any of these fronts will not be made by avoiding societal discourse on the issues.

In education specifically, the United States is in a period of significant retrenchment on critical issues such as these (Ujifusa, 2021). In our view, this makes it *more* important than ever, rather than *less* important, to push forward with critical research in education. Enduring problems and inequities in schools and other education settings will not be solved by ignoring or hiding them. As we've noted in earlier work, spontaneous outbreaks of equity in education simply do not happen (McKenzie & Skrla, 2011). Thus, critical research in education will continue to be needed. In this concluding chapter, we discuss our view of what critical research in education might look like in the future in three areas—turbulent state policy environments, effects of the pandemic, and use of big data.

TURBULENT STATE POLICY ENVIRONMENTS

Critical research in education will be needed, sorely needed, in the area of state policy environments. As of March 2022, 34 U.S. states had considered or adopted legislation targeting race education (Alfonseca, 2022). Many of these bills specifically prohibit the teaching of critical race theory (CRT), though they often miss what CRT actually is and misassign a whole host of other issues to CRT.

In addition to bills dealing with how race is taught, which are aimed at schools, universities, and other education settings (such as corporate training), other legislation has targeted LGBTQ topics and people. According to Sonoma (2022), "2022 has been a record-setting year for state legislation targeting LGBTQ adults and children. . . . Most bills (120) have targeted transgender people and youth, followed by a surge of school policy bills (83) banning class-room conversation and books about LGBTQ people" (para. 1–2).

Still other state legislation has aimed at multiple groups, who historically have been targeted for oppression, and has attempted to forbid businesses and schools from making people "feel bad" about past oppressions involving these groups. Perhaps the most notable of this type of legislation is Florida's Stop WOKE Act, which

> prohibits workplace training or school instruction that teaches that individuals are "inherently racist, sexist, or oppressive, whether consciously or unconsciously"; that people are privileged or oppressed based on race, gender, or national origin; or that a person "bears personal responsibility for and must feel guilt, anguish, or other forms of psychological distress" over actions committed in the past by mem-bers of the same race, gender, or national origin. (Reilly, 2022, para. 2)

This act broadly targets teaching and discussions of race, gender, and national origin in both schools and workplace training.

As these examples show, the past several years have seen a large increase in the volume and virulence of state policy actions designed to inhibit, prohibit, or call into question discussion, teaching, research, and action on several of the topics this critical research in education book is designed to help researchers do. This makes for a currently chilly policy climate in which to conduct such research, in addition to all the other intended and unintended policy and real-life consequences of such legislation.

Predictably, as of this book's writing in late summer 2022, some backlash has already begun. In late August 2022, a federal judge issued an injunction against Florida's Stop WOKE Act, calling it "bordering on unintelligible" and potentially in violation of the First Amendment (Atterbury, 2022, para. 2). Additionally, major corporations have staged public relations campaigns such as "Discrimination Is Bad for Business" against this type of legislation in states such as Florida and Texas (Gibson, 2022, para. 7). No doubt other forms of resistance, resilience, and pushback will arise and gather strength in the future.

All of these phases of the evolving state policy environments for critical research in education will need to be studied and evaluated. Thus, critical researchers in schools, universities, and other education settings will not find themselves short of topics or issues worthy of research. Those armed with in-formed understandings of the issues and able to take careful consideration of all the responsibilities involved in designing and conducting critical research in education will be ideally positioned to do the needed work.

EFFECTS OF THE PANDEMIC

A second area where critical research in education will be needed is what has occurred in schools, universities, and other educational settings as a result of dealing with the COVID-19 pandemic, which is in its third year as of this writing. Just about every chapter in this book addresses a population of parents and students disproportionately impacted by the pandemic: people of color; people living in poverty; women—especially women head of households; Tribal and Indigenous communities; and students with disabilities.

Virtually no aspect of education was left untouched by the pandemic and the response to it. It is clear that individuals, groups, schools, and communities that were already most vulnerable before the pandemic were disproportionately and negatively impacted by the response and aftermath (Schwartz, 2021). As a report from the U.S. Department of Education (2021) said,

> there are two headlines about COVID-19's impact on America's students: First, the pandemic posed profound challenges for nearly all students and schools in every part of our country; and second, the disparities in students' experiences are stark. Those who went into the pandemic with the fewest opportunities are at risk of leaving with even less. (p. 51)

And "COVID-19 appears to have deepened the impact of disparities in access and opportunity facing many students of color in public schools, including technological and other barriers that make it harder to stay engaged in virtual classrooms" (p. iv). So, again, critical research will be greatly needed. We suggest a few examples, but certainly there are more to come.

TribalCrit will be useful to study the impact of the pandemic on Native American and Indigenous Peoples to determine what has happened, is happening, and needs to happen with Native American and Indigenous school and university populations. The availability of and access to personal computers and broadband comes immediately to mind. While this adversely impacted the educational achievement of many communities and schools, the lack of computers and broadband chronically affects Native American and Indigenous students.

Inequity among communities leads us to another example. Some communities "are places where students and their families have both availability of and access to the resources and opportunities necessary for health and well-being"—the social determinants of health (McKenzie et al., 2020, p. 8). These include a livable income and availability of and access to affordable and safe housing, health care, and community resources like healthy food and green spaces (McKenzie et al., 2020). Other communities do not. This inequitable distribution of resources creates an opportunity gap. As noted by DeShano da Silva et al. (2007), "We must recognize that the gaps in educational achievement that we are so fond of discussing are produced by even more unwieldy gaps in opportunity" (p. 1).

Take, for example, socioeconomic status, which is the precursor for the other social determinants of health. Engle and Black (2008) noted that "children raised in low-income families are at risk for academic and social problems as well as poor health and well-being, which can in turn undermine educational achievement" (p. 244). In the first year of the pandemic, the poverty rate for non-Hispanic Whites and Hispanics increased, but while the poverty rate of non-Hispanic Whites was 8.2%, for Hispanics it was 17.0% (U.S. Census Bureau, 2021). Similarly, the poverty rate for families with a female head of household increased to 23.4%, while that for families with a male head of household remained unchanged at 11.4%.

Therefore, critical social epidemiological studies will be useful to study the impact of the pandemic on the opportunity gap and what effect this has had and is having on student achievement and mental health, as well as the mental health of the teachers and leaders who serve these communities.

One last example is critical research into the impact of the pandemic on students with disabilities, for which there is currently limited research. However,

> early evidence suggests widespread and lengthy interruptions in students' specialized services, which essentially disappeared overnight at the outset of the pandemic. [Moreover,] students with disabilities experienced higher rates of absenteeism, incomplete assignments and course failures compared to their typical peers [and] districts struggled most notably when trying to meet the needs of students who require more supports, including students with complex communication and learning disabilities. (Morando-Rhim & Ekin, 2021, pp. 5–6)

We don't yet know, however, "the true scope of the impacts of service interruptions in terms of students' progress including regression in basic skills among students with intensive needs [and] how the pandemic has affected the social and emotional development of students with disabilities" (p. 6). Therefore, the grave consequences of the pandemic for students with disabilities will require critical disability and DisCrit research in the near future.

USE OF BIG DATA

The third area of critical research in education that we see on the ascendency is research involving what is called *big data*. This term generally refers to datasets so large that they require advanced technology to manage and analyze them. In education, we are at the very beginning of studying what can be learned about all aspects of the field from the enormous amounts of information being collected all the time.

As we discussed in Chapter 12, big data use as a growth frontier for research guided by critical theory sensibilities may seem counterintuitive or antithetical. However, as was also pointed out, numbers are not inherently more or less biased or oppressive than words. It is in the awareness of the researchers where critical theory and quantitative methods intersect. Each decision is an opportunity to consider equity concerns, or not. Though big data was used as a cautionary tale by Gillborn et al., (2018) in their discussion of what a critical race theory for statistics might look like, we think that it could also be used as a powerful positive force in critical research in education.

Two highly influential researchers who are using big data in this way are Sean Reardon and Raj Chetty. Reardon is a professor in the Graduate School of Education at Stanford and senior fellow at the Stanford Institute for Economic Policy Research (SIEPR). One of Reardon and colleagues' current projects is a working paper for the Stanford Center for Education Policy Analysis titled "Is Separate Still Unequal? New Evidence on School Segregation and Racial Academic Achievement Gaps." In this work they sought to answer the question "does segregation of schools today limit Black and Hispanic students' educational opportunities?" (Reardon et al., 2021, p. 32). To answer the question, they "estimate[d] the effects of current-day school segregation on racial achievement gaps using 10 years of data from all public districts in the U.S." (p. 1). These data included "hundreds of millions of state accountability tests taken in the last decade . . . in thousands of school districts" (p. 32). They found

> a very strong link between racial school segregation and academic achievement gaps. More racially segregated school systems have larger achievement gaps, on average, and their gaps grow faster during elementary and middle schools than in less segregated school systems. Indeed, every school district in the U.S. where segregation is even moderately high has a large achievement gap. (pp. 32–33)

Raj Chetty is an economist and the William A. Ackman Professor of Public Economics at Harvard University. He is also the director of Opportunity Insights, "which uses 'big data' to understand how we can give children from disadvantaged backgrounds better chances of succeeding" (Harvard, Department of Economics, n.d., para. 1) and "whose mission is to train the next generation of researchers and policy leaders on methods to study and improve economic opportunity and related social problems" (Opportunity Insights, n.d., para 1). To address this mission, Chetty's course, *Using Big Data to Solve Economic and Social Problems*, and his lectures have been made public online. A sampling of the topics in the course include, "Higher Education and Upward Mobility, Primary Education, Racial Disparities in Economic Opportunity, The Geography of Upward Mobility in America, The Causal Effect of Colleges, [and] Teachers and Charter Schools" (Opportunity Insights, n.d., Lecture Materials). We encourage you to take a look at Chetty's website, as there are links to the valuable resources he offers.

We see the use of big data for critical research in education as a likely direction for future researchers. This, of course, will require continued work on resolving paradigmatic challenges between traditional views of scientific research involving data and statistics, on the one hand, and critical theories that foreground societal inequities and power differentials, on the other. Reardon and Chetty's work has done this and offers us examples of the power of big data for critical education research.

CONCLUSION

In this chapter we have discussed three areas that we see as sites in which critical researchers in education should engage in the future. These include turbulent state policy environments, effects of the pandemic, and use of big data. There are doubtless numerous other areas that critical research in education will focus on in the future that we have not foreseen or discussed here. Regardless of what those areas may turn out to be, we'd like to emphasize our point made at the beginning of the chapter: The current, extremely challenging circumstances faced by schools, universities, and other educational settings in the United States and across the globe make critical research in education more important than ever.

Endnotes

Preface

1. We use *results/findings* in that some researchers use *results* and others use *findings*. There is, however, controversy regarding using findings in qualitative research in that some contend that a "finding" is perceived as an indisputable truth and inconsistent with the tenets of qualitative research.

Chapter 4

1. This was the 1988 article that was republished in *Critical Race Theory: The Key Writings That Formed the Movement* (1995) that we quoted on page 44 and that laid out the challenges and agenda that led to CRT.

Chapter 7

1. The story of the Mattachine Foundation and Mattachine Society is complex, including other groups that evolved from the two—for example, One Inc. and *One Magazine,* the first pro-gay publication in the United States. Further reading should include *Sexual Politics, Sexual Communities: The Making of a Homosexual Minority in the United States* by John D'Emilio.

Chapter 11

1. Throughout this chapter the terms *critical policy studies*, *critical policy analysis*, and *critical policy scholarship* will be used interchangeably to accommodate the preferred term within the works we refer to or cite.

References

Alfonseca, K. (2022, March 24). Map: Where anti-critical race theory efforts have reached. *ABC News.* https://abcnews.go.com/Politics/map-anti-critical-race-theory -efforts-reached/story?id=83619715

Al-Khalili, J. (2009, January 4). *The 'first true scientist.'* http://news.bbc.co.uk/2/hi/science /nature/7810846.stm

American Psychological Association. (2020). *Publication manual of the American Psychological Association* (7th ed.). https://doi.org/10.1037/0000165-000

Anfara, V., & Mertz, M. (2006). *Theoretical frameworks in qualitative research.* Sage Publications.

Anyon, J. (2009). *Theory and educational research.* Routledge.

Apple, M. (1971). The hidden curriculum and the nature of conflict. *Interchange, 2*(4), 27–40. https://doi.org/10.1007/BF02287080

Apple, M. (1979). *Ideology and curriculum.* Routledge.

Apple, M. (2013). Between traditions: Stephen Ball and the critical sociology of education. *London Review of Education, 11*(3), 206–217. http://dx.doi.org/10.1080 /14748460.2013.840981

Apple, M. (2018). *The struggle for democracy in education.* Routledge.

Apple, M. (2019). On doing critical policy analysis. *Educational Policy, 33*(1), 276–287. https://doi.org/10.1177/0895904818807307

Archibeque, R., & Okhremtchouk, I. (2020). Understanding cultural differences: White teachers' perceptions and values in American Indian Schools. *Journal of American Indian Education, 59*(2 & 3), 75–98. https://doi.org/10.5749/jamerindieduc.59.2-3.fm

Arizona State University. (n.d.). *Bryan Brayboy.* https://search.asu.edu/profile/1148916

Atterbury, A. (2022, Aug. 18). Federal judge temporarily blocks DeSantis' 'Stop-WOKE' law. *Politico.* https://www.politico.com/news/2022/08/18/federal-judge-temporarily -blocks-desantis-stop-woke-law-00052768

Audi, R. (Ed.). (1999). *The Cambridge dictionary of philosophy* (2nd ed.). Cambridge University Press.

Ball, S. (2021). Response: Policy? Policy research? How absurd? *Critical Studies in Education, 62*(3), 387–393. https://doi.org/10.1080/17508487.2021.1924214

Ballotpedia. (2021). *Alabama separation of schools, Amendment 2.* https://ballotpedia .org/Alabama_Separation_of_Schools,_Amendment_2_(2004)

Banks, J. (2015). Gangsters and wheelchairs: Urban teachers' perceptions of disability, race and gender. *Disability and Society, 30*(4), 569–582. https://doi.org/10.1080/0968 7599.2015.1030066

Bartanen, B. (2020). Principal quality and student attendance. *Educational Researcher, 49*(2), 101–113. https://doi.org/10.3102/0013189X19898702

Bell, D. (1972). On meritocracy and equality. *The Public Interest, 29,* 29–68.

Bell, D. (1979). Bakke, minority admissions, and the usual price of racial remedies. *California Law Review, 67*, 3–19.

Bell, D. (1989). *And we are not saved: The elusive quest for social justice.* Basic Books.

Bell, D. (1995). Serving two masters: Integration ideals and client interests in school desegregation litigation. In K. Crenshaw, N. Gotanda, G. Peller, & K. Thomas (Eds.), *Critical race theory: The key writings that formed the movement* (pp. 5–19). The New Press. (Reprinted from "Serving Two Masters: Integration Ideals and Client Interests in School Desegregation Litigation," 1975, *Yale Law Journal, 85*, 470–516.)

Bernal, D. D. (1998). Using a Chicana feminist epistemology in educational research. *Harvard Educational Review, 68*(4), 555–583. https://doi.org/10.17763/haer.68.4.5wv 1034973g22q48

Besley, T. (2012). Why read Giroux? *Policy Futures in Education, 10*(6), 594–600. https://doi.org/10.2304/pfie.2012.10.6.594

Black, J., & Prince, J. (2019–present). *Performance, protest, and politics: The art of Gilbert Baker.* Exhibit LGBT Historical Society. https://www.glbthistory.org/gilbert -baker

Blumberg, N. (n.d.). Lile Elbi. *Britannica.* https://www.britannica.com/biography/Lili -Elbe

Bourassa, G. (2019). Educational biopolitics, innovation, and social reproduction. In M. Peters & R. Heraud (Eds.), *Encyclopedia of educational innovation* (pp. 1–6). Springer.

Bourdieu, P., & Passeron, J. C. (1977). *Reproduction in education, society, and culture.* Sage Publications.

Bowles, S., & Gintis, H. (1976). *Schooling in capitalist America: Educational reform and the contradictions of economic life.* Basic Books.

Braman, S. (Ed.). (2003). *Communication researchers and policy-making.* MIT Press.

Brayboy, B. M. J. (2006). Toward a tribal critical race theory in education. *Urban Review, 37*(5), 425–445. https://doi.org/10.1007/s11256-005-0018-y

Brayboy, B. M. J. (2013). Tribal critical race theory: An origin story and future directions. In M. Lynn & A. D. Dixson (Eds.), *Handbook of critical race theory in education* (pp. 88–100). Routledge.

Britannica. (n.d.). *Bakke decision.* https://www.britannica.com/event/Bakke-decision

Brush, S., Spencer, J. B., & Osler, M. (2019). Scientific revolution. *Britannica.* https://www.britannica.com/science/Scientific-Revolution

California Proposition 209. (1996). https://lao.ca.gov/ballot/1996/prop209_11_1996 .html#

Cannella, G. S., & Manuelito, K. D. (2008). Feminisms from unthought locations: Indigenous worldviews, marginalized feminisms, and revisioning social science. In N. K. Denzin, Y. S. Lincoln, & L. Tuhiwai Smith (Eds.), *Handbook of critical and indigenous methodologies* (pp. 45–60). Sage Publications.

Carle, S. (2009). Debunking the myth of civil rights liberalism: Visions of racial justice in the thought of T. Thomas Fortune, 1880–1890. *Fordham Law Review, 77*(4), 1479–153.

Carspecken, F. P. (2013). *Critical ethnography in educational research: A theoretical and practical guide* (2nd ed.). Routledge.

Castagno, A. E., & Brayboy, B. M. J. (2008). Culturally responsive schooling for Indigenous youth: A review of the literature. *Review of Educational Research, 78*(4), 941–993. https://doi.org/10.3102/0034654308323036

Centers for Disease Control and Prevention. (n.d.). *HIV surveillance report*. U.S. Department of Health and Human Services. https://www.cdc.gov/hiv/statistics/overview/index.html

Ching, C. D., Felix, E. R., Fernandez Castro, M., & Trinidad, A. (2020). Achieving racial equity from the bottom-up? The student equity policy in the California community colleges. *Educational Policy, 34*(6), 819–863. https://doi.org/10.1177/0895904818802092

Chiseri-Strater, E. (1996). Turning in upon ourselves: Positionality, subjectivity, and reflexivity in case study and ethnographic research. In P. Mortensen & G. Kirsch (Eds.), *Ethics and Representation in Qualitative Studies of Literacy* (pp. 115–133). National Council of Teachers of English.

Collins, P. H. (1990). *Black feminist thought: Knowledge, consciousness, and the politics of empowerment*. Routledge.

Collins, P. H., & Bilge, S. (2016). *Intersectionality*. Polity Press.

Connor, D. J., Ferri, B. A., & Annamma, S. A. (2021) From the personal to the global: Engaging with and enacting DisCrit theory across multiple spaces. *Race Ethnicity and Education, 24*(5), 597–606. https://doi.org/10.1080/13613324.2021.1918400

Cozby, P. (1993). *Methods in behavioral research* (5th ed.). Mayfield Publishing Company.

Crenshaw, K. (1989). Demarginalizing the intersection of race and sex: A black feminist critique of antidiscrimination doctrine, feminist theory and antiracist politics. *The University of Chicago Legal Forum, 140*, 139–167.

Crenshaw, K. (1991). Mapping the margins: Intersectionality, identity politics, and violence against women of color. *Stanford Law Review, 43*(6), 1241–1299.

Crenshaw, K. (1995). Race, reform, and retrenchment: Transformation and legitimation in antidiscrimination law. In K. Crenshaw, N. Gotanda, G. Peller, & K. Thomas (Eds.), *Critical race theory: The key writings that formed the movement* (pp.103–122). The New Press. (Reprinted from "Race, reform, and retrenchment: Transformation and legitimation in antidiscrimination law," 1988, *Harvard Law Review, 101*[7], 1331–1387.)

Crenshaw, K. (2002). The first decade: Critical reflections, or "A foot in the closing door." *UCLA Legal Review. 49*, 1343–1372.

Crenshaw, K., Gotanda, N., Peller, G., & Thomas, K. (Eds.). (1995). *Critical race theory. The key writings that formed the movement*. The New Press.

Creswell, J. (1994). *Research design*. Sage Publications.

Crotty, M. (2003). *The foundations of social research*. Sage Publications. (Original published in 1998)

Cynthia B. Dillard. http://cynthiabdillard.com/

DC.gov. (n.d.). *People first language*. Office of Disability Rights. https://odr.dc.gov/page/people-first-language

Delgado, R. (1984/1995). The imperial scholar: Reflections on a review of civil rights literature. In K. Crenshaw, N. Gotanda, G. Peller, & K. Thomas (Eds.), *Critical race theory: The key writings that formed the movement* (pp. 46–57). The New Press. (Reprinted from "The imperial scholar: Reflections on a review of civil rights literature," 1984, *University of Pennsylvania Law Review, 134*, 561–578.)

Delgado, R. (1989). Storytelling for oppositionists and others: A plea for narrative. *Michigan Law Review, 87*, 2411–2441.

Delgado, R. (1990). When a story is just a story: Does voice really matter? *Virginia Law Review*, 95–111.

Delgado, R. (1992). The imperial scholar revisited: How to marginalize outsider writing, ten years later. *University of Pennsylvania Law Review, 140*, 1349–1372.

Delgado, R., & Stefancic, J. (2001). *Critical race theory: An introduction.* New York University Press.

Delgado Bernal, D. (2002) Critical race theory, Latino critical theory, and critical raced-gendered epistemologies: Recognizing students of color as holders and creators of knowledge. *Qualitative Inquiry, 8*(1), 105–126. https://doi.org/10.1177/107780 040200800107

Denzin, N., & Lincoln, Y. (2005). Introduction: The discipline and practice of qualitative research. In N. Denzin & Y. Lincoln (Eds.), *The Sage handbook of qualitative research* (3rd ed., pp. 1–32). Sage Publications.

Denzin, N. K., & Lincoln, Y. S. (2008). Introduction. In N. K. Denzin, Y. S. Lincoln, & L. T. Smith (Eds.), *Handbook of critical and indigenous methodologies* (pp. 1–20). Sage Publications.

DeShano da Silva, C., Huguley, J., Kakli, Z, & Rao, R. (2007). *The opportunity gap: Achievement and inequality in education.* Harvard Education Publishing Group.

Diem, S., Young, M. D., & Sampson, C. (2019). Where critical policy meets the politics of education: An introduction. *Educational Policy, 33*(1), 3–15. https://doi.org/10 .1177/0895904818807317

Dimitriadis, G. & Kamberelis, G. (2006). *Theory for education.* Routledge.

Economic Innovation Group. (2016). *The 2016 Distressed Communities Index.* https:// eig.org/wp-content/uploads/2016/02/2016-Distressed-Communities-Index-Report .pdf

Eisner, E. (1993). Foreword. In D. Flinders & G. Mills (Eds.), *Theory and concepts in qualitative research: Perspectives from the field* (pp. 218–130). Teachers College Press.

Ellington, T. (2021). *A qualitative review of a culturally responsive education program for Native American Youth.* Doctoral dissertation, Utah State University. ProQuest. https://www.proquest.com/docview/2621371951?pq-origsite=gscholar&fromo penview=true

Ellsworth, E. (1989). Why doesn't this feel empowering? Working through the repressive myths of critical pedagogy. *Harvard Educational Review, 59*(3), 297–324. https://doi.org/10.17763/haer.59.3.058342114k266250

Engels, F. (1882). Engels to Eduard Bernstein in Zurich. *Marx/Engels Collected Works, 46*, p. 353. https://www.hekmatist.com/Marx%20Engles/Marx%20&%20Engels %20Collected%20Works%20Volume%2046_%20Ka%20-%20Karl%20Marx.pdf

Engle, P. L., & Black, M. M. (2008). The effect of poverty on child development and educational outcomes. *Annals of the New York Academy of Science, 1138*(10), 243–256. DOI: 10.1196/annals.1425.023

Ewald, W. (1988). Unger's philosophy: A critical legal study. *The Yale Law Review, 97*(5), 665–756.

Foley, D. (2005). Enrique Trueba: A Latino critical ethnographer for the ages. *Anthropology & Education Quarterly, 36*(4), 354–366. http://www.jstor.org/stable/36 51362

Fragile Families & Wellbeing Study. (2022). *About the fragile families and wellbeing study.* Princeton. https://fragilefamilies.princeton.edu/about

Freeman, A. (1995). Legitimizing racial discrimination law: A critical review of Supreme Court doctrine. In K. Crenshaw, N. Gotanda, G. Peller, & K. Thomas (Eds.), *Critical race theory: The key writings that formed the movement* (pp. 29–46). The New

Press. (Reprinted from "Legitimizing racial discrimination law: A critical review of Supreme Court doctrine," 1978, *Minnesota Law Review, 62*, 1049–1119.)

Freeman, E. (2019). Feminist theory and its use in qualitative research in education. *Oxford Encyclopedias-Education*. https://doi.org/10.1093/acrefore/9780190264093 .013.1193

Freire, P. (2002). *Pedagogy of the oppressed* (M. Ramos, Trans.; 30th Anniversary, ed.). Continuum. (Original work published 1970.)

Freyenhagen, F. (2018). Critical theory: Self-reflexive theorizing and struggles for emancipation. In W. Thompson (Ed.), *Oxford Research Encyclopedia of Politics*. Oxford University Press. https://doi.org/10.1093/acrefore/9780190228637.013.195

Garcia, N. M., López, N., & Vélez, V. N. (2018). QuantCrit: Rectifying quantitative methods through critical race theory. *Race Ethnicity and Education, 21*(2), 149–157. https://doi.org/10.1080/13613324.2017.1377675

Garlitz, D., & Kögler, H. (2015). Frankfurt School: Institute for Social Research. *International Encyclopedia of the Social & Behavioral Science* (2nd ed., (9), 380–386). https://doi.org/10.1016/B978-0-08-097086-8.61221-7

Gates, B. T. (1996). A root of ecofeminism: Ecoféminisme. *Interdisciplinary Studies in Literature and Environment, 3*(1), 7–16. http://www.jstor.org/stable/44085413

Gates, G. (2007). *The effects of "Don't Ask, Don't Tell" on retention among lesbian, gay, and bisexual military personnel.* https://williamsinstitute.law.ucla.edu/public ations/effect-data-retention-lgb-military/

Gibson, K. (2022, March 11). Florida and Texas governors face business backlash over anti-LGBTQ moves. *CBS News Moneywatch*. https://www.cbsnews.com/news/flo rida-texas-lgbtq-business-backlash/

Gillborn, D., Warmington, P., & Demack, S. (2018). QuantCrit: Education, policy, "big data" and principles for a critical race theory of statistics. *Race Ethnicity and Education, 21*(2), 158–179. https://doi.org/10.1080/13613324.2017.1377417

Ginsberg, R. B. (2004). *Brown v Board of Education in international context.* Columbia School of Law. https://www.supremecourt.gov/publicinfo/speeches/viewspeech /sp_10-25-04

Giroux, H. (1979a). Review of the book *Ideology and curriculum*, by Michael Apple. *The Journal of Education, 161*(4), 88–91. https://doi.org/10.1177/00220574791 6100408

Giroux, H. (1979b). Paulo Freire's approach to radical educational reform. *Curriculum Inquiry, 9*(3), 257–272. https://doi.org/10.2307/3202124

Giroux, H. (1980). Beyond the correspondence theory: Notes on the dynamics of educational reproduction and transformation. *Curriculum Inquiry, 10*(3), 225–247. https://doi.org/10.1080/03626784.1980.11075221

Giroux, H. (1983). Theories of reproduction and resistance in the New Sociology of Education: A critical analysis. *Harvard Educational Review, 53*(3), 257–293. https:// doi.org/10.17763/haer.53.3.a67x4u33g7682734

Giroux, H. (2010). Rethinking education as the practice of freedom: Paulo Freire and the promise of critical pedagogy. *Policy Futures in Education, 8*(6), 715–721. https:// doi.org/10.2304/pfie.2010.8.6.715

Gottesman, I. (2016). *The critical turn in education: From Marxist critique to poststructuralist feminism to critical theories of race.* Routledge.

Grimké, S. M. (2015). *Letters on the equality of the sexes, and the condition of women.* Good Books. (Original work published 1838)

Grubesic, T., & Matisziw, T. (2006). On the use of ZIP codes and ZIP code tabulation areas (ZCTAs) for the spatial analysis of epidemiological data. *International Journal of Health Geographics, 5*(58), 1–15. https://doi.org/10.1186/1476-072X-5-58

Guba, E., & Lincoln, Y. (2005). Paradigmatic controversies, contradictions, and emerging confluences. In N. Denzin & Y. Lincoln (Eds.), *The Sage handbook of qualitative research* (3rd ed., pp. 191–215). Sage Publications.

Habermas, J. (1972). *Knowledge and human interests* (J.J. Shapiro, Trans.). Beacon Press. (Original work published 1968)

Hall, M. C. (2019). Critical disability theory. In E. Zalta (Ed.), *The Stanford encyclopedia of philosophy*. Stanford University. https://plato.stanford.edu/archives/win2019/entries/disability-critical/

Harre, R. (1981). The positivist-empiricist approach and its alternative. In P. Reason & J. Rowan (Eds)., *Human inquiry: A sourcebook for new paradigm research* (pp. 3–17). John Wiley.

Harris, C. I. (1993). Whiteness as property. *Harvard Law Review, 106*(8), 1707–1791. https://harvardlawreview.org/1993/06/whiteness-as-property/

Harvard University Department of Economics. (n.d.) *Raj Chetty*. https://economics.harvard.edu/people/raj-chetty

Held, D. (1980). *Introduction to critical theory Horkheimer to Habermas*. University of California Press.

Henry, A. M. (2011). Feminist theories in education. In S. Tozer, B. P. Gallegos, A. M. Henry, M. B. Greiner, & P. G. Price (Eds.), *Handbook of research in the social foundations of education* (pp. 262–282). Routledge.

Heron, J., & Reason, P. (1997). A participatory inquiry paradigm. *Qualitative Inquiry, 3*(3), 274–294. https://doi.org/10.1177/107780049700300302

Hertz, R. (1997). Introduction: Reflexivity and voice. In R. Hertz (Ed.), *Reflexivity & Voice* (pp. vii-xvii). Sage Publications.

Holmes, A. (2020). Researcher positionality—A consideration of its influence and place in qualitative research—A new researcher guide. *Shanlax International Journal of Education, 8*(4), 1–10. https://doi.org/10.34293/education.v8i4.3232

Honjo, K. (2004). Social epidemiology: Definition, history, and research examples. *Environmental Health and Preventive Medicine, 9*, 193–199. doi: 10.1007/BF02898100

hooks, b. (2000). *Feminism is for everybody: Passionate politics*. South End Press.

Hsu, J., Qin, X., Beavers, S., & Mirabelli, M. (2016). Asthma-related school absenteeism, morbidity, and modifiable factors. *American Journal of Preventive Medicine, 51*(1), 23–32. DOI: 10.1016/j.amepre.2015.12.012

Jackson, P. W. (1968). *Life in classrooms*. Teachers College Press.

Jeffries, S. (2016). *Grand hotel abyss: The lives of the Frankfurt School*. Verso.

Katz, J. (n.d.). ENGL 003.401 & GSWS 003.401—*Intro to Queer Studies* [Syllabus]. Department of English & Department of Gender, Sexuality and Women's Studies, University of Pennsylvania. https://www.english.upenn.edu/courses/undergraduate/2019/spring/engl003.401

Kepner, J., & Murray, S. (2002). Henry Gerber (1895–1972): Grandfather of the American gay movement. In V. Bullough (Ed.), *Before Stonewall: Activists for gay and lesbian rights in historical context* (pp. 24–34). Haworth Press.

Krieger, N. (2001). Theories for social epidemiology in the 21st century: An ecosocial perspective. *International Journal of Epidemiology, 30*(4), 668–677. https://doi.org/10.1093/ije/30.4.668

Krieger, N. (2014). Got theory? On the 21st c. CE rise of explicit use of epidemiologic theories of disease distribution: A review and ecosocial analysis. *Current Epidemiology Reports, 1*(1), 45–56. https://doi.org/10.1007/s40471-013-0001-1

Kuhn, T. (1996). *Structure of scientific knowledge* (3rd ed.). University of Chicago Press. (Original work published in 1962)

Ladson-Billings, G. (1995). Toward a theory of culturally relevant pedagogy. *American Educational Research Journal, 32*(3), 465–491. https://doi.org/10.3102/00028312 032003465

Ladson-Billings, G. (1997). I know why this doesn't feel empowering: A critical *race* analysis of critical pedagogy. *Counterpoints, 60,* 127–141. https://www.jstor.org /stable/45135945

Ladson-Billings, G. (1998). Just what is critical race theory and what's it doing in a nice field like education? *International Journal of Qualitative Studies in Education, 11*(1), 7–24. https://doi.org/10.1080/095183998236863

Ladson-Billings, G. (1999). Preparing teachers for diverse student populations: A critical race theory perspective. *Review of Research in Education, 24*(1), 211–247. https:// doi.org/10.2307/1167271

Ladson-Billings, G., & Tate, W. (1995). Toward a critical race theory of education. *Teachers College Record, 97*(1), 47–68. https://doi.org/10.1177/016146819509 700104

Lasswell, H. (2009). *Power and personality.* Transaction Publishers. (Original work published 1948)

Lather, P. (1986). Research as praxis. *Harvard Educational Review, 56*(3), 257–277. https://doi.org/10.17763/haer.56.3.bj2h231877069482

Lather, P. (1991). *Getting smart: Feminist research and pedagogy with/in the postmodern.* Routledge.

Leonardo, Z., & Broderick, A. (2011). Smartness as property: A critical exploration of the intersections between whiteness and disability studies. *Teachers College Record, 113*(10), 2206–2232. https://doi.org/10.1177/016146811111301008

Lincoln, Y., & Guba, E. (1985). *Naturalistic inquiry.* Sage Publications.

Lincoln, Y., & Guba, E. (2000). Paradigmatic controversies and emerging confluences. In N. Denson & Y. Lincoln (Eds.), *The handbook of qualitative research* (2nd ed.), pp. 163–188. Sage Publications.

Lincoln, Y., & Guba, E. (2013). *The constructivist credo.* Left Coast Press.

LinkedIn. (December 17, 2021). *William Tate, profile.* https://www.linkedin.com/in /williamftateiv/

Little, D. (n.d.). *Marxism and method.* http://www-personal.umd.umich.edu/~delittle /Marxism%20and%20Method%203.htm

Macías, L. F. (2018). The scheme game: How DACA recipients navigate barriers to higher education. *Educational Studies, 54*(6), 609–628. https://doi.org/10.1080/00131946 .2018.1530236

Marx, K. (1843). Marx to Ruge. *Letters from the Deutsch-Französische Jahrbücher.* https://www.marxists.org/archive/marx/works/1843/letters/43_05.htm

Marx, K. (1846). *The German ideology.* https://www.marxists.org/archive/marx/works /1845/german-ideology/ch01b.htm

Marx, K., & Engels, F. (1848). *The Communist manifesto* (S. Moore, Trans.). World Public Library.

Matsuda, M., Lawrence III, C., Delgado, R., & Crenshaw, K. (1993). *Words that wound. Critical race theory, assaultive speech, and the First Amendment.* Westview Press.

McKenzie, K., Gunn, J. M., Agan T., Campbell, B., & Herrera-Evan, A. (2020). *Community equity audits: Communities and schools working together to eliminate the opportunity gap* (2nd ed.). McKenzie-Gunn Educational Consulting.

McKenzie, K., & Phillips, G. (2016). Equity traps then and now: Deficit thinking, racial erasure and naïve acceptance of meritocracy. *Whiteness and Education, 1*(1), 26–38. https://doi.org/10.1080/23793406.2016.1159600

McKenzie, K., & Scheurich, J. (2004). The corporatizing and privatizing of schooling: A call for grounded critical praxis. *Educational Theory, 54*(4), 345–450. https://doi.org/10.1111/j.0013-2004.2004.00029.x

McKenzie, K., & Skrla, L. (2011). *Using equity audits in the classroom to reach and teach all students.* Corwin Press.

McNaron, T. A. H. (1997). *Poisoned ivy: Lesbian and gay academics confronting homophobia.* Temple University Press.

McNeil, L. (1981). On the possibility of teachers as the source of an emancipatory pedagogy: A response to Henry Giroux. *Curriculum Inquiry, 11*(3), 205–210. https://doi.org/10.1080/03626784.1981.11075252

Meeker, M. (2001). Behind the mask of respectability: Reconsidering the Mattachine Society and male homophile practice, 1950s and 1960s. *Journal of the History of Sexuality, 10*(1), 78–116. 10.1353/sex.2001.0015

Meekosha, H., & Shuttleworth, R. P. (2009). What's so "critical" about critical disability studies? *Australian Journal of Human Rights, 15*(1), 47–75. https://doi.org/10.1080/1323238X.2009.11910861

Mensah, F. M. (2019). Finding voice and passions: Critical race theory methodology in science teacher education. *American Educational Research Journal, 56*(4), 1412–1456. https://doi.org/10.3102/0002831218818093

Merriam, S. (2001). *Qualitative research and case study applications in education.* Jossey-Bass.

Merriam, S., & Tisdell, E. (2016). *Qualitative research.* Jossey-Bass.

Moghadam, V. (2022). Varieties of feminist activism. In B. G. Smith & N. Robinson (Eds.), *The Routledge global history of feminism* (pp. 37–55). Routledge. https://doi.org/10.4324/9781003050049

Molla, T. (2021). Critical policy scholarship in education: An overview. *Education Policy Analysis Archives, 29*(2), 1–26. https://doi.org/10.14507/epaa.29.5655

Morando-Rhim, L., & Ekin, S., (2021). *How has the pandemic affected students with disabilities? A review of the evidence to date.* Center for Reinventing Public Education. https://crpe.org/how-has-the-pandemic-affected-students-with-disabilities-a-review-of-the-evidence-to-date/

National Native American Boarding School Coalition. (n.d.). *US Indian Boarding School History.* https://boardingschoolhealing.org/education/us-indian-boarding-school-history/

National Women's History Museum. (2021). *Feminism: The first wave.* https://www.womenshistory.org/exhibits/feminism-first-wave-0

Noddings, N. (1993). *Caring: A relational approach to ethics and moral education.* University of California Press.

Obergefell v. Hodges, 576 U.S. ___(2015). https://supreme.justia.com/cases/federal/us/576/14-556/

Olesen, V. (1994). Feminisms and models of qualitative research. In N. K. Denzin & Y. S. Lincoln (Eds.), *Handbook of qualitative research* (pp. 158–174). Sage Publications, Inc.

Olesen, V. (2018). Feminist qualitative research in the millennium's first decade: Development, challenges, prospects. In N. K. Denzin & Y. S. Lincoln (Eds.), *Sage Publications handbook of qualitative research* (5th ed., pp. 264–316). Sage Publications.

Oliven, J. (1965). *Sexual hygiene and pathology* (2nd ed.). Lippincott and Company.

Opportunity Insights. (n.d.). *Using big data to solve economic and social problems.* https://opportunityinsights.org/course/

Parkhouse, H. (2016). *Critical pedagogy in US history classrooms: Conscientization and contradictory consciousness* (Publication No. 10119798). Doctoral dissertation, The University of North Carolina at Chapel Hill. ProQuest Dissertations Publishing.

Parkhouse, H. (2018). Pedagogies of naming, questioning, and demystification: A study of two critical U.S. history classrooms. *Theory and Research in Social Education, 46*(2), 277–317. https://doi.org/10.1080/00933104.2017.1389327

Parkin, A. (1996). On the practical relevance of Habermas's theory of communicative action. *Social Theory and Practice, 22*(3), 417–441. https://www.jstor.org/stable/23559058

Pascale, C. (2011). *Cartographies of knowledge.* Sage Publications.

Payne, E. C., & Smith, M. J. (2018). Refusing relevance: School administrator resistance to offering professional development addressing LGBTQ issues in schools. *Educational Administration Quarterly, 54*(2), 183–215. https://doi.org/10.1177/0013161X17723426

Penn State College of Education. (n.d.). *Dr. Edward Fuller.* https://ed.psu.edu/directory/dr-edward-j-fuller

Pérez Huber, L., Vélez, V. N., & Solórzano, D. (2018). More than 'papelitos': A Quant-Crit counterstory to critique Latina/o degree value and occupational prestige. *Race Ethnicity & Education, 21*(2), 208–230. https://doi.org/10.1080/13613324.2017.1377416

Perouse-Harvey, E. (2022). Seeing the unseen: Applying intersectionality and disability critical race theory (DisCrit) frameworks in preservice teacher education. *Teachers College Record, 124*(7), 51–81. https://doi.org/10.1177/01614681221111429

Pillow, W. (2003). Confession, catharsis, or cure? Rethinking the uses of reflexivity as methodological power in qualitative research. *International Journal of Qualitative Studies in Education, 16*(2), 175–196. https://doi.org/10.1080/0951839032000060635

Pratt, H. R. (1892, June 23–29). *The advantages of mingling Indians with Whites* [speech]. The National Conference of Charities and Corrections, Denver, CO. https://carlisleindian.dickinson.edu/sites/default/files/docs-resources/CIS-Resources_1892-PrattSpeech.pdf

Public Broadcasting System (PBS). (2005, April 22). Interview: Kimberlé Williams Crenshaw. *Frontline.* https://www.pbs.org/wgbh/pages/frontline/oj/interviews/crenshaw.html

Reardon, S. F., Weathers, E. S., Fahle, E. M., Jang, H., & Kalogrides, D. (2021). Is separate still unequal? New evidence on school segregation and racial academic achievement. (CEPA working paper no. 19.06.) *Stanford Center for Education Policy Analysis.* https://cepa.stanford.edu/sites/default/files/wp19-06-v092021.pdf

Reilly, K. (2022, April 22). Florida's governor just signed the 'Stop Woke Act.' Here's what it means for schools and businesses. *Time.* https://time.com/6168753/florida-stop-woke-law/

Ruhsam, J. (2017). *WGSS 392Q—Introduction to Queer Theory* [Syllabus]. Department of Women, Gender, and Sexual Studies, University of Massachusetts. https://

www.umass.edu/wgss/sites/default/files/assets/wgss/ruhsam_-_wgss_392q_-_spring
_2017_0.pdf

Rutgers University. (n.d.). *Catherine Lugg*. https://gse.rutgers.edu/faculty/catherine-lugg/

Sablan, J. R. (2019). Can you really measure that? Combining critical race theory and quantitative methods. *American Educational Research Journal, 56*(1), 178–203. https://doi.org/10.3102/0002831218798325

Sage Publishing. (n.d.). *Catherine Marshall*. https://us.sagepub.com/en-us/nam/author/catherine-marshall

Savage, S. (2019). Exploring the intergenerational responsibility of musical mothering and morality. *International Journal of Community Music, 12*(1), 111–128. https://doi.org/10.1386/ijcm.12.1.111_1

Schwandt, T. (1993). Theory for the moral sciences. In D. Flinders & G. Mills (Eds.), *Theory and concepts in qualitative research: Perspectives from the field* (pp. 5–23). Teachers College Press.

Schwandt, T. (2015). *The Sage dictionary of qualitative inquiry* (2nd ed.). Sage Publications.

Schwartz, G., Leifheit, K., Chen, J., Arcaya, M., & Berkman, L. (2022). Childhood eviction and cognitive development: Developmental timing-specific associations in an urban birth cohort. *Social Science & Medicine, 292*, 1–10. https://doi.org/10.1016/j.socscimed.2021.114544

Schwartz, S. (2021, Dec. 14). The pandemic hit vulnerable students hardest. Now, schools have to reckon with the effects. *Education Week*. https://www.edweek.org/leadership/the-pandemic-hit-vulnerable-students-hardest-now-schools-have-to-reckon-with-the-effects/2021/12

Sikes, P. (2013). Working together for critical research ethics. *Compare: A Journal of Comparative and International Education, 43*(4), 516–536. https://doi.org/10.1080/03057925.2013.797765

Smith, L. T. (1999). *Decolonizing methodologies*. Zed Books.

Soedirgo, J., & Glas, A. (2020). Toward active reflexivity: Positionality and practice in the production of knowledge. *Political Science & Politics, 53*(3), 527–531. https://doi.org/10.1017/S1049096519002233

Solórzano, D. G., & Yosso, T. J., (2001). Critical race and LatCrit theory and method: Counter-storytelling. *International Journal of Qualitative Studies in Education, 14*(4), 471–495. https://doi.org/10.1080/09518390110063365

Sonoma, S. (2022, Aug. 18). *Guide for media covering state legislation targeting LGBTQ people*. GLAAD. https://www.glaad.org/blog/guide-media-covering-state-legislation-targeting-lgbtq-people

Spivak, G. C. (1988). Can the subaltern speak? In C. Nelson & L. Groberg (Eds.), *Marxism and the interpretation of culture* (pp. 271–313). University of Illinois Press.

Stage, F. K. (2007). Answering critical questions using quantitative data. *New Directions for Institutional Research, 2007*(133), 5–16. https://doi.org/10.1002/ir.200

Stage, F. K., & Wells, R. S. (2014), Critical quantitative inquiry in context. *New Directions for Institutional Research, 2013*(158), 1–7. https://doi.org/10.1002/ir.20041

Stanford Encyclopedia of Philosophy. (n.d.). *William Whewell*. Plato.Stanford.edu. https://plato.stanford.edu/entries/whewell/

Stefancic, J. (1997). Latino and Latina critical theory: An annotated bibliography. *California Law Review, 85*(5), 1509–1584. https://doi.org/10.2307/3481065

Strunk, K. K., & Locke, L. A. (2019). *Research methods for social justice and equity in education*. Palgrave Macmillan.

Struthers, R. (2001). Conducting sacred research: An indigenous experience. *Wicazo Sa Review, 16*(1), 125–133. https://www.jstor.org/stable/i261467

Tate, W. (1994). From inner city to ivory tower: Does my voice matter in the academy? *Urban Education, 29*(3), 245–269. https://doi.org/10.1177/0042085994029003002

Tate, W. (1997). Critical race theory and education: History, theory, and implications. *Review of Research in Education, 22*(1), 195–347. https://doi.org/10.3102/0091732 X022001195

Tate, W. (2003). The 'race' to theorize education: Who is my neighbor? *International Journal of Qualitative Studies in Education, 16*(1), 121–126. https://doi.org/10.1080 /0951839032000033563

Tate, W. (2005). Ethics, engineering and the challenge of racial reform in education. *Race Ethnicity and Education, 8*(1), 121–127. https://doi.org/10.1080/1361332052000 341033

Tate, W., & Striley, C. (2010). Epidemiology and education research: Dialoguing about disparities. *Teachers College Record.* https://www.tcrecord.org/content.asp?contentid =16036

Taylor & Francis. (2020). Aims and scope. *Disability & Society.* https://www.tandfonline .com/action/journalInformation?show=aimsScope&journalCode=cdso20

Teranishi, R. T. (2007). Race, ethnicity, and higher education policy: The use of critical quantitative research. *New Directions for Institutional Research, 2007*(133), 37–49. https://doi.org/10.1002/ir.203

Torgerson, D. (2017). Policy sciences and democracy: A reexamination. *Policy Sciences, 50*(3), 339–350.

Tufts University School of Arts and Sciences. (n.d.). *Shameka Powell.* https://as.tufts.edu /education/people/faculty/shameka-powell

Ujifusa, A. (2021, May 26). Critical race theory puts educators at the center of a frustrating cultural fight once again. *Education Week.* https://www.edweek.org/leader ship/critical-race-theory-puts-educators-at-center-of-a-frustrating-cultural-fight-once -again/2021/05

University of Birmingham. (n.d.). *Professor David Gillborn.* https://www.birmingham .ac.uk/staff/profiles/education/gillborn-david.aspx

University of Pennsylvania School of Sociology. (n.d.). *Tukufu Zuberi.* https://sociology .sas.upenn.edu/people/tukufu-zuberi

University of Wisconsin-Madison. (n.d.). *Michael W. Apple.* https://lacis.wisc.edu/staff /apple-michael-w/

U.S. Census Bureau. (2021). *Income and poverty in the United States: 2020.* https://www .census.gov/library/publications/2021/demo/p60-273.html

U.S. Department of Education, Office of Civil Rights. (2021). *Education in a pandemic: The disparate impacts of COVID-19 on America's students.* https://www2.ed.gov /about/offices/list/ocr/docs/20210608-impacts-of-covid19.pdf

Valdés, F., & Bender, S. W. (2021). *LatCrit: From critical legal theory to academic activism.* NYU Press.

Valencia, R. R. (1997). *Evolution of deficit thinking: Educational thought and practice.* Routledge.

Vehmas, S., & Watson, N. (2014). Moral wrongs, disadvantages, and disability: A critique of critical disability studies. *Disability & Society, 29*(4), 638–650.

Vélez, V., & Solórzano, D. G. (2017). Critical race spatial analysis: Conceptualizing GIS as a tool for critical race research in education. *Critical race spatial analysis: Mapping to understand and address educational inequity*, 8–31.

Vox. (2019). *The intersectionality wars.* https://www.vox.com/the-highlight/2019/5/20
/18542843/intersectionality-conservatism-law-race-gender-discrimination

Wiener, J. (2021, July 5). The predictable backlash to critical race theory: A Q & A with Kimberlé Crenshaw. *The Nation.* https://www.thenation.com/article/politics/critical
-race-kimberle-crenshaw/

Winerip, M. (1985, May 13). School integration in Buffalo is hailed as a model for U.S. *The New York Times.* https://www.nytimes.com/1985/05/13/nyregion/school
-integration-in-buffalo-is-hailed-as-a-model-for-us.html

World Health Organization. (2022). *Social determinants of health.* https://www.who.int
/health-topics/social-determinants-of-health#tab=tab_1

Young, M. D., & Diem, S. (2017). Introduction: Critical approaches to education policy analysis. In M. D. Young & S. Diem (Eds.), *Critical approaches to education policy analysis* (pp. 1–13). Springer.

Index

About the Authors

Kathryn Bell McKenzie is professor emerita of educational leadership at both Texas A&M University and California State University. She received her PhD in educational leadership from The University of Texas at Austin. At Texas A&M she was coordinator of the PhD in K–12 educational leadership and affiliated faculty in Women and Gender Studies; at California State University she was the director of the EdD program in educational leadership. Her scholarship focuses on the social and political structures and policies within schools and communities that limit opportunities for students and families who have historically been marginalized and ways to address them. She typically employs critical qualitative methods and recently critical descriptive social epidemiology. She has numerous published peer-reviewed articles and book chapters and three coauthored books on equity audits. Both K–12 schools and universities use her work on equity traps and equity audits. She is also an educational consultant working in both the United States and internationally with schools, school districts, universities, and nonprofits. Prior to becoming a professor, she was a public school educator serving as a teacher, curriculum specialist, and principal.

Linda Skrla is professor emerita at Texas A&M University. A former public school teacher and administrator, she earned her PhD in educational administration at The University of Texas at Austin. She has 25 years of experience as a researcher, teacher, and doctoral mentor in higher education. Skrla is a past vice president of Division A of the American Educational Research Association and former editor of *Educational Administration Quarterly*. The University Council for Educational Administration awarded her its Culbertson, Mawhinney, and Bridges awards for distinguished service and research.